MASTER THE MILLER ANALOGIES TEST®

2002

TEACHER-TESTED STRATEGIES AND TECHNIQUES FOR SCORING HIGH

ARCO
THOMSON LEARNING

Australia • Canada • Mexico • Singapore • Spain • United Kingdom • United States

An ARCO Book

ARCO is a registered trademark of Thomson Learning, Inc., and is used herein under license by Peterson's.

About Peterson's

Founded in 1966, Peterson's, a division of Thomson Learning, is the nation's largest and most respected provider of lifelong learning online resources, software, reference guides, and books. The Education Supersite[SM] at petersons.com—the Web's most heavily traveled education resource—has searchable databases and interactive tools for contacting U.S.-accredited institutions and programs. CollegeQuest® (CollegeQuest.com) offers a complete solution for every step of the college decision-making process. GradAdvantage[TM] (GradAdvantage.org), developed with Educational Testing Service, is the only electronic admissions service capable of sending official graduate test score reports with a candidate's online application. Peterson's serves more than 55 million education consumers annually.

Thomson Learning is among the world's leading providers of lifelong learning, serving the needs of individuals, learning institutions, and corporations with products and services for both traditional classrooms and for online learning. For more information about the products and services offered by Thomson Learning, please visit www.thomsonlearning.com. Headquartered in Stamford, Connecticut, with offices worldwide, Thomson Learning is part of The Thomson Corporation (www.thomson.com), a leading e-information and solutions company in the business, professional, and education marketplaces. The Corporation's common shares are listed on the Toronto and London stock exchanges.

For more information, contact Peterson's, 2000 Lenox Drive, Lawrenceville, NJ 08648; 800-338-3282; or find us on the World Wide Web at: www.petersons.com/about

COPYRIGHT © 2001 Petersons, a division of Thomson Learning, Inc.
Thomson Learning[TM] is a trademark used herein under license.

Previous editions © 1982, 1985, 1989, 1991, 1993, 1995, 1998, 2000.

ALL RIGHTS RESERVED. No part of this work covered by the copyright herein may be reproduced or used in any form or by any means—graphic, electronic, or mechanical, including photocopying, recording, taping, Web distribution, or information storage and retrieval systems—without the prior written permission of the publisher.

For permission to use material from this text or product, contact us by
Phone: 800-730-2214
Fax: 800-730-2215
Web: www.thomsonrights.com

ISSN: International Standard Serial Number information available upon request.
ISBN: 0-7689-0641-5

Printed in the United States of America

10 9 8 7 6 5 4 3 2 1   03 02

MASTER THE MILLER ANALOGIES TEST— THE MOST COMMON ANALOGY CATEGORIES

Type	Example	Explanation
SYNONYMS OR SIMILAR CONCEPTS	DELIVERANCE : (a) rescue, (b) oration, (c) liberate, (d) demise :: EXERCISE : PRACTICE	The relationship between the C and D words is that they are synonyms. So what you're looking for is a synonym for the A word, DELIVERANCE. (a) RESCUE fills the bill.
ANTONYMS OR CONTRASTING CONCEPTS	(a) hostel, (b) hostile, (c) amenable, (d) amoral : AMICABLE :: CHASTE : LEWD	The relationship between CHASTE (pure or decent) and LEWD (obscene or salacious) is that they are opposites. The opposite of AMICABLE is (b) HOSTILE.
CAUSE AND EFFECT	HEREDITY : ENVIRONMENT :: (a) influenza, (b) pneumonia, (c) hemophilia, (d) roseola : RUBELLA	This is an A : C :: B : D relationship. Something present in the ENVIRONMENT (a virus) causes RUBELLA. To balance the analogy, look for something that is caused by HEREDITY, which would be (c) HEMOPHILIA.
PART TO WHOLE	LEAF : TREE :: KEY : (a) lock, (b) door, (c) typewriter, (d) car	It's clear that a LEAF is part of a TREE. While a key can be used to open a lock, it is not a part of that lock. A KEY is, however, a part of a (c) TYPEWRITER.
PART TO PART	FATHER : DAUGHTER :: GILL : (a) fish, (b) fin, (c) lung, (d) wattle	FATHER and DAUGHTER are each part of a family. GILL and (b) FIN are each part of a fish. While GILL and FISH might seem to be a match, they represent a part-to-whole relationship.
PURPOSE OR USE	GLOVE : BALL :: HOOK : (a) coat, (b) line, (c) fish, (d) curve	A GLOVE catches a BALL, and a HOOK catches a (c) FISH. Even though a HOOK could possibly catch or hold a coat, it's not as close to the initial relationship.
ACTION TO OBJECT	PITCH : FIRE :: (a) coal, (b) ball, (c) sound, (d) slope : GUN	At first glance this looks like a synonym. The answer choices, however, don't complete the match. Instead, this becomes an A : C :: B : D relationship—you FIRE a GUN and PITCH a (b) BALL.
OBJECT TO ACTION	SPRAIN : (a) ankle, (b) joint, (c) twist, (d) swell :: BITE : ITCH	This one can be problematic until you figure out that SPRAIN and BITE are being used as nouns rather than verbs, and that ITCH is a verb. Then you can use the verb (d) SWELL to complete the relationship of an object causing an action.
PLACE	PARAGUAY : BOLIVIA :: SWITZERLAND : (a) Afghanistan, (b) Poland, (c) Hungary, (d) Bulgaria	Paraguay, Bolivia, and Switzerland are all landlocked countries. Since two of the answer choices, Afghanistan and Hungary, are also landlocked, you have to narrow the relationship. Paraguay and Bolivia are landlocked countries on the same continent. Only (c) HUNGARY is on the same continent as Switzerland; Afghanistan is in Asia.

Type	Example	Explanation
ASSOCIATION	MOZART : MUSIC :: PEI : (a) painting, (b) architecture, (c) sculpture, (d) dance	The composer MOZART is associated with MUSIC in the same way that PEI is associated with (b) ARCHITECTURE.
SEQUENCE OR TIME	SAIL : STEAM :: PROPELLER : (a) plane, (b) engine, (c) jet, (d) wing	Ships were propelled by SAIL, then they were propelled by STEAM. The matching relationship is that planes were propelled by PROPELLER and then by a (c) JET engine.
CHARACTERISTIC OR DESCRIPTION	(a) scream, (b) ear, (c) shrill, (d) vocal : PIERCING :: CRY : PLAINTIVE	Just as a CRY can be called PLAINTIVE, a SCREAM can be called PIERCING. In this analogy, it might help to reverse the order of the pairs.
DEGREE	WARM : HOT :: BRIGHT : (a) dark, (b) dim, (c) genius, (d) illuminate	WARM is a lesser degree of temperature than HOT. Think of BRIGHT as a degree of intelligence rather than of light; (c) GENIUS. While ILLUMINATE might be tempting, it doesn't fit the relationship.
MEASUREMENT	ODOMETER : (a) speed, (b) distance, (c) pressure, (d) temperature :: CLOCK : TIME	There's no surprise here. A CLOCK measures TIME as an ODOMETER measures (b) DISTANCE.
GRAMMATICAL	BROKE : BROKEN :: (a) fled, (b) flight, (c) flew, (d) flung : FLOWN	In this case, BROKE and BROKEN are the past tense and the past participle of the verb *break*. FLOWN is the past participle of *fly*, and the past tense is (c) FLEW. MAT grammar analogies can also present parts of speech and plurals.
MATHEMATICAL	$12\frac{1}{2}\%$: (a) $\frac{1}{4}$, (b) $\frac{1}{5}$, (c) $\frac{1}{8}$, (d) $\frac{1}{3}$: $16\frac{2}{3}\%$: $\frac{1}{6}$	Mathematical MAT analogies can deal with geometrical and numerical relationships, as well as equalities. Percents are really fractions with denominators of 100, so $16\frac{2}{3}\%$ equals $16\frac{2}{3}$ divided by 100, which is $\frac{1}{6}$. The matching relationship is $12\frac{1}{2}\% = 12\frac{1}{2} \div 100 =$ (c) $\frac{1}{8}$.
WORKER TO TOOL	PHYSICIAN : (a) hospital, (b) patient, (c) surgeon, (d) X ray :: ACTUARY : STATISTICS	An ACTUARY is a worker who uses STATISTICS as a tool to calculate insurance premiums. A PHYSICIAN is a worker who uses an X RAY as a tool to diagnose and treat a patient.
NONSEMANTIC (Sound)	HOE : ROE :: THOUGH : (a) rough, (b) flood, (c) flow, (d) how	The strongest relationship among all the words is that they rhyme. This leads you to (c) FLOW as the best answer.
NONSEMANTIC (Arrangement)	EVIL : LIVE :: STEP : (a) stand, (b) stop, (c) post, (d) pest	The arrangement and rearrangement of letters in the word creates the relationship. EVIL and LIVE have the same letters in different arrangements. By rearranging the letters in STEP, you'll come up with (d) PEST as the correct choice.

CONTENTS

PART 1 MAT BASICS 1

Chapter 1 All About the MAT 3
Meet the MAT 3
Registering for the MAT 3
Understanding the MAT 4
How MAT Scores Are Reported 4
Retaking the MAT 4
Timecruncher Study Plans 5

Chapter 2 All About Analogies 7
Solving MAT Analogies 8
The Most Common Analogy Categories 10
The Most Common Analogy Subject Areas 13
Traps to Avoid 13
What Smart Test Takers Know 14

PART 2 15 ANALOGY TYPES BY CATEGORY 17

Chapter 3 Analogy Tests by Category 23
Group A: Tests 1–5 24
  Test 1: Synonyms and Definitions 24
  Test 2: Antonyms 26
  Test 3: Cause and Effect 28
  Test 4: Part to Whole 30
  Test 5: Part to Part 31
Group B: Tests 6–10 33
  Test 6: Purpose, Use, or Function 33
  Test 7: Action to Object 34
  Test 8: Actor to Object 36
  Test 9: Place 37
  Test 10: Association 39
Group C: Tests 11–15 41
  Test 11: Sequence 41
  Test 12: Characteristic 42
  Test 13: Degree 44
  Test 14: Grammatical 46
  Test 15: Miscellaneous 47

Chapter 4 Answer Key—Analogy Tests by Category 49
Test 1: Synonyms and Definitions 49
Test 2: Antonyms 50
Test 3: Cause and Effect 51
Test 4: Part to Whole 53

Test 5: Part to Part 54
Test 6: Purpose, Use, or Function 56
Test 7: Action to Object 57
Test 8: Actor to Object 58
Test 9: Place 59
Test 10: Association 60
Test 11: Sequence 62
Test 12: Characteristic 63
Test 13: Degree 64
Test 14: Grammatical 65
Test 15: Miscellaneous 66

PART 3 7 SAMPLE MATS 69

Chapter 5 Sample Test 1 73
Answer Key 78
Explanatory Answers 79

Chapter 6 Sample Test 2 91
Answer Key 96
Explanatory Answers 97

Chapter 7 Sample Test 3 109
Answer Key 114
Explanatory Answers 115

Chapter 8 Sample Test 4 127
Answer Key 132
Explanatory Answers 133

Chapter 9 Sample Test 5 145
Answer Key 150
Explanatory Answers 151

Chapter 10 Sample Test 6 163
Answer Key 168
Explanatory Answers 169

Chapter 11 Sample Test 7 181
Answer Key 186
Explanatory Answers 187

PART 4 GRE VERBAL ANALOGIES 197

Chapter 12 Practice for the GRE 199
Test 1 203
Test 2 205
Test 3 207
Test 4 209
Test 5 211
Test 6 213
Test 7 215

Answer Key 217
Explanatory Answers 219

PART 5: APPENDIXES   225

Appendix A: Mythology 227
Appendix B: Nations of the World 231
Appendix C: Mathematics 235

Before You Start

HOW TO USE THIS BOOK

Congratulations! You've just picked up the best Miller Analogies Test (MAT) preparation guide you can buy. This book has all the answers to your questions about the MAT. It includes a wealth of practice questions, sample exams, and solid test-taking advice. Here's how you can use it to get your best MAT score—and get into the graduate program of your choice:

- Start by reading Part 1, "MAT Basics." Although this part is not very long, it's full of answers to all your questions about the test itself and about how to solve analogy questions. You'll learn what the test looks like, where you can take it, and how it is scored. You'll also learn what subjects are covered, what the common question categories are, and what traps to watch out for.

- Next, work your way through Part 2, "15 Analogy Types by Category." This part provides you with plenty of practice in many formats and with many relationships. In addition to the correct answer choice for each analogy, you'll usually find a simple sentence that could be used to find the answer. Also, wherever it's appropriate, you'll find an explanation of the thinking process that was followed to choose the correct answer. By studying these explanations, you'll upgrade your analytical skills.

- When you come to Part 3, "7 Sample MATs," you've reached the heart of the preparation program. Each test is as close as you can get to the real thing. Take as many as your time allows. Remember—practice makes perfect!

- In Part 4, "GRE Verbal Analogies," you'll find a different type of analogy, the paired analogy. This will be particularly helpful if you are also planning to take the GRE. Even if you are taking only the MAT, try some of these. The experience and explanations could turn out to be very helpful.

- The appendixes contain lists of terms that frequently appear in MAT analogies but that could be unfamiliar to some test-takers. These lists cover Greek and Roman mythology, nations of the world, and key math terms. Use the appendixes as well as other sources to learn or review as much material as possible. The more you know, the less you'll have to guess.

PART 1

MAT Basics

PREVIEW

CHAPTER 1   *All About the MAT*

CHAPTER 2   *All About Analogies*

Chapter

All About the MAT

MEET THE MAT

The MAT, officially known as the Miller Analogies Test, is a high-level test of mental ability and critical-thinking skills. The test is required by many graduate schools as part of the admissions process for a master's or a doctoral program. It also can be used as a basis for granting financial aid for graduate students. Some employers require the test when recruiting for jobs that require high levels of critical thinking and problem-solving ability.

REGISTERING FOR THE MAT

The MAT is given at local Controlled Testing Centers, which are generally located at colleges and universities. The MAT is not given on a particular date; instead, the testing centers set their own dates and fees. Controlled Testing Centers are located throughout the United States and in Puerto Rico, Canada, Great Britain, Japan, Venezuela, Saudi Arabia, and the Philippines.

The testing centers are listed in the *Miller Analogies Test Candidate Information Booklet,* which is published by the Psychological Corporation, the maker and grader of the test. To obtain a copy of this booklet, contact the Psychological Corporation at the following address:

Miller Analogies Test Coordinator
The Psychological Corporation
555 Academic Court
San Antonio, TX 78204-3956
(800) 622-3231 or (210) 921-8801

If you live more than 100 miles from a testing center, or if there is no testing center in your country, the Psychological Corporation can make special testing arrangements.

At the testing center, you must present two forms of personal identification, one of which must be a government- or school-issued photo ID with your signature. You also will need to bring your own number 2 pencils with erasers.

ROAD MAP

- *Meet the MAT*
- *Registering for the MAT*
- *Understanding the MAT*
- *How MAT Scores Are Reported*
- *Retaking the MAT*
- *Timecruncher Study Plans*

UNDERSTANDING THE MAT

The Miller Analogies Test won't take up your whole day. It has only 100 questions—mostly verbal—which you're given 50 minutes to answer. These 100 questions cover a broad range of subjects. While an extensive vocabulary is essential, the questions also assume a better-than-average grasp of literature, social studies, mathematics, and science.

Generally, the questions are arranged with the easiest first, becoming more difficult as you proceed through the test. However, if you aren't familiar with the topic of the question, even an obvious analogy becomes difficult. It is helpful to know, though, that all questions carry equal weight and that there's no penalty for an incorrect response. So, it is definitely worth your time to work through all the questions and answer as many as you can as quickly as you can. Then, you can go back and answer the questions you skipped, even if your answer is a guess. When your time is up, your answer sheet should be filled in completely.

HOW MAT SCORES ARE REPORTED

When you take the MAT, you are entitled to a personal score report and as many as three additional responses sent to institutions you designate. After the test date, you may have more reports sent out, but there is an additional fee for each report.

The test score report contains three scores:

1. Your raw score, which is the number of correct answers
2. Your percentile score relative to other test-takers in your intended major
3. Your percentile score relative to all MAT takers

The Psychological Corporation doesn't provide any analysis or norms. Each report recipient does its own analysis based on its own criteria, standards, or norms.

If you decide during the exam that you do not wish to have your score reported, you can choose to cancel your score on the spot. If you do so, your score will not be reported to any recipient, and there will be no record that you have taken the MAT. However, be aware that you cannot reinstate a canceled score at a later time.

RETAKING THE MAT

You can indeed take the test again. In fact, if you need to submit scores more than two years after taking the test, you should take the test again. If more than five years have passed since you took the MAT, you *must* take the test again. The Psychological Corporation won't report scores that are more than five years old.

NOTE
Percentile scores indicate how well you did in comparison to other test-takers. For example, a score in the 85th percentile means that you did better than 85 percent of the other people taking the test.

When you take the MAT, your score report will include a retest admission ticket. You must present this ticket when you retake the test in order to ensure that you are not given the same test form that you took before. If you are given the same test form, the retest score will be voided and you will have to make new arrangements to retake the test.

TIMECRUNCHER STUDY PLANS

PLAN A: ACCELERATED

Are you starting to prepare a little later than you had planned? Don't get upset—it happens. You might have to cut some corners, but you can still prepare. Follow this plan if you have at least two weeks and can give it an hour a day:

- *Skim* Chapter 1, "All About the MAT"
- *Study* Chapter 2, "All About Analogies"
- *Work through* Chapter 3, "Analogy Tests by Category"
- *Take* all seven sample MATs and study the explanations
- *Skip* Chapter 12, "Practice for the GRE"
- *Skim* the appendixes

PLAN B: TOP SPEED

If the calendar says that your MAT is coming up in fewer than ten days, go for this superconcentrated study plan:

- *Skip* Chapter 1, "All About the MAT"
- *Study* Chapter 2, "All About Analogies"
- *Read* Chapter 3, "Analogy Tests by Category"
- *Take* as many sample MATs as time allows
- *Study* explanations for the sample MATs you took
- *Skip* the rest of the book

TIP
What is a good score? That depends. On recent tests, a raw score of 65 would have put you in the 85th percentile compared to all test-takers. However, it would have put you in the 75th percentile compared to all humanities majors.

Chapter

All About Analogies

When you get right down to it, analogies are about relationships. They test your ability to see a relationship between two words and to recognize a similar relationship between two other words. The key to analogy success is being able to express the relationship between the words in a pair.

In a MAT analogy question, you are given three capitalized words. Two of the words have a relationship. The task is to find a word among the answer choices that has the same relationship to the third capitalized word.

MAT analogies are presented in a kind of mathematical shorthand. For example, you may see:

DAY : SUN :: NIGHT : (A. ray, B. cold, C. moon, D. dark)

The : sign is read as *is to,* and the :: sign is read as *as*. So, the analogy reads "day is to sun as night is to?" The correct answer is C, *moon*, because that makes a pair in which the two words are related in the same way as day and sun.

If you substitute letters for the words in this analogy, it might read, "A is to B as C is to D." However, this is not the only possible relationship in MAT analogies. In some questions, the relationship will be "A is to C as B is to D." That means that when you're solving a MAT analogy, if you can't find a relationship between the first and second words (A and B), look for a relationship between the first and third words (A and C).

It also helps to remember that the relationship of the words in the analogy is the same on both sides of the "equation." For example, if the pattern is A → B, and if A is a part of B, then the second relationship has to be C → D, and C is a part of D. Here's an illustration:

MINUTE : HOUR :: MONTH : (A. week, B. year, C. time, D. calendar)

The minute-to-hour relationship is a part-to-whole relationship. Looking at the answer choices, you might be tempted to choose answer A, *week*. However, that would reverse the relationship, making it month-to-week, or whole-to-part. The correct choice, B, *year,* completes the analogy with an equal part-to-whole relationship.

ROAD MAP

- *Solving MAT Analogies*
- *The Most Common Analogy Categories*
- *The Most Common Analogy Subject Areas*
- *Traps to Avoid*
- *What Smart Test Takers Know*

8 Master the Miller Analogies Test

TIP

What if the first two words don't seem to be related at all? A MAT question may be based on the relationship between the first and third words and the second and fourth words.

CAUTION

If none of the answer choices seems exactly right, remember that the directions tell you to choose the best answer. The correct answer won't necessarily be a perfect fit, but it will work better than the other choices.

SOLVING MAT ANALOGIES

With MAT analogies, your first order of business is to determine what the analogy is all about. That is, you'll want to define the terms that are given. Take a look at the words in the analogy and review what they mean. Sometimes, two of the words will help you define an unfamiliar third word; sometimes, the answer choices will clarify a mystery word. In any case, you need to know the meanings of the words so that you can figure out the relationship in the analogy.

After you've read the analogy carefully, follow these five steps:

1. Find a relationship between two of the capitalized words.
2. Make up a sentence that expresses the relationship.
3. Try out your sentence by substituting the third capitalized word and each of the answer choices.
4. If more than one answer seems to work, go back and make your sentence express a more specific relationship.
5. Choose the best answer. If none of the choices works exactly, choose the one that works best.

Now use the five-step method to solve the following examples.

DOCTOR : SYMPTOM :: DETECTIVE : (A. mystery, B. crime, C. police, D. clue)

In this analogy, it's pretty clear that there is a strong relationship between the first two words (A and B). A symptom gives a doctor an idea about how to identify an illness. You then know that a similar relationship should exist between words three and four (C and D). So, while a detective knows that a crime has been committed, what's really needed is an idea about how to identify a solution: a clue. So, the answer is D, *clue*.

DOCTOR : DETECTIVE :: SYMPTOM : (A. illness, B. mystery, C. crime, D. clue)

If the analogy were presented this way, you would not be able to establish a relationship between A and B, but you could find one instead between A and C. This tells you that the companion relationship is between B and D. The correct answer, *clue,* is the same.

PLAY : AUDIENCE :: BOOK : (A. writer, B. publisher, C. plot, D. reader)

There is a clear relationship between *play* and *audience:* A play entertains an audience. Now substitute the third word and each answer choice in the same sentence.

(A) A *book* entertains a *writer*. Possible, but that's not the main purpose of a book.

(B) A *book* entertains a *publisher*. Again, possible, but not the main purpose.

(C) A *book* entertains a *plot*. This makes no sense at all, so it can be eliminated right away.

(D) A *book* entertains a *reader*. This is the answer. The sentence parallels the original sentence and also is true.

BRIM : HAT :: HAND : (A. glove, B. finger, C. foot, D. arm)

A brim is part of a hat, so you could say that this is a part-to-whole relationship. This is probably enough to complete the analogy, but if the choices don't work, you need to go back and make the relationship more specific. You might rephrase your sentence as "brim is the outside part of a hat," or "brim is not a necessary part of a hat." Once you have a solid relationship, move on to the third word and the answer choices.

By process of elimination, work with the answer choices to establish a relationship that's parallel to the one between *brim* and *hat*. If you can glance at the choices and eliminate one immediately, do it. In this example, though, each choice has to be considered, keeping the part-to-whole criterion in mind. The first choice, *glove,* certainly has an association with HAND, but it's not a part of *hand*. This can be eliminated.

Now take a look at *finger*. At first glance, *finger* looks pretty good; after all, it is a part of *hand*. However, the relationship you're working with is part-to-whole. Ask yourself, "Does HAND : FINGER match part-to-whole?" No! This follows a whole-to-part relationship, and you know that both sides of the analogy must have the same relationship. Therefore, *finger* is out as a possible choice.

The relationship of *hand* to *foot* is that they are both parts, but not part-to-whole. As you move over to *arm,* it becomes clear why answer D is the best answer: A hand is indeed part of an arm. This parallels the part-to-whole BRIM : HAT relationship.

When you're solving analogies, be prepared to be flexible. Consider this example:

LETTER : WORD :: SONG : (A. story, B. music, C. note, D. orchestra)

Your first thought is that a letter is a part of a word, so this is another part-to-whole relationship. While all the choices have some logical relationship with *song,* none of the choices completes a part-to-whole relationship. Now you must go back and rethink the relationship. Ask yourself, "How else can *letter* and *word* be connected?" If *letter* is not a part of a word but rather a form of written communication, then it's clear that a word is part of a letter. Now the relationship correctly becomes whole-to-part. When you go back and review the choices, you'll find that as *song* becomes the whole, then *note* becomes the part. You now have your parallel relationship on both sides of the analogy.

TIP
Think up a simple sentence to express the relationship between the words in an analogy pair. Then use the sentence to try out answer choices until you find one that fits.

CAUTION
Order counts! If the sentence you create reverses the order of terms in a pair, remember to reverse the order of the terms in your answer pair as well.

If you're really having trouble finding the correct relationship, it might help to read the analogy backward. Be careful, though; if you do determine the relationship this way, remember to make the third and fourth words match the direction of the initial relationship.

The examples you've worked with so far have been A → B / C → D relationships. Let's take a look at an analogy with an A → C / B → D relationship.

HAIL : HALE :: (A. farewell, B. greet, C. hearty, D. taxi) : STRONG

Because *hail* and *hale* are homonyms (they sound alike but are spelled differently), that's probably the relationship you want to go with. However, there's no homonym for *strong*, so you have to go back and look at the relationship again. There really is no other viable relationship between *hail* and *hale*, but there certainly is one between *hale* and *strong*, your B and D words: They are synonyms. Now that you have a valid relationship, it's time to take a look at the choices.

While the phrase "hail and farewell" probably comes to mind, it does not match the synonym relationship. After looking at the others, the only synonym is answer B, *greet*. The analogy is now balanced—there is a parallel relationship between words on both sides.

THE MOST COMMON ANALOGY CATEGORIES

Most MAT analogies fall into one of the following categories. Knowing what these categories are and looking for them as you tackle each problem will make your job much easier. Here's the list, with samples of each type:

TIP
Memorize the categories. By knowing what types of relationships to look for, you can switch gears more quickly if your first thought doesn't pan out.

1. Synonyms or similar concepts

   DELIVERANCE : (A. rescue, B. oration, C. liberate, D. demise) :: EXERCISE : PRACTICE

   To solve this problem, note that the relationship between the C and D words is that they are synonyms. So, what you're looking for is a synonym for the A word, *deliverance*. Answer A, *rescue*, fills the bill.

2. Antonyms or contrasting concepts

   (A. hostel, B. hostile, C. amenable, D. amoral) : AMICABLE :: CHASTE : LEWD

   The relationship between *chaste* (pure or decent) and *lewd* (obscene or salacious) is that they are opposites. The opposite of *amicable* is B, *hostile*.

3. Cause and effect

   HEREDITY : ENVIRONMENT :: (A. influenza, B. pneumonia, C. hemophilia, D. roseola) : RUBELLA

   This is an A : C :: B : D relationship. Something present in the environment (a virus) causes rubella. To balance the analogy, look for something that is caused by heredity, which would be C, *hemophilia*.

4. Part to whole

    LEAF : TREE :: KEY : (A. lock, B. door, C. typewriter, D. car)

    It's clear that a leaf is part of a tree. While a key can be used to open a lock, it is not a part of that lock. However, a key is a part of answer C, *typewriter*.

5. Part to part

    FATHER : DAUGHTER :: GILL : (A. fish, B. fin, C. lung, D. wattle)

    Father and *daughter* are each part of a family. *Gill* and B, *fin,* are each part of a fish. While *gill* and *fish* might seem to be a match, they represent a part-to-whole relationship.

6. Purpose or use

    GLOVE : BALL :: HOOK : (A. coat, B. line, C. fish, D. curve)

    A glove catches a ball, and a hook catches answer C, *fish*. Even though a hook could possibly catch or hold a coat, it's not as close to the initial relationship.

7. Action to object

    PITCH : FIRE :: (A. coal, B. ball, C. sound, D. slope) : GUN

    At first glance, this looks like a synonym relationship between *pitch* and *fire*. The answer choices, however, don't complete the match. Instead, this becomes an A : C :: B : D relationship—you fire a gun and pitch a B, *ball*.

8. Object to action

    SPRAIN : (A. ankle, B. joint, C. twist, D. swell) :: BITE : ITCH

    This one can be problematic until you figure out that *sprain* and *bite* are being used as nouns rather than verbs, and that *itch* is a verb. Then, you can use D, the verb *swell,* to complete the relationship of an object causing an action.

9. Place

    PARAGUAY : BOLIVIA :: SWITZERLAND : (A. Afghanistan, B. Poland, C. Hungary, D. Bulgaria)

    Paraguay, Bolivia, and Switzerland are all landlocked countries. Because two of the answer choices, *Afghanistan* and *Hungary,* are also landlocked, you have to narrow the relationship. Paraguay and Bolivia are landlocked countries on the same continent. Only C, *Hungary,* is on the same continent as Switzerland; Afghanistan is in Asia.

10. Association

    MOZART : MUSIC :: PEI : (A. painting, B. architecture, C. sculpture, D. dance)

    The composer Mozart is associated with music in the same way that Pei is associated with B, *architecture*.

11. Sequence or time

    SAIL : STEAM :: PROPELLER : (A. plane, B. engine, C. jet, D. wing)

    Ships were propelled by sail, and then they were propelled by steam. The matching relationship is that planes were propelled by propeller and then by C, a *jet* engine.

NOTE

If you can't find a pair of relationships, change your definition of one or more capitalized words.

12. Characteristic or description

    (A. scream, B. ear, C. shrill, D. vocal) : PIERCING :: CRY : PLAINTIVE

    Just as a cry can be called plaintive, a *scream* can be called piercing. In this analogy, it might help to reverse the order of the pairs, placing *piercing* first, followed by the answer choices, and then by *plaintive* and *cry*. This makes it easier to find the relationship and keeps both sides balanced.

13. Degree

    WARM : HOT :: BRIGHT : (A. dark, B. dim, C. genius, D. illuminate)

    Warm is a lesser degree of temperature than hot. If you think of *bright* as a degree of intelligence rather than of light, then it is a lesser degree of intelligence than C, *genius*. While *illuminate* might be tempting, it doesn't fit the relationship.

14. Measurement

    ODOMETER : (A. speed, B. distance, C. pressure, D. temperature) :: CLOCK : TIME

    There's no surprise here. A clock measures time as an odometer measures B, *distance*.

15. Grammatical

    BROKE : BROKEN :: (A. fled, B. flight, C. flew, D. flung) : FLOWN

    In this case, *broke* and *broken* are the past tense and the past participle of the verb *break*. *Flown* is the past participle of *fly*, and the past tense is C, *flew*. MAT grammar analogies can also present parts of speech and plurals.

16. Mathematical

    $12\frac{1}{2}\%$: (A. $\frac{1}{4}$, B. $\frac{1}{5}$, C. $\frac{1}{8}$, D. $\frac{1}{3}$) :: $16\frac{2}{3}\%$: $\frac{1}{6}$

    Mathematical MAT analogies can deal with geometrical and numerical relationships as well as equalities, which this analogy covers. Percents are really fractions with denominators of 100, so $16\frac{2}{3}\%$ equals $16\frac{2}{3}$ divided by 100, which is $\frac{1}{6}$. The matching relationship is $12\frac{1}{2}\% = 12\frac{1}{2} \div 100 = C, \frac{1}{8}$.

17. Worker to tool

    PHYSICIAN : (A. hospital, B. patient, C. surgeon, D. X-ray) :: ACTUARY : STATISTICS

    An actuary is a worker who uses statistics as a tool to calculate insurance premiums. A physician is a worker who uses an X-ray as a tool to diagnose and treat a patient.

18. Nonsemantic

    Here are two types of nonsemantic analogies to work with.

    HOE : ROE :: THOUGH : (A. rough, B. flood, C. flow, D. how)

    This is an analogy that relies on sound rather than on meaning. The strongest relationship among all the words is that they rhyme. This leads you to C, *flow*, as the best answer.

    EVIL : LIVE :: STEP : (A. stand, B. stop, C. post, D. pest)

    In this analogy, the arrangement and rearrangement of letters in the word create the relationship. *Evil* and *live* have the same letters in different arrangements. By rearranging the letters in *step*, you'll come up with D, *pest*, as the correct choice.

THE MOST COMMON ANALOGY SUBJECT AREAS

MAT analogies are not like the analogies you may have seen on the SAT or the GRE. Those analogies tested your verbal reasoning ability, but MAT analogies go beyond mere vocabulary to test your knowledge of the arts, the humanities, and the natural and social sciences. The terms used in MAT analogies can be drawn from specific college courses or general background knowledge. Because the questions cover so many subjects, there is only a handful of questions in any one area. So, even if you never took chemistry, for example, there will be enough questions in subjects you did study to enable you to do well.

Most MAT analogies are based on one of these subject areas:

General knowledge—Sports terminology; relationships between common words; frequently used abbreviations; parts of buildings; universally accepted concepts, such as the relationship between crime and punishment; common metaphors, proverbs, and sayings

Vocabulary—Words usually not used in ordinary conversation but which would be familiar through education and reading

Literature—Mythology, Shakespeare, ancient and modern drama and poetry, classic and current novels

Music—Musical terms, composers and their works, instruments

Art—Artists and their works, artistic periods

History—Ancient world history, modern world history, United States history, documents, people, historians

Geography—Ancient and modern place names, place characteristics

Sciences—Biology, chemistry, physics, medicine, terminology, concepts, people

Mathematics—Algebra, geometry, calculus, terminology, equivalencies, simple calculations

Grammar—Singular and plural nouns, adjective and adverb endings, tenses, participles

Word study—Spelling, anagrams, homophones, synonyms and antonyms, rhymes, configurations

Philosophy

Psychology

NOTE
Play the odds. If you can eliminate one answer choice when you need to guess, you have a one-in-three chance of guessing correctly. If you can eliminate two choices, you have a 50–50 chance of getting it right.

TRAPS TO AVOID

You can raise your MAT score if you watch out for these common analogy traps:

- Some answers may reverse the sequence of the relationship. Part-to-whole is not the same as whole-to-part. Cause-to-effect is not the same as effect-to-cause. Smaller-to-larger is not the same as larger-to-smaller. Action-to-object is not the same as object-to-action.

CAUTION
Don't let unfamiliar terms bog you down. Remember that on the MAT you get only 30 seconds per question. That's why it's a mistake to let unfamiliar terms stop you. If you don't recognize the terms in the analogy, make your guess and keep going. Save your time for figuring out relationships between terms that you know.

NOTE
Know the analogy equations. Remember that there are two possible analogy equations:
A : B :: C : **D** or
A : C :: B : D.

- Some answers confuse the nature of the relationship. Part-to-part [geometry : calculus] is not the same as part-to-whole [algebra : mathematics]. Cause and effect [fire : smoke] is not the same as association [walk : limp]. Degree [drizzle : downpour] is not the same as antonyms [dry : wet]. Association [walk : limp] is not the same as synonyms [eat : consume].

- Some answers create a grammatical inconsistency. The initial grammatical relationship has to be repeated when the analogy is completed. In the analogy IMPRISONED : LION :: CAGE : PARROT, the relationship is the same on both sides, but the grammatical construction is not the same. In order to be correct, the analogy should read either PRISON : LION :: CAGE : PARROT or IMPRISONED : LION :: CAGED : PARROT. In both examples, the grammatical construction is balanced on both sides of the analogy.

- Some answers focus on the wrong relationship. Given an analogy that begins FEATHERS : BEAK, you might think "bird" instead of "part-to-part relationship." To complete the analogy with *wing* and answer choices that include *bird* and *tail*, you might incorrectly choose bird rather than the best answer, *tail*.

TIP
Note that the directions ask you to choose the *best* answer. That's why you should always read all the answer choices before you make your final selection.

WHAT SMART TEST TAKERS KNOW

MAT questions go from easiest to most difficult. You should, too. Work your way through the earlier, easier questions as quickly as you can. That way, you'll have more time for the later, more difficult questions.

The analogy equation can take two forms. If you can't see a relationship between the first two terms, A and B, try to form a relationship between the first and third terms, A and C. Remember that the analogy equation can be either A is to B as C is to D, *or* A is to C as B is to D.

It's wise to read all the answer choices. Don't choose the first answer you come to that seems right—there may be a better one listed. That's why it always pays to read all the choices before selecting the one that's best.

A word can have more than one meaning. If you can't see a connection between two of the capitalized terms, try to think of another meaning for one of the words. Often, a question is based on a secondary or less common meaning of one of the words. For example, *play* may be a verb meaning "to take part in a game or sport," or it may be a noun meaning "a dramatic production." If one meaning doesn't work, try another.

CAUTION
Time is of the essence. The MAT is a high-speed test. You get only 50 minutes to answer 100 questions. That's 30 seconds per question, so make sure you keep up the pace!

The part of speech of analogy terms is an important clue. In MAT analogies, the correct answer choice will be the same part of speech as the corresponding word in the original pair. In other words, if your original word pair is NOUN : VERB and the third capitalized word is another noun, you know you must look for a verb as the correct answer choice.

Easy questions count just as much as hard ones, so it's in your best interest to answer as many as you can. Don't stop to ponder difficult questions until you've answered every one that's easy for you. Save a little time at the end of the test to go back and rethink any questions you skipped. If you still can't answer a question, remember that there's no penalty for a wrong answer, and take your best guess. If you can eliminate one or more answer choices, you can improve your chances of guessing correctly.

It's smart to keep moving. You have 50 minutes to answer 100 questions—you do the math. Don't spend time dissecting difficult analogies. If the answer doesn't come to you right away, guess, mark the question, and move on. If you think you're running out of time, mark all the remaining questions with the same answer choice—you just might get lucky!

A watch is a must. On the MAT, time is critical. It's much faster for you to glance at your watch (especially if it has a stopwatch function) than to search around the room for a clock.

Summary: What You Must Know About the MAT

- The MAT is a test of mental ability and critical-thinking skills.
- The test consists of 100 questions that you must answer in 50 minutes.
- The questions are arranged in order from easiest to hardest.
- Remember that the analogy equation can take two forms: A : B :: C : D, *or* A : C :: B : D.
- There's no penalty for guessing, so answer every question.
- If you don't know the answer, eliminate obviously wrong choices and make an educated guess.
- These steps will help you solve a MAT analogy:

    1. Find a relationship between two of the capitalized words.
    2. Make up a sentence that expresses the relationship.
    3. Try out your sentence, substituting the third capitalized word and each of the answer choices.
    4. If more than one answer seems to work, go back and make your sentence express a more specific relationship.
    5. Choose the best answer. If none of the choices works exactly, choose the one that works best.

PART 2

15 Analogy Types by Category

CHAPTER 3

CHAPTER 4

PREVIEW

Analogy Tests by Category

Answer Key—Analogy Tests by Category

ANSWER SHEET

ANALOGY TESTS BY CATEGORY

Test 1. Synonyms And Definitions

1. ⓐⓑⓒⓓ   8. ⓐⓑⓒⓓ   15. ⓐⓑⓒⓓ   22. ⓐⓑⓒⓓ
2. ⓐⓑⓒⓓ   9. ⓐⓑⓒⓓ   16. ⓐⓑⓒⓓ   23. ⓐⓑⓒⓓ
3. ⓐⓑⓒⓓ   10. ⓐⓑⓒⓓ 17. ⓐⓑⓒⓓ   24. ⓐⓑⓒⓓ
4. ⓐⓑⓒⓓ   11. ⓐⓑⓒⓓ 18. ⓐⓑⓒⓓ   25. ⓐⓑⓒⓓ
5. ⓐⓑⓒⓓ   12. ⓐⓑⓒⓓ 19. ⓐⓑⓒⓓ   26. ⓐⓑⓒⓓ
6. ⓐⓑⓒⓓ   13. ⓐⓑⓒⓓ 20. ⓐⓑⓒⓓ
7. ⓐⓑⓒⓓ   14. ⓐⓑⓒⓓ 21. ⓐⓑⓒⓓ

Test 2. Antonyms

1. ⓐⓑⓒⓓ   8. ⓐⓑⓒⓓ   15. ⓐⓑⓒⓓ   22. ⓐⓑⓒⓓ
2. ⓐⓑⓒⓓ   9. ⓐⓑⓒⓓ   16. ⓐⓑⓒⓓ   23. ⓐⓑⓒⓓ
3. ⓐⓑⓒⓓ   10. ⓐⓑⓒⓓ 17. ⓐⓑⓒⓓ   24. ⓐⓑⓒⓓ
4. ⓐⓑⓒⓓ   11. ⓐⓑⓒⓓ 18. ⓐⓑⓒⓓ   25. ⓐⓑⓒⓓ
5. ⓐⓑⓒⓓ   12. ⓐⓑⓒⓓ 19. ⓐⓑⓒⓓ   26. ⓐⓑⓒⓓ
6. ⓐⓑⓒⓓ   13. ⓐⓑⓒⓓ 20. ⓐⓑⓒⓓ
7. ⓐⓑⓒⓓ   14. ⓐⓑⓒⓓ 21. ⓐⓑⓒⓓ

Test 3. Cause And Effect

1. ⓐⓑⓒⓓ   8. ⓐⓑⓒⓓ   15. ⓐⓑⓒⓓ   22. ⓐⓑⓒⓓ
2. ⓐⓑⓒⓓ   9. ⓐⓑⓒⓓ   16. ⓐⓑⓒⓓ   23. ⓐⓑⓒⓓ
3. ⓐⓑⓒⓓ   10. ⓐⓑⓒⓓ 17. ⓐⓑⓒⓓ   24. ⓐⓑⓒⓓ
4. ⓐⓑⓒⓓ   11. ⓐⓑⓒⓓ 18. ⓐⓑⓒⓓ   25. ⓐⓑⓒⓓ
5. ⓐⓑⓒⓓ   12. ⓐⓑⓒⓓ 19. ⓐⓑⓒⓓ   26. ⓐⓑⓒⓓ
6. ⓐⓑⓒⓓ   13. ⓐⓑⓒⓓ 20. ⓐⓑⓒⓓ
7. ⓐⓑⓒⓓ   14. ⓐⓑⓒⓓ 21. ⓐⓑⓒⓓ

Test 4. Part to Whole

1. ⓐⓑⓒⓓ   8. ⓐⓑⓒⓓ   15. ⓐⓑⓒⓓ   22. ⓐⓑⓒⓓ
2. ⓐⓑⓒⓓ   9. ⓐⓑⓒⓓ   16. ⓐⓑⓒⓓ   23. ⓐⓑⓒⓓ
3. ⓐⓑⓒⓓ   10. ⓐⓑⓒⓓ 17. ⓐⓑⓒⓓ   24. ⓐⓑⓒⓓ
4. ⓐⓑⓒⓓ   11. ⓐⓑⓒⓓ 18. ⓐⓑⓒⓓ   25. ⓐⓑⓒⓓ
5. ⓐⓑⓒⓓ   12. ⓐⓑⓒⓓ 19. ⓐⓑⓒⓓ   26. ⓐⓑⓒⓓ
6. ⓐⓑⓒⓓ   13. ⓐⓑⓒⓓ 20. ⓐⓑⓒⓓ
7. ⓐⓑⓒⓓ   14. ⓐⓑⓒⓓ 21. ⓐⓑⓒⓓ

TEAR

Test 5. Part to Part

1. ⓐ ⓑ ⓒ ⓓ
2. ⓐ ⓑ ⓒ ⓓ
3. ⓐ ⓑ ⓒ ⓓ
4. ⓐ ⓑ ⓒ ⓓ
5. ⓐ ⓑ ⓒ ⓓ
6. ⓐ ⓑ ⓒ ⓓ
7. ⓐ ⓑ ⓒ ⓓ
8. ⓐ ⓑ ⓒ ⓓ
9. ⓐ ⓑ ⓒ ⓓ
10. ⓐ ⓑ ⓒ ⓓ
11. ⓐ ⓑ ⓒ ⓓ
12. ⓐ ⓑ ⓒ ⓓ
13. ⓐ ⓑ ⓒ ⓓ
14. ⓐ ⓑ ⓒ ⓓ
15. ⓐ ⓑ ⓒ ⓓ
16. ⓐ ⓑ ⓒ ⓓ
17. ⓐ ⓑ ⓒ ⓓ
18. ⓐ ⓑ ⓒ ⓓ
19. ⓐ ⓑ ⓒ ⓓ
20. ⓐ ⓑ ⓒ ⓓ
21. ⓐ ⓑ ⓒ ⓓ
22. ⓐ ⓑ ⓒ ⓓ
23. ⓐ ⓑ ⓒ ⓓ
24. ⓐ ⓑ ⓒ ⓓ
25. ⓐ ⓑ ⓒ ⓓ
26. ⓐ ⓑ ⓒ ⓓ

Test 6. Purpose, Use, or Function

1. ⓐ ⓑ ⓒ ⓓ
2. ⓐ ⓑ ⓒ ⓓ
3. ⓐ ⓑ ⓒ ⓓ
4. ⓐ ⓑ ⓒ ⓓ
5. ⓐ ⓑ ⓒ ⓓ
6. ⓐ ⓑ ⓒ ⓓ
7. ⓐ ⓑ ⓒ ⓓ
8. ⓐ ⓑ ⓒ ⓓ
9. ⓐ ⓑ ⓒ ⓓ
10. ⓐ ⓑ ⓒ ⓓ
11. ⓐ ⓑ ⓒ ⓓ
12. ⓐ ⓑ ⓒ ⓓ
13. ⓐ ⓑ ⓒ ⓓ
14. ⓐ ⓑ ⓒ ⓓ
15. ⓐ ⓑ ⓒ ⓓ
16. ⓐ ⓑ ⓒ ⓓ
17. ⓐ ⓑ ⓒ ⓓ
18. ⓐ ⓑ ⓒ ⓓ
19. ⓐ ⓑ ⓒ ⓓ
20. ⓐ ⓑ ⓒ ⓓ
21. ⓐ ⓑ ⓒ ⓓ
22. ⓐ ⓑ ⓒ ⓓ
23. ⓐ ⓑ ⓒ ⓓ
24. ⓐ ⓑ ⓒ ⓓ
25. ⓐ ⓑ ⓒ ⓓ
26. ⓐ ⓑ ⓒ ⓓ

Test 7. Action to Object

1. ⓐ ⓑ ⓒ ⓓ
2. ⓐ ⓑ ⓒ ⓓ
3. ⓐ ⓑ ⓒ ⓓ
4. ⓐ ⓑ ⓒ ⓓ
5. ⓐ ⓑ ⓒ ⓓ
6. ⓐ ⓑ ⓒ ⓓ
7. ⓐ ⓑ ⓒ ⓓ
8. ⓐ ⓑ ⓒ ⓓ
9. ⓐ ⓑ ⓒ ⓓ
10. ⓐ ⓑ ⓒ ⓓ
11. ⓐ ⓑ ⓒ ⓓ
12. ⓐ ⓑ ⓒ ⓓ
13. ⓐ ⓑ ⓒ ⓓ
14. ⓐ ⓑ ⓒ ⓓ
15. ⓐ ⓑ ⓒ ⓓ
16. ⓐ ⓑ ⓒ ⓓ
17. ⓐ ⓑ ⓒ ⓓ
18. ⓐ ⓑ ⓒ ⓓ
19. ⓐ ⓑ ⓒ ⓓ
20. ⓐ ⓑ ⓒ ⓓ
21. ⓐ ⓑ ⓒ ⓓ
22. ⓐ ⓑ ⓒ ⓓ
23. ⓐ ⓑ ⓒ ⓓ
24. ⓐ ⓑ ⓒ ⓓ
25. ⓐ ⓑ ⓒ ⓓ
26. ⓐ ⓑ ⓒ ⓓ

Test 8. Actor to Object

1. ⓐ ⓑ ⓒ ⓓ
2. ⓐ ⓑ ⓒ ⓓ
3. ⓐ ⓑ ⓒ ⓓ
4. ⓐ ⓑ ⓒ ⓓ
5. ⓐ ⓑ ⓒ ⓓ
6. ⓐ ⓑ ⓒ ⓓ
7. ⓐ ⓑ ⓒ ⓓ
8. ⓐ ⓑ ⓒ ⓓ
9. ⓐ ⓑ ⓒ ⓓ
10. ⓐ ⓑ ⓒ ⓓ
11. ⓐ ⓑ ⓒ ⓓ
12. ⓐ ⓑ ⓒ ⓓ
13. ⓐ ⓑ ⓒ ⓓ
14. ⓐ ⓑ ⓒ ⓓ
15. ⓐ ⓑ ⓒ ⓓ
16. ⓐ ⓑ ⓒ ⓓ
17. ⓐ ⓑ ⓒ ⓓ
18. ⓐ ⓑ ⓒ ⓓ
19. ⓐ ⓑ ⓒ ⓓ
20. ⓐ ⓑ ⓒ ⓓ
21. ⓐ ⓑ ⓒ ⓓ
22. ⓐ ⓑ ⓒ ⓓ
23. ⓐ ⓑ ⓒ ⓓ
24. ⓐ ⓑ ⓒ ⓓ
25. ⓐ ⓑ ⓒ ⓓ
26. ⓐ ⓑ ⓒ ⓓ

TEAR

Test 9. Place

1. ⓐ ⓑ ⓒ ⓓ
2. ⓐ ⓑ ⓒ ⓓ
3. ⓐ ⓑ ⓒ ⓓ
4. ⓐ ⓑ ⓒ ⓓ
5. ⓐ ⓑ ⓒ ⓓ
6. ⓐ ⓑ ⓒ ⓓ
7. ⓐ ⓑ ⓒ ⓓ
8. ⓐ ⓑ ⓒ ⓓ
9. ⓐ ⓑ ⓒ ⓓ
10. ⓐ ⓑ ⓒ ⓓ
11. ⓐ ⓑ ⓒ ⓓ
12. ⓐ ⓑ ⓒ ⓓ
13. ⓐ ⓑ ⓒ ⓓ
14. ⓐ ⓑ ⓒ ⓓ
15. ⓐ ⓑ ⓒ ⓓ
16. ⓐ ⓑ ⓒ ⓓ
17. ⓐ ⓑ ⓒ ⓓ
18. ⓐ ⓑ ⓒ ⓓ
19. ⓐ ⓑ ⓒ ⓓ
20. ⓐ ⓑ ⓒ ⓓ
21. ⓐ ⓑ ⓒ ⓓ
22. ⓐ ⓑ ⓒ ⓓ
23. ⓐ ⓑ ⓒ ⓓ
24. ⓐ ⓑ ⓒ ⓓ
25. ⓐ ⓑ ⓒ ⓓ
26. ⓐ ⓑ ⓒ ⓓ

Test 10. Association

1. ⓐ ⓑ ⓒ ⓓ
2. ⓐ ⓑ ⓒ ⓓ
3. ⓐ ⓑ ⓒ ⓓ
4. ⓐ ⓑ ⓒ ⓓ
5. ⓐ ⓑ ⓒ ⓓ
6. ⓐ ⓑ ⓒ ⓓ
7. ⓐ ⓑ ⓒ ⓓ
8. ⓐ ⓑ ⓒ ⓓ
9. ⓐ ⓑ ⓒ ⓓ
10. ⓐ ⓑ ⓒ ⓓ
11. ⓐ ⓑ ⓒ ⓓ
12. ⓐ ⓑ ⓒ ⓓ
13. ⓐ ⓑ ⓒ ⓓ
14. ⓐ ⓑ ⓒ ⓓ
15. ⓐ ⓑ ⓒ ⓓ
16. ⓐ ⓑ ⓒ ⓓ
17. ⓐ ⓑ ⓒ ⓓ
18. ⓐ ⓑ ⓒ ⓓ
19. ⓐ ⓑ ⓒ ⓓ
20. ⓐ ⓑ ⓒ ⓓ
21. ⓐ ⓑ ⓒ ⓓ
22. ⓐ ⓑ ⓒ ⓓ
23. ⓐ ⓑ ⓒ ⓓ
24. ⓐ ⓑ ⓒ ⓓ
25. ⓐ ⓑ ⓒ ⓓ
26. ⓐ ⓑ ⓒ ⓓ

Test 11. Sequence

1. ⓐ ⓑ ⓒ ⓓ
2. ⓐ ⓑ ⓒ ⓓ
3. ⓐ ⓑ ⓒ ⓓ
4. ⓐ ⓑ ⓒ ⓓ
5. ⓐ ⓑ ⓒ ⓓ
6. ⓐ ⓑ ⓒ ⓓ
7. ⓐ ⓑ ⓒ ⓓ
8. ⓐ ⓑ ⓒ ⓓ
9. ⓐ ⓑ ⓒ ⓓ
10. ⓐ ⓑ ⓒ ⓓ
11. ⓐ ⓑ ⓒ ⓓ
12. ⓐ ⓑ ⓒ ⓓ
13. ⓐ ⓑ ⓒ ⓓ
14. ⓐ ⓑ ⓒ ⓓ
15. ⓐ ⓑ ⓒ ⓓ
16. ⓐ ⓑ ⓒ ⓓ
17. ⓐ ⓑ ⓒ ⓓ
18. ⓐ ⓑ ⓒ ⓓ
19. ⓐ ⓑ ⓒ ⓓ
20. ⓐ ⓑ ⓒ ⓓ
21. ⓐ ⓑ ⓒ ⓓ
22. ⓐ ⓑ ⓒ ⓓ
23. ⓐ ⓑ ⓒ ⓓ
24. ⓐ ⓑ ⓒ ⓓ
25. ⓐ ⓑ ⓒ ⓓ
26. ⓐ ⓑ ⓒ ⓓ

Test 12. Characteristic

1. ⓐ ⓑ ⓒ ⓓ
2. ⓐ ⓑ ⓒ ⓓ
3. ⓐ ⓑ ⓒ ⓓ
4. ⓐ ⓑ ⓒ ⓓ
5. ⓐ ⓑ ⓒ ⓓ
6. ⓐ ⓑ ⓒ ⓓ
7. ⓐ ⓑ ⓒ ⓓ
8. ⓐ ⓑ ⓒ ⓓ
9. ⓐ ⓑ ⓒ ⓓ
10. ⓐ ⓑ ⓒ ⓓ
11. ⓐ ⓑ ⓒ ⓓ
12. ⓐ ⓑ ⓒ ⓓ
13. ⓐ ⓑ ⓒ ⓓ
14. ⓐ ⓑ ⓒ ⓓ
15. ⓐ ⓑ ⓒ ⓓ
16. ⓐ ⓑ ⓒ ⓓ
17. ⓐ ⓑ ⓒ ⓓ
18. ⓐ ⓑ ⓒ ⓓ
19. ⓐ ⓑ ⓒ ⓓ
20. ⓐ ⓑ ⓒ ⓓ
21. ⓐ ⓑ ⓒ ⓓ
22. ⓐ ⓑ ⓒ ⓓ
23. ⓐ ⓑ ⓒ ⓓ
24. ⓐ ⓑ ⓒ ⓓ
25. ⓐ ⓑ ⓒ ⓓ
26. ⓐ ⓑ ⓒ ⓓ

TEAR

Test 13. Degree

1. ⓐⓑⓒⓓ   8. ⓐⓑⓒⓓ   15. ⓐⓑⓒⓓ   22. ⓐⓑⓒⓓ
2. ⓐⓑⓒⓓ   9. ⓐⓑⓒⓓ   16. ⓐⓑⓒⓓ   23. ⓐⓑⓒⓓ
3. ⓐⓑⓒⓓ   10. ⓐⓑⓒⓓ   17. ⓐⓑⓒⓓ   24. ⓐⓑⓒⓓ
4. ⓐⓑⓒⓓ   11. ⓐⓑⓒⓓ   18. ⓐⓑⓒⓓ   25. ⓐⓑⓒⓓ
5. ⓐⓑⓒⓓ   12. ⓐⓑⓒⓓ   19. ⓐⓑⓒⓓ   26. ⓐⓑⓒⓓ
6. ⓐⓑⓒⓓ   13. ⓐⓑⓒⓓ   20. ⓐⓑⓒⓓ
7. ⓐⓑⓒⓓ   14. ⓐⓑⓒⓓ   21. ⓐⓑⓒⓓ

Test 14. Grammatical

1. ⓐⓑⓒⓓ   8. ⓐⓑⓒⓓ   15. ⓐⓑⓒⓓ   22. ⓐⓑⓒⓓ
2. ⓐⓑⓒⓓ   9. ⓐⓑⓒⓓ   16. ⓐⓑⓒⓓ   23. ⓐⓑⓒⓓ
3. ⓐⓑⓒⓓ   10. ⓐⓑⓒⓓ   17. ⓐⓑⓒⓓ   24. ⓐⓑⓒⓓ
4. ⓐⓑⓒⓓ   11. ⓐⓑⓒⓓ   18. ⓐⓑⓒⓓ   25. ⓐⓑⓒⓓ
5. ⓐⓑⓒⓓ   12. ⓐⓑⓒⓓ   19. ⓐⓑⓒⓓ   26. ⓐⓑⓒⓓ
6. ⓐⓑⓒⓓ   13. ⓐⓑⓒⓓ   20. ⓐⓑⓒⓓ
7. ⓐⓑⓒⓓ   14. ⓐⓑⓒⓓ   21. ⓐⓑⓒⓓ

Test 15. Miscellaneous

1. ⓐⓑⓒⓓ   8. ⓐⓑⓒⓓ   15. ⓐⓑⓒⓓ   22. ⓐⓑⓒⓓ
2. ⓐⓑⓒⓓ   9. ⓐⓑⓒⓓ   16. ⓐⓑⓒⓓ   23. ⓐⓑⓒⓓ
3. ⓐⓑⓒⓓ   10. ⓐⓑⓒⓓ   17. ⓐⓑⓒⓓ   24. ⓐⓑⓒⓓ
4. ⓐⓑⓒⓓ   11. ⓐⓑⓒⓓ   18. ⓐⓑⓒⓓ   25. ⓐⓑⓒⓓ
5. ⓐⓑⓒⓓ   12. ⓐⓑⓒⓓ   19. ⓐⓑⓒⓓ   26. ⓐⓑⓒⓓ
6. ⓐⓑⓒⓓ   13. ⓐⓑⓒⓓ   20. ⓐⓑⓒⓓ
7. ⓐⓑⓒⓓ   14. ⓐⓑⓒⓓ   21. ⓐⓑⓒⓓ

TEAR

Chapter 3

Analogy Tests by Category

Start your preparation for the MAT by taking each of the tests that follow. These tests provide intensive practice with the category technique for solving analogy problems. Each test consists of 26 questions that are indicative of the range of possibilities within a given category. The 13-minute time limit for each test simulates the pace of the MAT, a pace that requires quick decisions and allows for no dawdling over elusive relationships.

The fifteen short practice tests by category have been divided into three groups. The categories in Group A are the most frequently used, and Group C categories are the least often seen. Each 26-question test is discrete in itself. You need not answer the 15 tests in any order, nor must you complete one group before going on to another. Just be sure to do each 26-question test in the 13 minutes allowed.

When you have completed these tests, check your answers with the correct answers in the next chapter. Read through all the explanations. If you are not satisfied with your performance on the practice tests, try them again. When your scores show that you have a good grasp of the analogy question, move on to tackle the seven full-length sample exams that follow.

The sample exams contain a mixture of analogy problems very much like the mixture on the actual MAT. In addition to correct answers, explanations are provided after each exam to show you where and how you might have gone astray in answering each question. Take time to read these explanations because they could help keep you from making some of the more common errors on your exam.

ROAD MAP

- *Group A: Tests 1-5*
- *Group B: Tests 6-10*
- *Group C: Tests 11-15*

GROUP A: TESTS 1–5

TEST 1: SYNONYMS AND DEFINITIONS

26 Questions • 13 Minutes

CAUTION

Don't skip this section! You might wonder why you should bother with the analogy questions when the nature of the relationship is given. By knowing what the relationship must be, however, you can concentrate on choosing words that fit into the proper relationship.

TIP

Be flexible. If you can't find a synonym for the third word, try to redefine it using another part of speech.

Directions: Each of these test questions consists of three capitalized words and four lettered words enclosed in parentheses. Two of the capitalized words are related in some way. Find the two related words, and establish the nature of the relationship. Then study the four words lettered A, B, C, and D. Select the one lettered word that is related to the remaining capitalized word in the same way that the first two capitalized words are related. Mark the answer sheet for the letter preceding the word you select.

1. DILIGENT : UNREMITTING :: DIAMETRIC : (A. pretentious, B. geographical, C. adamant, D. opposite)

2. FRAUDULENT : (A. deceitful, B. slander, C. incorrigible, D. plausible) :: REMUNERATIVE : PROFITABLE

3. EXTORT : WREST :: CONSPIRE : (A. entice, B. plot, C. deduce, D. respire)

4. DOWAGER : WIDOW :: (A. enemy, B. constable, C. consort, D. distaff) : COMPANION

5. GAUDY : OSTENTATIOUS :: DEJECTED : (A. oppressed, B. informed, C. rejected, D. depressed)

6. (A. intermediate, B. feminine, C. alto, D. high) : SOPRANO :: LOW : BASS

7. LUXURY : EXTRAVAGANCE :: (A. penury, B. misery, C. poorhouse, D. hunger) : POVERTY

8. CUNNING : SLY :: INEPT : (A. incompetent, B. artistic, C. tricky, D. insatiable)

9. REGALE : (A. endure, B. remain, C. entertain, D. cohere) :: REGISTER : ENROLL

10. BEGIN : (A. murky, B. seasonal, C. equinoctial, D. nightly) :: ESTABLISH : NOCTURNAL

11. STREW : STRAY :: DISPERSE : (A. deviate, B. utter, C. dredge, D. relegate)

12. VERTICAL : (A. circular, B. plumb, C. horizontal, D. inclined) :: PROSTRATE : FLAT

13. (A. indigenous, B. barbaric, C. foreign, D. godly) : NATIVE :: REMOTE : DISTANT

14. BLAST : GUST :: BLARE : (A. uncover, B. roar, C. blaze, D. icicle)

15. (A. slavery, B. wrong, C. disengage, D. end) : DAILY :: ABOLISH : DIURNAL

16. BEGINNING : INCIPIENT :: (A. irrelevant, B. corresponding, C. reflexive, D. congregated) : CONGRUENT

17. SUFFICIENT : INTRODUCTION :: ENOUGH : (A. salute, B. lecturer, C. conclusion, D. prologue)

18. DIN : NOISE :: CONTORTION : (A. disease, B. twisting, C. exploitation, D. contingency)

19. RESTRAINT : CONTINENCE :: (A. fissure, B. glacier, C. depth, D. mountain) : RIFT

20. REFINED : URBANE :: EQUITABLE : (A. equine, B. just, C. recurrent, D. ambiguous)

21. FINIAL : PEDIMENT :: PINNACLE : (A. basement, B. lineage, C. gable, D. obstruction)

22. HISTORY : (A. fact, B. war, C. peace, D. geography) :: FABLE : FICTION

23. JABBER : GIBBERISH :: QUIDNUNC : (A. quisling, B. busybody, C. theorist, D. testator)

24. DIAPASON : (A. diaphragm, B. clef, C. chord, D. organ) :: KEYNOTE : TONIC

25. PALLID : BLANCHED :: (A. form, B. sum, C. purpose, D. begin) : INSTITUTE

26. CREPUSCULAR : CURSORY :: DIM : (A. profane, B. egregious, C. superficial, D. unique)

TEST 2: ANTONYMS

26 Questions • 13 Minutes

Directions: Each of these test questions consists of three capitalized words and four lettered words enclosed in parentheses. Two of the capitalized words are related in some way. Find the two related words, and establish the nature of the relationship. Then study the four words lettered A, B, C, and D. Select the one lettered word that is related to the remaining capitalized word in the same way that the first two capitalized words are related. Mark the answer sheet for the letter preceding the word you select.

1. SUNDER : CONSOLIDATE :: TANGIBLE : (A. abstract, B. tasty, C. possible, D. tangled)

2. ACCORD : BREACH :: CONNECTION : (A. tie, B. dissociation, C. association, D. distrust)

3. BIRTH : JEER :: DEATH : (A. oblivion, B. drink, C. cheer, D. discussion)

4. GENEROSITY : TOLERANCE :: PARSIMONY : (A. advocacy, B. totality, C. urgency, D. bigotry)

5. (A. elongated, B. useless, C. everlasting, D. heavenly) : DERISION :: EPHEMERAL : APPROBATION

6. (A. clumsy, B. clandestine, C. graceful, D. lugubrious) : GAUCHE :: WEALTHY : INDIGENT

7. MATURE : COUNTERFEIT :: (A. spotted, B. rotten, C. unripe, D. grown) : REAL

8. MANIFEST : (A. latent, B. destiny, C. obvious, D. manipulated) :: INQUISITIVE : INCURIOUS

9. IDIOT : GENIUS :: VALLEY : (A. plateau, B. moron, C. mountain, D. field)

10. MISCELLANEOUS : PERMANENT :: (A. motley, B. undetermined, C. righteous, D. single) : TEMPORARY

11. IMPROMPTU : (A. ad lib, B. memorized, C. verbose, D. prolific) :: SPONTANEOUS : CALCULATED

CAUTION
Stay alert. Antonyms are opposites. Do not choose a synonym.

12. MEDLEY : (A. victory, B. enjoyment, C. criticize, D. succeed) :: ONE : PRAISE

13. WHITE : VALOR :: (A. color, B. dim, C. pigment, D. black) : COWARDICE

14. HYPOCRISY : HONESTY :: HOSTILITY : (A. war, B. amity, C. enmity, D. hostage)

15. PLETHORA : CUNNING :: DEARTH : (A. dull, B. earthy, C. foxy, D. cute)

16. PERTINENT : (A. pert, B. cloudy, C. irrelevant, D. perceptive) :: INCLEMENT : CLEAR

17. BOMBASTIC : (A. stringent, B. medicinal, C. fishy, D. filthy) :: PLAINSPOKEN : LAX

18. (A. pursue, B. abstain, C. hunt, D. find) : INDULGE :: AVOID : SEEK

19. DISHONESTY : OBVIOUS :: INTEGRITY : (A. oblong, B. invidious, C. surreptitious, D. honest)

20. REVERE : (A. composed, B. reprehensible, C. completed, D. inscrutable) :: BLASPHEME : COMPREHENSIBLE

21. IMMATURITY : (A. anger, B. childhood, C. adulthood, D. incompatibility) :: COMPETITION : MONOPOLY

22. REPUGN : COMPROMISE :: RESCIND : (A. refuse, B. rest. C. decipher, D. validate)

23. DEGRADE : MARTIAL :: LAUD : (A. military, B. noisy, C. worried, D. halcyon)

24. SCARCE : WARLIKE :: (A. fear, B. hardly, C. few, D. abundant) : PEACEFUL

25. INTIMIDATE : ENCOURAGE :: (A. interdict, B. comply, C. expect, D. continue) : ALLOW

26. COSTLY : TRIUMPHANT :: CHEAP : (A. vanquished, B. tinny, C. difficult, D. puny)

TEST 3: CAUSE AND EFFECT

26 Questions • 13 Minutes

Directions: Each of these test questions consists of three capitalized words and four lettered words enclosed in parentheses. Two of the capitalized words are related in some way. Find the two related words, and establish the nature of the relationship. Then study the four words lettered A, B, C, and D. Select the one lettered word that is related to the remaining capitalized word in the same way that the first two capitalized words are related. Mark the answer sheet for the letter preceding the word you select.

NOTE
Shift gears. It is often easier to recognize a cause-and-effect relationship by reversing the order of the terms.

1. CURIOSITY : ENLIGHTENMENT :: VERACITY : (A. credulousness, B. credibility, C. validity, D. cognizance)

2. PERSISTENCE : (A. adversity, B. antagonism, C. attainment, D. lassitude) :: MONOTONY : BOREDOM

3. SATISFACTION : GOOD DEED :: IMPROVEMENT : (A. sin, B. criticism, C. diligence, D. kindness)

4. (A. yolk, B. crack, C. bird, D. shell) : EGG :: PLANT : SEED

5. CARE : (A. avoidance, B. accident, C. fruition, D. safety) :: ASSIDUITY : SUCCESS

6. GRAPE : (A. vintage, B. vine, C. wine, D. fruit) :: WHEAT : FLOUR

7. WAR : GRIEF :: (A. joy, B. peace, C. soldier, D. finish) : HAPPINESS

8. SUN : LIGHT :: ECLIPSE : (A. violence, B. darkness, C. cruelty, D. whistling)

9. WATER : (A. sky, B. rain, C. lake, D. H_2O) :: HEAT : FIRE

10. SCAR : WOUND :: (A. damage, B. case, C. car, D. murder) : ACCIDENT

11. HEALTH : DISEASE :: SANITATION : (A. filth, B. measles, C. indifference, D. illness)

12. COLD : (A. water, B. ice, C. gas, D. crystals) :: HEAT : STEAM

13. LAZINESS : STRATEGY :: FAILURE : (A. mentality, B. brutality, C. company, D. victory)

14. (A. starvation, B. indigestion, C. energy, D. life) : FOOD :: SUFFOCATION : AIR

15. RESPONSE : (A. answer, B. stimulus, C. correct, D. effect) :: PREDICAMENT : CARELESSNESS

16. PAIN : (A. punishment, B. crime, C. defiance, D. distress) :: FALL : DISOBEDIENCE

17. FAITH : DESPERATION :: PRAYER : (A. blasphemy, B. crime, C. salvation, D. insularity)

18. FANATICISM : (A. infirmity, B. criticism, C. intolerance, D. restlessness) :: BIGOTRY : HATRED

19. CONVICTION : (A. revenge, B. contrition, C. justice, D. vindication) :: GUILT : INNOCENCE

20. LIQUOR : ALCOHOLISM :: FOOD : (A. confectionery, B. blemish, C. obesity, D. overindulgence)

21. TAXATION : (A. rebellion, B. slavery, C. prohibition, D. cotton) :: REVOLUTION : CIVIL WAR

22. FIRE : SMOKE :: PROFLIGACY : (A. debt, B. prodigality, C. profit, D. deceit)

23. WORK : (A. employment, B. entertainment, C. office, D. income) :: FOOD : GROWTH

24. ERROR : (A. recklessness, B. caution, C. indifference, D. accident) :: INEXPERIENCE : CARELESSNESS

25. OPPRESSION : PRISON :: (A. democracy, B. tyranny, C. economy, D. disrespect) : CRIME

26. FLAME : BURN :: INSULT : (A. inanity, B. anger, C. reparation, D. approbation)

TEST 4: PART TO WHOLE

26 Questions • 13 Minutes

Directions: Each of these test questions consists of three capitalized words and four lettered words enclosed in parentheses. Two of the capitalized words are related in some way. Find the two related words, and establish the nature of the relationship. Then study the four words lettered A, B, C, and D. Select the one lettered word that is related to the remaining capitalized word in the same way that the first two capitalized words are related. Mark the answer sheet for the letter preceding the word you select.

CAUTION
Don't switch directions midstream. The relationship must be in the same direction on both sides of the analogy. Beware of shifting from part : whole to whole : part.

1. VERSAILLES : PALACE :: BASTILLE : (A. parkway, B. Paris, C. prison, D. France)

2. PLAY : PROLOGUE :: CONSTITUTION : (A. preamble, B. laws, C. article, D. amendment)

3. SENTENCE : (A. structure, B. word, C. composition, D. correctness) :: PARAGRAPH : SENTENCE

4. BEAD : (A. ball, B. iron, C. link, D. strength) :: NECKLACE : CHAIN

5. PEACH : PIT :: (A. planet, B. moon, C. orbit, D. solar system) : SUN

6. SLICE : LOAF :: ISLAND : (A. land, B. archipelago, C. peninsula, D. ocean)

7. PEAK : (A. water, B. storm, C. crest, D. ocean) :: MOUNTAIN : WAVE

8. (A. carpenter, B. market, C. roast, D. cowboy) : MEAT :: RANCH : STEER

9. INGREDIENT : COLOR :: RECIPE : (A. black, B. spectrum, C. composition, D. age)

10. (A. crystallization, B. mine, C. foliage, D. forest) : QUARRY :: WOOD : STONE

11. GRANITE : MARBLE :: (A. hardness, B. polish, C. quartz, D. fragility) : LIMESTONE

12. STEEL : ALLOY :: IRON : (A. compound, B. element, C. alloy, D. mixture)

13. MAN : (A. wound, B. woman, C. fist, D. shield) :: BEE : STINGER

14. PART : (A. United States, B. Lake Erie, C. Ontario, D. North America) :: WHOLE : CANADA

15. CADET : WEST POINT :: (A. sergeant, B. plebe, C. ensign, D. Navy) : ANNAPOLIS

Analogy Tests by Category   31

16. BOOK : HOTEL :: PREFACE : (A. room, B. guest, C. manager, D. lobby)

17. ORCHESTRA : CONDUCTOR :: (A. speaker, B. orator, C. assembly, D. speech) : CHAIRMAN

18. POETRY : SONNET :: (A. symphony, B. song, C. music, D. etude) : CONCERTO

19. (A. coat, B. rabbit, C. warm, D. women) : FLOWER :: FUR : PETAL

20. CHEMISTRY : ELEMENTS :: GRAMMAR : (A. teacher, B. English, C. subject, D. parts of speech)

21. PINE : (A. Christmas, B. tree, C. fir, D. loss) :: POINSETTIA : FLOWER

22. CARROT : COW :: PLANT : (A. meat, B. herd, C. animal, D. stockyard)

23. CORPORATION : (A. mayor, B. state, C. nation, D. government) :: PRESIDENT : GOVERNOR

24. (A. face, B. eye, C. head, D. brain) : TEAM :: EAR : PLAYER

25. CLARINET : WOODWIND :: TROMBONE (A. musician, B. percussion, C. brass, D. copper)

26. WHEAT : (A. bushel, B. chaff, C. stalk, D. bread) :: WINE : DREGS

TEST 5: PART TO PART

26 Questions • 13 Minutes

Directions: Each of these test questions consists of three capitalized words and four lettered words enclosed in parentheses. Two of the capitalized words are related in some way. Find the two related words, and establish the nature of the relationship. Then study the four words lettered A, B, C, and D. Select the one lettered word that is related to the remaining capitalized word in the same way that the first two capitalized words are related. Mark the answer sheet for the letter preceding the word you select.

1. NEPHEW : NIECE :: UNCLE : (A. man, B. relative, C. father, D. aunt)

2. HAND : ELBOW :: FOOT : (A. muscle, B. knee, C. leg, D. toe)

3. SNEAKER : SHOE :: (A. hand, B. foot, C. mitten, D. boot) : GLOVE

4. CONTRALTO : (A. opera, B. soprano, C. woman, D. song) :: BARITONE : TENOR

5. CARDINAL : (A. St. Bernard, B. calico, C. redbreast, D. duck) :: BLUE JAY : SPANIEL

CAUTION
Keep your eye on the relationship. Part to part is *not* the same as part to whole. Don't be led astray by meanings instead of relationships.

6. HEART : LUNGS :: BRAIN : (A. appendix, B. intelligence, C. liver, D. breathing)

7. LAWNMOWER : MOP :: (A. fertilizer, B. rake, C. gardener, D. grass) : BUCKET

8. HIGH JUMP : LONG JUMP :: HOCKEY : (A. bowling, B. surfing, C. soccer, D. tennis)

9. PEN : (A. ink, B. paper, C. point, D. chalk) :: PAPER : BOARD

10. NICOTINE : MILK :: (A. alcohol, B. cigarettes, C. cancer, D. tobacco) : ORANGE JUICE

11. PERCH : TROUT :: PUPPY : (A. Great Dane, B. wolf, C. dog, D. kitten)

12. CARROT : LETTUCE :: POTATO : (A. grape, B. cabbage, C. radish, D. onion)

13. FORWARD : (A. batter, B. referee, C. goaltender, D. quarterback) :: GUARD : PUNTER

14. (A. box, B. Egypt, C. pentagon, D. triangle) : SQUARE :: PYRAMID : CUBE

15. GOOSE : GANDER :: (A. cow, B. hog, C. pig, D. lamb) : BULL

16. SENEGAL : TUNISIA :: (A. Brazil, B. Bolivia, C. Suriname, D. Guyana) : COLOMBIA

17. FOOT : (A. pound, B. degree, C. kilometer, D. ampere) :: INCH : CENTIMETER

18. OPHELIA : HAMLET :: PORTIA : (A. Shylock, B. Macbeth, C. Iago, D. Henry VIII)

19. (A. cob, B. corn, C. swan, D. bitch) : DOE :: COCK : EWE

20. CLAM : OYSTER :: COW : (A. pig, B. sheep, C. dog, D. squirrel)

21. AIRPLANE : (A. kite, B. ship, C. bird, D. helicopter) :: BUS : TRAIN

22. GELDING : CAPON :: (A. stallion, B. waterfowl, C. steer, D. mongrel) : EUNUCH

23. EYE : SHIRT :: EAR : (A. button, B. pants, C. cotton, D. clothing)

24. FINGER : PALM :: (A. shoe, B. foot, C. sole, D. limb) : HEEL

25. (A. car, B. bicycle, C. bumper, D. night) : SEAM :: HEADLIGHT : BUTTON

26. WING : BEAK :: PAW : (A. tail, B. foot, C. cat, D. dog)

GROUP B: TESTS 6–10

TEST 6: PURPOSE, USE, OR FUNCTION

26 Questions • 13 Minutes

> **Directions:** Each of these test questions consists of three capitalized words and four lettered words enclosed in parentheses. Two of the capitalized words are related in some way. Find the two related words, and establish the nature of the relationship. Then study the four words lettered A, B, C, and D. Select the one lettered word that is related to the remaining capitalized word in the same way that the first two capitalized words are related. Mark the answer sheet for the letter preceding the word you select.

1. HORSE : HITCHING POST :: CRAFT : (A. parapet, B. moorage, C. running, D. vessel)

2. BALL : BAT :: SHUTTLECOCK : (A. battledore, B. badminton, C. plumage, D. game)

3. WIRELESS : (A. message, B. speed, C. transoceanic, D. communication) :: AIRPLANE : TRANSPORTATION

4. CALF : GOOSE :: SHOE : (A. gander, B. pillow, C. roast, D. feathers)

5. (A. wood, B. chair, C. house, D. cloth) : CURTAIN :: TABLE : WINDOW

6. EXERCISE : (A. action, B. drama, C. stage, D. performance) :: GYMNASIUM : THEATER

7. CRATER : VOLCANO :: CHIMNEY : (A. fire, B. house, C. flue, D. smoke)

8. SIPHON : (A. shovel, B. pipette, C. sponge, D. spoon) :: GASOLINE : COAL

9. ARCHAEOLOGIST : ANTIQUITY :: ICHTHYOLOGIST : (A. theology, B. marine life, C. horticulture, D. mysticism)

10. SCOPE : (A. tele, B. enlarge, C. see, D. range) :: METER : MEASURE

11. (A. leather, B. cow, C. animal, D. farm) : BEEF :: PIG : PORK

12. PRINT : PRESS :: (A. efface, B. board, C. chalk, D. rubber) : ERASER

13. AGAR : (A. jelly, B. skin, C. culture, D. medium) :: BREAD : MOLD

14. MENU : MEAL :: MAP : (A. road, B. survey, C. trip, D. scale)

15. HEW : AX :: (A. punch, B. tack, C. clear, D. auger) : AWL

TIP
Ask yourself questions. One question to ask is, "What is the purpose or use for this item?"

16. CONE : PINE :: ACORN : (A. nut, B. squirrel, C. tree, D. oak)

17. GUN : HOLSTER :: SWORD : (A. pistol, B. scabbard, C. warrior, D. slay)

18. PORTER : LETTER CARRIER :: (A. beer, B. baggage, C. steak, D. complicated) : MAIL

19. BANDAGE : ROOF :: WOUND : (A. house, B. shingle, C. window, D. top)

20. (A. tobacco, B. fire, C. flame, D. flue) : SIPHON :: SMOKE : LIQUID

21. MAN : BREAD :: HORSE : (A. stable, B. duck, C. barn, D. hay)

22. HANG : (A. gallows, B. nail, C. murderer, D. picture) :: BEHEAD : GUILLOTINE

23. BARREL : SILO :: WINE : (A. horses, B. toss, C. grain, D. refuse)

24. HAIR : (A. grass, B. fish, C. scales, D. orangutan) :: FEATHER : OSTRICH

25. (A. steel, B. head, C. combat, D. football) : FACE :: HELMET : MASK

26. WING : BIRD :: (A. gill, B. tail, C. fin, D. scales) : FISH

TEST 7: ACTION TO OBJECT

26 Questions • 13 Minutes

Directions: Each of these test questions consists of three capitalized words and four lettered words enclosed in parentheses. Two of the capitalized words are related in some way. Find the two related words, and establish the nature of the relationship. Then study the four words lettered A, B, C, and D. Select the one lettered word that is related to the remaining capitalized word in the same way that the first two capitalized words are related. Mark the answer sheet for the letter preceding the word you select.

TIP
Don't give up. If one sentence doesn't work, try another.

1. HEAR : SOUND :: SEE : (A. move, B. taste, C. picture, D. artistry)

2. MOP : VACUUM :: FLOOR : (A. sweep, B. carpet, C. kitchen, D. cleanse)

3. BANANA : (A. sea, B. fish, C. sand, D. oyster) :: PEEL : SHUCK

4. (A. book, B. remodeling, C. correction, D. content) : REVISION :: GARMENT : ALTERATION

5. SCENE : VIEW :: (A. taste, B. concert, C. odor, D. color) : HEAR

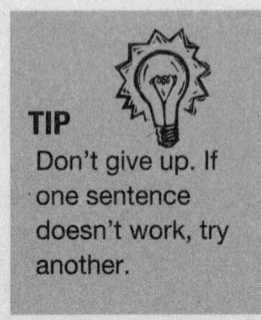

Analogy Tests by Category

6. STUDY : TRY :: LEARN : (A. begin, B. attempt, C. tail, D. succeed)

7. DREDGE : SCOOP :: SILT : (A. ladle, B. ice cream, C. shovel, D. newspaper)

8. (A. store, B. coat, C. wool, D. sheep) : BREAD :: WEAR : EAT

9. HONE : WHET :: (A. hunger, B. knife, C. meat, D. fork) : APPETITE

10. PRESIDE : (A. court, B. jury, C. judge, D. subject) :: REIGN : KING

11. OVERLOOK : MISTAKE :: ADVOCATE : (A. recommend, B. cause, C. consideration, D. error)

12. ASSUAGE : (A. appease, B. reassure, C. fear, D. joy) :: PROFESS : LOVE

13. KNOWLEDGE : (A. culture, B. erudition, C. deception, D. debt) :: ASSIMILATE : ASSUME

14. THWART : ASPIRATIONS :: STIFLE : (A. heat, B. air, C. anger, D. sense)

15. (A. reject, B. contend, C. love, D. reply) : HATE :: FRIEND : ENEMY

16. CHECK : FORGERY :: COPYRIGHT : (A. bank, B. infringement, C. book, D. author)

17. DECAY : (A. dampness, B. rust, C. steel, D. ore) :: WOOD : IRON

18. (A. college, B. research, C. library, D. paper) : THESIS :: ANALYSIS : DIAGNOSIS

19. SHIP : ARMY :: MUTINY : (A. court-martial, B. desertion, C. officer, D. navy)

20. IRRIGATION : (A. oxygen, B. respiration, C. ventilation, D. atmosphere) :: WATER : AIR

21. (A. wardrobes, B. tears, C. silverware, D. fall) : CLOTHING :: BREAK : DISHES

22. TONE : HEARING :: COLOR : (A. pigment, B. sight, C. melody, D. picture)

23. GRIND : (A. wear, B. tear, C. see, D. darn) :: KNIFE : STOCKING

24. PLAY : REHEARSE :: GAME : (A. football, B. practice, C. coach, D. players)

25. (A. buying, B. cheating, C. bravery, D. praying) : SELLING :: FAME : PROFIT

26. MARBLE : (A. palace, B. engraving, C. agate, D. quarry) :: SALT : MINE

TEST 8: ACTOR TO OBJECT

26 Questions • 13 Minutes

Directions: Each of these test questions consists of three capitalized words and four lettered words enclosed in parentheses. Two of the capitalized words are related in some way. Find the two related words, and establish the nature of the relationship. Then study the four words lettered A, B, C, and D. Select the one lettered word that is related to the remaining capitalized word in the same way that the first two capitalized words are related. Mark the answer sheet for the letter preceding the word you select.

NOTE
The question you must ask is, "What does this person or thing do?"

1. SALESMAN : PRODUCT :: TEACHER : (A. principal, B. English, C. pupils, D. subject)

2. EARTH : (A. Mars, B. moon, C. sky, D. sun) :: MOON : EARTH

3. TEACHER : (A. parent, B. dolly, C. youngster, D. obey) :: PUPIL : CHILD

4. BARK : ROAR :: DOG : (A. lion, B. snake, C. lamb, D. train)

5. (A. vocalist, B. singing, C. chorus, D. music) : ACTRESS :: SING : ACT

6. COACH : PLAYER :: COUNSELOR : (A. tutor, B. supervisor, C. leader, D. student)

7. MUSIC : (A. typewriter, B. book, C. piano, D. character) :: COMPOSER : AUTHOR

8. WITHER : BLOOM :: PASS : (A. time, B. study, C. fail, D. excuse)

9. CONSTITUTION : MISTAKE :: (A. preamble, B. amendment, C. law, D. unconstitutional) : ERASER

10. DOCTOR : (A. operation, B. disease, C. poverty, D. therapy) :: PSYCHIATRIST : DISORDER

11. POLISH : MANICURIST :: TRIM : (A. barber, B. ship, C. buff, D. nail)

12. COMMAND : OBEY :: (A. performance, B. parents, C. armor, D. result) : CHILDREN

13. WOODSMAN : (A. cut, B. hew, C. plumber, D. cobbler) :: AX : AWL

14. (A. fish, B. pool, C. pier, D. boat) : MAN :: SWIMS : WALKS

15. SCALPEL : SURGEON :: (A. mallet, B. cleaver, C. chisel, D. wrench) : BUTCHER

16. HEAL : LEND :: PHYSICIAN : (A. money, B. banker, C. give, D. bank)

17. MAN : (A. ditty, B. bird, C. communication, D. tune) :: SPEECH : SONG

18. (A. house, B. wall, C. lodge, D. trowel) : MASON :: SAW : CARPENTER

19. TAILOR : PATTERN :: ARCHITECT : (A. house, B. drawing board, C. plan, D. artist)

20. SEED : EGG :: (A. sow, B. pollinate, C. germinate, D. plant) : HATCH

21. VIBRATION : TONE :: REFRACTION : (A. light, B. noise, C. rays, D. color)

22. REFEREE : RULES :: CONSCIENCE : (A. thought, B. regulations, C. morals, D. Freud)

23. FORMALDEHYDE : FREON :: (A. insulation, B. preservation, C. levitation, D. aggravation) : REFRIGERATION

24. CELL : (A. mitosis, B. organism, C. phone, D. prisoner) :: CORRAL : LIVESTOCK

25. MUTE : CUSHION :: HORN : (A. chair, B. padding, C. soften, D. pillow)

26. WATER : (A. wet, B. ink, C. water, D. fuel) :: CORK : OIL

TEST 9: PLACE

26 Questions • 13 Minutes

Directions: Each of these test questions consists of three capitalized words and four lettered words enclosed in parentheses. Two of the capitalized words are related in some way. Find the two related words, and establish the nature of the relationship. Then study the four words lettered A, B, C, and D. Select the one lettered word that is related to the remaining capitalized word in the same way that the first two capitalized words are related. Mark the answer sheet for the letter preceding the word you select.

1. THIMBLE : FINGER :: SOCK : (A. band, B. felt, C. hat rack, D. foot)

2. KING : PEASANT :: (A. queen, B. royalty, C. serf, D. palace) : HOVEL

3. BODY : (A. arteries, B. hands, C. brain, D. muscles) :: COUNTRY : RAILROADS

4. BANK : (A. intelligence, B. blackboard, C. books, D. riches) :: MONEY : KNOWLEDGE

5. RACE : TRACK :: SWIM : (A. stroke, B. breathe, C. meet, D. pool)

NOTE
Think before you choose. It's easy to lose sight of the relationship in analogies based on place or location.

6. LAND : (A. captain, B. ravage, C. bounty, D. sea) :: GENERAL : ADMIRAL

7. TREE : VINE :: (A. limb, B. sap, C. pear, D. earth) : MELON

8. SUBMARINE : FISH :: AIRPLANE : (A. aquarium, B. bird, C. wing, D. hangar)

9. BLOOD : (A. corpuscle, B. body, C. vein, D. plasma) :: WATER : AQUEDUCT

10. (A. pizza, B. Mexico, C. pestle, D. England) : *PESO* :: FRANCE : *FRANC*

11. FJORD : PENINSULA :: MAINLAND : (A. boats, B. sea, C. cape, D. Massachusetts)

12. ILLINOIS : CHICAGO :: MASSACHUSETTS : (A. Boston, B. Kentucky, C. Kennedy, D. Europe)

13. SHANGRI-LA : (A. Tibet, B. *Prometheus Unbound*, C. *Lost Horizon*, D. paradise) :: XANADU : *KUBLA KHAN*

14. (A. sail, B. sea, C. yacht, D. plane) : BOAT :: AIR : WATER

15. CARRIAGE : BABY :: (A. woman, B. automobile, C. child, D. adult) : MAN

16. FRANCE : (A. Norway, B. Hungary, C. Spain, D. Portugal) :: THAILAND : CAMBODIA

17. HOSPITAL : NURSE :: SCHOOL : (A. student, B. apple, C. test, D. teacher)

18. (A. engineer, B. driver, C. butler, D. servant) : CHAUFFEUR :: TRAIN : AUTOMOBILE

19. BAGPIPE : (A. harp, B. guitar, C. piano, D. trumpet) :: SCOTLAND : SPAIN

20. CAPE : CONTINENT :: GULF : (A. ocean, B. lake, C. reservoir, D. water)

21. LONDON : (A. Florence, B. Madrid, C. Milan, D. Rome) :: GLOBE THEATER : LA SCALA

22. UKRAINE : STEPPES :: ARGENTINA : (A. mountains, B. pampas, C. tundra, D. valleys)

23. (A. scientist, B. beaker, C. fume, D. chemical) : LABORATORY :: MANAGER : OFFICE

24. FACULTY : STAFF :: UNIVERSITY : (A. intern, B. patient, C. workers, D. hospital)

25. EAGLE : (A. eaglet, B. aerie, C. hawk, D. rabbit) :: RABBIT : BURROW

26. TRAIN : (A. steamer, B. pier, C. water, D. track) :: STATION : WHARF

TEST 10: ASSOCIATION

26 Questions • 13 Minutes

Directions: Each of these test questions consists of three capitalized words and four lettered words enclosed in parentheses. Two of the capitalized words are related in some way. Find the two related words, and establish the nature of the relationship. Then study the four words lettered A, B, C, and D. Select the one lettered word that is related to the remaining capitalized word in the same way that the first two capitalized words are related. Mark the answer sheet for the letter preceding the word you select.

1. SILK : RAYON :: BUTTER : (A. margarine, B. oil, C. cream, D. bread)

2. BOAT : (A. rescue, B. sink, C. life preserver, D. safety) :: AIRPLANE : PARACHUTE

3. NUTRITION : (A. vision, B. bulb, C. electricity, D. watt) :: FOOD : LIGHT

4. (A. deed, B. recommendation, C. person, D. thanks) : FAVOR :: FEE : SERVICE

5. ELECTROCUTION : RUBBER :: DISEASE : (A. sickness, B. heat, C. vaccine, D. death)

6. (A. horse, B. hoof, C. neigh, D. army) : FOOT :: CAVALRY : INFANTRY

7. REWARD : PRESENT :: (A. accomplishment, B. punishment, C. medal, D. money) : BIRTHDAY

8. BALLET : TERPSICHORE :: POETRY : (A. Zeus, B. music, C. Mount Olympus, D. Erato)

9. HOSTAGE : (A. criminal, B. ransom, C. murder, D. threat) :: LAWBREAKER : BAIL

10. LIBRARY : GYMNASIUM :: (A. sick, B. school, C. books, D. knowledge) : HEALTH

11. PEAS : CARROTS :: MEAT : (A. dinner, B. bird, C. potatoes, D. beef)

12. (A. vote, B. freedom, C. people, D. republic) : DEMOCRACY :: KING : MONARCHY

13. APARTHEID : SOUTH AFRICA :: (A. miscegenation, B. collectivism C. segregation, D. libertarianism) : SOVIET UNION

14. SORROW : (A. joy, B. smile, C. girls, D. sadness) :: TEARS : LAUGHTER

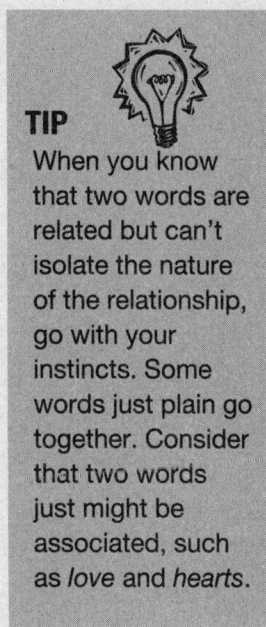

TIP
When you know that two words are related but can't isolate the nature of the relationship, go with your instincts. Some words just plain go together. Consider that two words just might be associated, such as *love* and *hearts*.

15. ROBIN : SPRING :: (A. bear, B. leaves, C. frost, D. equinox) : WINTER

16. BIBLIOPHILE : PHILATELIST :: BOOKS : (A. pharmacy, B. coins, C. stamp, D. jewelry)

17. NAIAD : WATER :: DRYAD : (A. land, B. tree, C. elm, D. wringer)

18. (A. river, B. irrigation, C. dam, D. water) : FOOD :: DROUGHT : FAMINE

19. ROYAL : SAD :: PURPLE : (A. white, B. chartreuse, C. pauper, D. blue)

20. THIRTEEN : BLACK CAT :: (A. broken mirror, B. rabbit's foot, C. will-o'-the-wisp, D. cat-o'-nine-tails) : IDES OF MARCH

21. HALF-MAST : ELEGY :: UPSIDE DOWN (A. excitement, B. error, C. confusion, D. distress)

22. (A. October, B. autumn, C. season, D. sadness) : SPRING :: LEAVES : FEVER

23. WET SUIT : SCUBA :: TUTU : (A. church, B. Africa, C. snorkel, D. ballet)

24. CULINARY : (A. bedroom, B. closet, C. knife, D. kitchen) :: ECUMENICAL : CHURCH

25. (A. teacher, B. player, C. actor, D. surgeon) : TEAM :: OSCAR™ : PENNANT

26. MIDAS : BRYAN :: GOLD : (A. silver, B. politician, C. miser, D. tail)

GROUP C: TESTS 11–15

TEST 11: SEQUENCE

26 Questions • 13 Minutes

> **Directions:** Each of these test questions consists of three capitalized words and four lettered words enclosed in parentheses. Two of the capitalized words are related in some way. Find the two related words, and establish the nature of the relationship. Then study the four words lettered A, B, C, and D. Select the one lettered word that is related to the remaining capitalized word in the same way that the first two capitalized words are related. Mark the answer sheet for the letter preceding the word you select.

1. MAY : FEBRUARY :: NOVEMBER : (A. August, B. January, C. October, D. July)

2. THIRD : FIRST :: JEFFERSON : (A. Washington, B. White House, C. president, D. Jackson)

3. G : (A. K, B. C, C. D, D. F) :: Q : M

4. EFH : ABD :: (A. MNO, B. NOP, C. NOO, D. MNP) : IJL

5. (A. Sunday, B. Monday, C. Wednesday, D. Friday) : SATURDAY :: THURSDAY : TUESDAY

6. MIDDLE AGES : RENAISSANCE :: 1700 : (A. Dark Ages, B. 1500, C. ancient Greece, D. 21st century)

7. TALKIES : (A. tube, B. broadcast, C. television, D. space travel) :: SILENTS : RADIO

8. (A. bone, B. bark, C. pup, D. kennel) : LAMB :: DOG : SHEEP

9. TODAY : YESTERDAY :: PRESENT : (A. yesterday, B. tomorrow, C. past, D. now)

10. STALLION : (A. water, B. river, C. brook, D. puddle) :: COLT : STREAM

11. (A. child, B. grandfather, C. boy, D. father) : SON :: MOTHER : DAUGHTER

12. DUSK : (A. twilight, B. dawn, C. night, D. rain) :: ELDERLINESS : INFANCY

13. SPRING : WINTER :: (A. end, B. continuation, C. birth, D. sorrow) : DEATH

14. APRIL : JUNE :: JANUARY : (A. November, B. March, C. February, D. August)

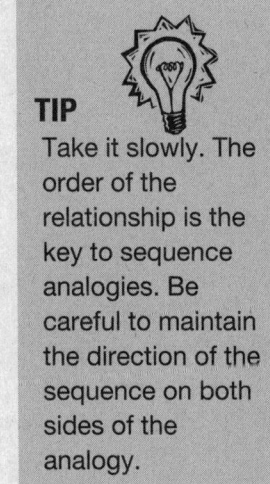

TIP
Take it slowly. The order of the relationship is the key to sequence analogies. Be careful to maintain the direction of the sequence on both sides of the analogy.

15. MATURITY : ADOLESCENCE :: CHILDHOOD : (A. manhood, B. infancy, C. school, D. immaturity)

16. INTERN : APPRENTICE :: PHYSICIAN : (A. doctor, B. lawyer, C. trade, D. craftsman)

17. (A. individual, B. baby, C. adult, D. male) : OAK :: INFANT : ACORN

18. HANDPLOW : (A. building, B. skyscraper, C. stairs, D. feet) :: TRACTOR : ELEVATOR

19. TOMORROW : YESTERDAY :: FUTURE : (A. present, B. unknown, C. year, D. past)

20. HORSE : (A. telephone, B. letter, C. communication, D. transportation) :: AUTOMOBILE : TELEGRAM

21. (A. eat, B. money, C. dough, D. yeast) : COAL :: BREAD : COKE

22. INFANT : TODDLER :: ADOLESCENT : (A. tyke, B. adult, C. youngster, D. masculine)

23. CLUB : (A. prehistoric, B. cave, C. cannon, D. rampage) :: GUN : HOUSE

24. (A. throne, B. prince, C. kingdom, D. majesty) : FILLY :: KING : MARE

25. TWIG : (A. thorn, B. branch, C. leaf, D. rose) :: BUD : FLOWER

26. MOTORCYCLE : BICYCLE :: AUTOMOBILE : (A. bus, B. airplane, C. transportation, D. wagon)

TEST 12: CHARACTERISTIC

26 Questions • 13 Minutes

Directions: Each of these test questions consists of three capitalized words and four lettered words enclosed in parentheses. Two of the capitalized words are related in some way. Find the two related words, and establish the nature of the relationship. Then study the four words lettered A, B, C, and D. Select the one lettered word that is related to the remaining capitalized word in the same way that the first two capitalized words are related. Mark the answer sheet for the letter preceding the word you select.

1. RICH : OWN :: WISE : (A. know, B. teach, C. divulge, D. save)

2. LION : (A. kingly, B. animal, C. carnivorous, D. omnipotent) :: MAN : OMNIVOROUS

3. SWALLOW : MIGRATION :: (A. chicken, B. lobster, C. bear, D. hummingbird) : HIBERNATION

4. IRON : (A. steak, B. crowd, C. humor, D. diamond) :: COMMON : RARE

5. (A. complaining, B. weakness, C. insistence, D. solitude) : STINGINESS :: HERMIT : MISER

6. NOISE : AUDIBLE :: (A. picture, B. honesty, C. distance, D. heaven) : VISIBLE

7. ALERT : (A. strong, B. cruel, C. kind, D. steady) :: PILOT : MARKSMAN

8. LOUD : THUNDER :: LARGE : (A. monkey, B. midget, C. whale, D. blatancy)

9. (A. coat, B. industry, C. fur, D. mammal) : BEAVER :: WISDOM : OWL

10. SUGAR : (A. malaria, B. quinine, C. saccharine, D. acidity) :: SWEET : BITTER

11. CLOUD : FEVER :: (A. sky, B. cold, C. storm, D. weather) : SICKNESS

12. (A. harmful, B. loud, C. orchestrated, D. pleasing) : HARMONY :: DISTRACTING : NOISE

13. GOURMET : DISCRIMINATION :: GLUTTON : (A. excess, B. food, C. charity, D. obesity)

14. (A. traffic, B. direct, C. speed, D. distance) : MEANDERING :: HIGHWAY : STREAM

15. RAIN : SNOW :: (A. wet, B. summer, C. cold, D. flood) : WINTER

16. NOVICE : EXPERT :: INSECURITY : (A. tools, B. confidence, C. difficulty, D. money)

17. IRON : (A. bread, B. penicillin, C. virus, D. disease) :: RUST : MOLD

18. SINKS : ROCK :: FLOATS : (A. feather, B. light, C. flies, D. drowns)

19. SAGE : FOX :: (A. brains, B. student, C. school, D. wisdom) : CUNNING

20. BUOYANT : CORK :: (A. jewel, B. watch, C. brilliant, D. extravagant) : DIAMOND

21. SHIVER : COLD :: TREMBLE : (A. hot, B. happiness, C. fear, D. intelligence)

22. TUNDRA : DESERT :: (A. exotic, B. dry, C. salty, D. frozen) : DRY

NOTE
Trust yourself. If an analogy seems easy, it probably is. Move quickly if you recognize an analogy based on well-known characteristics.

23. INGENUE : KNAVE :: NAIVETÉ : (A. chivalry, B. chicanery, C. morality, D. subtlety)

24. SEER : (A. auctioneer, B. dissembler, C. mendicant, D. philanthropist) :: PRESCIENCE : CHARITY

25. HERO : VALOR :: HERETIC : (A. dissent, B. bravado, C. reverence, D. discretion)

26. (A. loud, B. resounding, C. response, D. echo) : BALL :: RESONANT : RESILIENT

TEST 13: DEGREE

26 Questions • 13 Minutes

Directions: Each of these test questions consists of three capitalized words and four lettered words enclosed in parentheses. Two of the capitalized words are related in some way. Find the two related words, and establish the nature of the relationship. Then study the four words lettered A, B, C, and D. Select the one lettered word that is related to the remaining capitalized word in the same way that the first two capitalized words are related. Mark the answer sheet for the letter preceding the word you select.

1. POSSIBLE : PROBABLE :: HOPE : (A. expect, B. deceive, C. resent, D. prove)

2. GRAY : BLACK :: DISCOMFORT : (A. green, B. pain, C. hospital, D. mutilation)

3. BANQUET : (A. festival, B. party, C. ball, D. snack) :: ORATION : CHAT

4. HUT : INCH :: (A. foundation, B. skyscraper, C. building, D. abode) : MILE

5. (A. rain, B. sunshine, C. climate, D. cyclone) : CLOUDBURST :: BREEZE : SHOWER

6. MONTH : WEEK :: WEEK : (A. day, B. month, C. year, D. hour)

7. EAGLE : (A. forest, B. mountain, C. grass, D. tree) :: HUMMINGBIRD : SHRUB

8. (A. eagle, B. whale, C. giant, D. elephant) : HORSEFLY :: MINNOW : FLEA

9. CENTURY : DECADE :: DIME : (A. lucre, B. cent, C. age, D. nickel)

10. SQUARE INCH : (A. inch, B. cubic inch, C. foot, D. yard) :: INCH : SQUARE INCH

11. SLEET : MIST :: (A. breathe, B. gulp, C. chew, D. devour) : SIP

12. PLEAD : (A. beggar, B. selfishness, C. charity, D. philanthropist) :: BEG : ALMS

13. (A. pronunciation, B. stammer, C. crutch, D. speech) : LIMP :: TALK : WALK

14. NONE : LITTLE :: NEVER : (A. maybe, B. frequently, C. negative, D. seldom)

15. WORSE : (A. bad, B. good, C. best, D. better) :: WORST : WORSE

16. (A. heat, B. molecules, C. ice, D. matter) : WATER :: WATER : STEAM

17. RAGE : (A. irk, B. annoy, C. anger, D. mischief) :: DEMONIC : NAUGHTY

18. HOUR : MINUTE :: MINUTE : (A. time, B. day, C. second, D. moment)

19. LAUGH : (A. bathe, B. lather, C. water, D. dry) :: SMILE : WASH

20. RUN : WALK :: (A. number, B. total, C. multiply, D. subtract) : ADD

21. GUSH : (A. torpid, B. torrid, C. lukewarm, D. comfortable) :: TRICKLE : TEPID

22. WEEK : DAY :: DAY : (A. month, B. second, C. hour, D. night)

23. (A. guess, B. value, C. calculate, D. worth) : RECOMMEND :: ESTIMATE : SUGGEST

24. PRAISE : (A. exhort, B. exclaim, C. extort, D. extol) :: DRONE : DECLAIM

25. QUART : PINT :: GALLON : (A. inch, B. gram, C. liter, D. quart)

26. COVET : (A. acquire, B. want, C. possess, D. pretext) :: GRIEF : DISTRESS

NOTE
Degree analogies are similar to sequence analogies—the same cautions apply. Be sure to maintain the same direction on both sides of the analogy.

TEST 14: GRAMMATICAL

26 Questions • 13 Minutes

Directions: Each of these test questions consists of three capitalized words and four lettered words enclosed in parentheses. Two of the capitalized words are related in some way. Find the two related words, and establish the nature of the relationship. Then study the four words lettered A, B, C, and D. Select the one lettered word that is related to the remaining capitalized word in the same way that the first two capitalized words are related. Mark the answer sheet for the letter preceding the word you select.

TIP

Look at the whole question. If you don't see an immediate relationship between two words, scan the entire question for grammatical relationships among the terms.

1. SPRING : SPRUNG :: LIE : (A. lie, B. lain, C. lies, D. lay)

2. ROSE : RISE :: WENT : (A. going, B. gone, C. go, D. return)

3. SHABBILY : (A. harp, B. harmonica, C. harmoniously, D. harmony) :: SHABBY : HARMONIOUS

4. INFAMY : (A. infamous, B. inflammatory, C. infernal, D. infantile) :: PLAUSIBILITY : PLAUSIBLE

5. (A. you, B. your, C. ladies, D. we) : THEIR :: BABIES' : ITS

6. SHEEP : ALUMNUS :: EWE : (A. alumna, B. alumni, C. alumnae, D. alumnas)

7. RAT : RATS :: MOUSE : (A. mouses, B. mice, C. cats, D. trap)

8. I : (A. mine, B. they, C. us, D. we) :: MOOSE : MOOSE

9. LIES : DRINKS :: LAIN : (A. drunk, B. drink, C. drinked, D. drank)

10. HIM : (A. me, B. us, C. them, D. you) :: HE : WE

11. (A. fourth, B. third, C. second, D. first) : ONE :: THIRD : THREE

12. SPOKE : SPEAK :: (A. sang, B. talk, C. told, D. tale) : TELL

13. REVERT : REVERSION :: SYMPATHIZE : (A. sympathetic, B. symposium, C. sympathy, D. sympathizer)

14. LB. : CAPT. :: (A. building, B. lawyer, C. pound, D. ton) : CAPTAIN

15. DOWN : DOWNY :: HISTORY : (A. aging, B. historic, C. historian, D. time)

16. REGRESS : (A. sterilization, B. sterilize, C. sterility, D. sterilizer) :: REGRESSIVE : STERILE

17. (A. men, B. his, C. man's, D. mine) : MINE :: MAN : I

18. LAY : LIES :: ATE : (A. eater, B. eats, C. eating, D. eat)

19. (A. their, B. your, C. we're, D. one's) : THEY'RE :: NE'ER : E'ER

20. HIS : (A. its, B. it's, C. her's, D. their's) :: MINE : YOURS

21. RELIEF : BELIEVE :: RECEIVE : (A. friend, B. deceit, C. belief, D. brief)

22. LEAF : (A. leafs, B. leave, C. left, D. leaves) :: MEDIUM : MEDIA

23. LIVES : LIFE :: (A. brother-in-laws, B. brothers-in-law, C. brother-in-law's, D. brother's-in-law) : BROTHER-IN-LAW

24. BRING : BROUGHT :: WRITE : (A. wrought, B. writer, C. writing, D. wrote)

25. (A. radii, B. radial, C. radices, D. radiums) : ANALYSES :: RADIUS : ANALYSIS

26. SIMPLEST : (A. fewest, B. myriad, C. more, D. most) :: SIMPLE : MANY

TEST 15: MISCELLANEOUS

26 Questions • 13 Minutes

Directions: Each of these test questions consists of three capitalized words and four lettered words enclosed in parentheses. Two of the capitalized words are related in some way. Find the two related words, and establish the nature of the relationship. Then study the four words lettered A, B, C, and D. Select the one lettered word that is related to the remaining capitalized word in the same way that the first two capitalized words are related. Mark the answer sheet for the letter preceding the word you select.

1. ALVA : (A. Benjamin, B. stove, C. lightning, D. Delano) :: THOMAS : FRANKLIN

2. DIED : FREEDOM FIGHTER :: (A. passed away, B. dye, C. comatose, D. underprivileged) : REBEL

3. (A. 11, B. 13, C. 14, D. 17) : 3 :: SONNET : HAIKU

4. JENNY LIND : TOM THUMB :: *THE GREATEST SHOW ON EARTH* : (A. circus, B. *The Ten Commandments,* C. *Gone with the Wind,* D. P.T. Barnum)

5. ELLERY QUEEN, JR. : (A. Ellery Queen, B. Upton Sinclair, C. Samuel Clemens, D. Agatha Christie) :: FRANKLIN W. DIXON : CAROLYN KEENE

6. (A. COD, B. RFD, C. CIA, D. SOS) : LAX :: FBI : JFK

48 Master the Miller Analogies Test

> **TIP**
>
> Even if you can't find one, there is a relationship in each analogy. Some relationships are very obscure, and Miscellaneous is a true catchall category. Draw on your store of general knowledge—guess if you must. Do not dwell on the "impossible."

7. *SILENT SPRING* : (A. *Pride and Prejudice*, B. *Of Human Bondage*, C. *The Way of All Flesh*, D. *Uncle Tom's Cabin*) :: ENVIRONMENTAL EXPLOITATION : BLACK EXPLOITATION

8. (A. fry, B. bake, C. braise, D. stew) : SAUTÉ :: BOIL : STEAM

9. MUHAMMAD ALI : CASSIUS CLAY :: (A. Matthew Henson, B. Malcolm X, C. Kareem Abdul-Jabbar, D. Adam Clayton Powell) : LEW ALCINDOR

10. πr^2 : $\frac{bh}{2}$ :: CIRCLE : (A. trapezoid, B. rhombus, C. pyramid, D. triangle)

11. SAMSON : ACHILLES :: (A. lion, B. hair, C. Delilah, D. pillars) : HEEL

12. BRACES : (A. suspenders, B. belt, C. band, D. tram) :: LORRY : TRUCK

13. ENGLAND : DENMARK :: (A. Sweden, B. China, C. France, D. Thailand) : ISRAEL

14. JELLO™ : GELATIN :: XEROX™ : (A. IBM™, B. carbon paper, C. toner, D. photocopier)

15. AK : MN :: (A. AS, B. AZ, C. NB, D. IO) : PA

16. ETYMOLOGY : WORDS :: HAGIOLOGY : (A. saints, B. senility, C. selling, D. writing)

17. (A. Apollo, B. Janus, C. Eros, D. Jupiter) : JUNO :: ZEUS : HERA

18. *GESUNDHEIT* : *AL DENTE* :: *CAVEAT EMPTOR* : (A. buyer beware, B. *amicus curiae*, C. *savoir faire*, D. thank goodness)

19. HEW : (A. hewn, B. mow, C. toe, D. hue) :: BLEW : BLUE

20. *PASTORALE* : *EMPEROR* :: *EROICA* : (A. *Brandenburg*, B. *Egmont*, C. *The Nutcracker*, D. Beethoven)

21. (A. proboscis, B. smell, C. olfactory, D. redolent) : TACTILE :: NOSE : FINGER

22. KOESTLER : (A. Kreisler, B. Hemingway, C. Rhineland, D. Beethoven) :: DARKNESS : MOONLIGHT

23. (A. Jacob, B. Benjamin, C. Isaac, D. David) : JOSEPH :: GEORGE V : ELIZABETH II

24. TOFU : BROCCOLI :: (A. potato chips, B. liver, C. caviar, D. bread) : JELLY BEANS

25. TANZANIA : UNITED ARAB EMIRATES :: ESTONIA : (A. England, B. Laos, C. Brazil, D. Armenia)

26. CARTON : DARNAY :: DAMON : (A. Runyan, B. Heloise, C. Romeo, D. Pythias)

Chapter 4

Answer Key—Analogy Tests by Category

TEST 1: SYNONYMS AND DEFINITIONS

1. D	8. A	15. D	22. A
2. A	9. C	16. B	23. B
3. B	10. D	17. D	24. C
4. C	11. A	18. B	25. D
5. D	12. B	19. A	26. C
6. D	13. A	20. B	
7. A	14. B	21. C	

ROAD MAP

- *Test 1: Synonyms and Definitions*
- *Test 2: Antonyms*
- *Test 3: Cause and Effect*
- *Test 4: Part to Whole*
- *Test 5: Part to Part*
- *Test 6: Purpose, Use, or Function*
- *Test 7: Action to Object*
- *Test 8: Actor to Object*
- *Test 9: Place*
- *Test 10: Association*
- *Test 11: Sequence*
- *Test 12: Characteristic*
- *Test 13: Degree*
- *Test 14: Grammatical*
- *Test 15: Miscellaneous*

EXPLANATORY ANSWERS

1. (**D**) *Diligent* means *unremitting; diametric* means *opposite*.
2. (**A**) *Fraudulent* means *deceitful; remunerative* means *profitable*.
3. (**B**) To *extort* is to *wrest;* to *conspire* is to *plot*.
4. (**C**) A *dowager* (by one definition) is a *widow;* a *consort* is a *companion*.
5. (**D**) That which is *gaudy* is *ostentatious;* one who is *dejected* is *depressed*.
6. (**D**) This analogy is more easily read and solved in a B : A :: D : C sequence. A *soprano* voice is *high;* a *bass* voice is *low*.
7. (**A**) *Luxury* is *extravagance; penury* is *poverty*.
8. (**A**) *Cunning* means *sly;* an *inept* person is *incompetent*.
9. (**C**) To *regale* is to *entertain;* to *register* is to *enroll*.
10. (**D**) This is an A : C :: B : D relationship. To *begin* is to *establish*. *Nocturnal* means *nightly* or *at night*. While there is absolutely no relationship between the two pairs of words, each pair represents a pair of true synonyms.
11. (**A**) With this analogy, you have no choice but A : C :: B : D. To *strew* is to *disperse;* to *stray* is to *deviate*.
12. (**B**) *Vertical* means *plumb* or *straight up and down; prostrate* means *flat*.
13. (**A**) Read B : A :: D : C. *Native* means *indigenous; distant* means *remote*.
14. (**B**) A *blast* is a *gust* (as in wind); a *blare* is a *roar* (as in noise).
15. (**D**) *Diurnal* means *daily;* to *abolish* is to *end*. Do not get involved in the significance of words; concentrate on relationships.

16. **(B)** *Beginning* means *incipient; corresponding* means *congruent*.
17. **(D)** *Sufficient* means *enough*. A prologue is an introduction.
18. **(B)** *Din* means *noise; contortion* means *twisting*.
19. **(A)** *Continence* means *restraint* or holding back; a rift (in rock) is a fissure.
20. **(B)** A refined person is urbane or extremely polished; an equitable person is just.
21. **(C)** Actually, all four terms in this analogy are synonyms or near synonyms. A finial is a top ornament. A pediment is the triangular space that forms a gable. A pinnacle is a lofty peak or a church spire. A gable is the triangular end at the top of a building. The other three choices do not refer to the uppermost portions of a structure.
22. **(A)** History is fact; a fable is fiction.
23. **(B)** Jabber and gibberish are both nonsense; quidnunc is a busybody.
24. **(C)** Diapson is the full range of harmonic sound, hence a chord played on an organ. The tonic, also known as keynote, is the first note of a diatonic scale.
25. **(D)** *Pallid* means *blanched* or *pale;* to begin is to institute.
26. **(C)** *Crepuscular* means *dim; cursory* means *superficial*. The analogy reads A : C :: B : D.

TEST 2: ANTONYMS

1. A	8. A	15. A	22. D
2. B	9. C	16. C	23. D
3. C	10. D	17. A	24. D
4. D	11. B	18. B	25. A
5. C	12. C	19. C	26. A
6. C	13. D	20. D	
7. C	14. B	21. C	

EXPLANATORY ANSWERS

1. **(A)** To sunder is the opposite of to consolidate; tangible is the opposite of abstract.
2. **(B)** The opposite of accord is breach; the opposite of connection is dissociation.
3. **(C)** Birth is clearly the opposite of death. To jeer is to speak or shout derisively, whereas to cheer is to shout approval or encouragement.
4. **(D)** The only relationship here is A : C :: B : D. Generosity is the opposite of parsimony; tolerance is the opposite of bigotry.
5. **(C)** Derision expresses disapproval, while approbation expresses warm approval. That which is ephemeral is temporary and therefore is not everlasting.
6. **(C)** Graceful is the opposite of gauche, which means *crude;* wealthy is the opposite of indigent, which means *poor*.
7. **(C)** Mature is the opposite of unripe; counterfeit is the opposite of real.
8. **(A)** Ordinarily, the prefix *in* means *not,* but in the word *inquisitive,* the prefix *in* means *into,* so the meaning of *inquisitive* is *questioning*. In the word *incurious,* the prefix *in* does indeed mean *not,* hence the meaning *not curious*. Obviously, manifest is the opposite of latent, meaning *dormant* or *hidden;* inquisitive is the opposite of incurious.

9. **(C)** An idiot is the opposite of a genius; a valley, in its depth, is the opposite of a mountain, in its height.

10. **(D)** That which is permanent is not temporary. *Miscellaneous* has to do with many different things, while *single* has to do with only one. When you know that the analogy will be based upon antonyms, it is easy to answer. When your analogies are unclassified, you must look harder to determine whether your answer depends on an A : B :: C : D relationship or an A : C :: B : D relationship.

11. **(B)** That which is impromptu has not been memorized; that which is spontaneous has not been calculated.

12. **(C)** That which is a medley is a mixture of many things, the opposite of *one*. To praise is the opposite of to criticize.

13. **(D)** White is the opposite of black; valor is the opposite of cowardice.

14. **(B)** Hypocrisy is the opposite of honesty; hostility is the opposite of amity, which means *friendship*. *Enmity* is a synonym of *hostility*.

15. **(A)** *Plethora* means *excess;* its opposite, *dearth,* means *lack. Cunning* means *clever,* clearly the opposite of *dull*.

16. **(C)** Pertinent is the opposite of irrelevant; inclement weather is not clear.

17. **(A)** A bombastic speech is inflated and pretentious and is not plainspoken; one who is stringent and strict in observance is not lax.

18. **(B)** To abstain is precisely the opposite of to indulge; to avoid is the exact opposite of to seek.

19. **(C)** Dishonesty is clearly the opposite of integrity; that which is obvious is the opposite of that which is surreptitious or secret.

20. **(D)** To revere is to be respectful, while to blaspheme is to revile; to be inscrutable is the opposite of being comprehensible.

21. **(C)** Immaturity is a trait associated with childhood, which makes it a near opposite of adulthood; competition is a trait associated with open trade and hence is a near opposite of a monopoly. If the terms of the initial pair are not exact opposites, the second pair need not be exact opposites either, but their relationship must parallel the relationship of the first pair.

22. **(D)** Repugn, meaning *oppose,* is the opposite of compromise; *rescind,* meaning *take back,* is the opposite of *validate,* meaning *confirm*.

23. **(D)** To degrade is the opposite of to laud; *martial,* meaning *military,* is the opposite of *halcyon,* meaning *peaceful*.

24. **(D)** Warlike is the opposite of peaceful; scarce is the opposite of abundant.

25. **(A)** To intimidate is to discourage, which is the opposite of encourage; to interdict is to prohibit, which is the opposite of to allow.

26. **(A)** That which is costly is not cheap; one who is triumphant is not vanquished.

TEST 3: CAUSE AND EFFECT

1. B	8. B	15. B	22. A
2. C	9. B	16. A	23. D
3. C	10. A	17. B	24. D
4. C	11. A	18. C	25. B
5. D	12. B	19. D	26. B
6. C	13. D	20. C	
7. B	14. A	21. B	

EXPLANATORY ANSWERS

1. **(B)** One's curiosity (when acted upon) leads to one's enlightenment; one's veracity (when recognized by others) leads to one's credibility.
2. **(C)** Persistence leads to attainment; monotony leads to boredom.
3. **(C)** One's own good deed gives one a feeling of satisfaction; one's own diligence leads to one's improvement. Criticism also might lead one to improvement, but criticism comes from someone else. In creating analogies, look for the greatest number of parallelisms.
4. **(C)** A bird comes from an egg; a plant comes from a seed.
5. **(D)** Taking care leads to safety; assiduity or diligence leads to success. Taking care also might lead to avoidance of misfortune, but care's leading to safety is a more positive statement in line with assiduity's leading to success.
6. **(C)** Wine is made from the grape; flour is made from wheat.
7. **(B)** War causes grief; peace causes happiness.
8. **(B)** When the sun is shining, we have light; during an eclipse, there is darkness.
9. **(B)** Heat comes directly from fire; water comes directly from rain.
10. **(A)** A scar is caused by a wound; damage is caused by an accident.
11. **(A)** This is a C : A :: D : B analogy. Sanitation leads to health; filth leads to disease. You might refuse to accept this as a cause-and-effect relationship and simply call it association. How you personally categorize a relationship does not matter. The only requirement is that you choose the right answer.
12. **(B)** Cold creates ice; heat creates steam. When speaking of the action of temperature upon water, you might correctly state that cold creates crystals, but ice is a collection of crystals as steam is a collection of droplets.
13. **(D)** A : C :: B : D. Laziness leads to failure, as having a strategy leads to victory.
14. **(A)** Lack of food leads to starvation; lack of air leads to suffocation.
15. **(B)** A stimulus leads to a response; carelessness may well land one in a predicament. The terms on one side of the equation are in no way related to the terms on the other side, but the relationship within each pair is the same—cause and effect.
16. **(A)** C : A :: D : B. A fall leads to pain; disobedience leads to punishment.
17. **(B)** Faith leads one to prayer; desperation may well lead one to crime.
18. **(C)** Fanaticism is excessive enthusiasm, and it leads to intolerance; bigotry is excessive belief in the superiority of one's own group, and it leads to hatred.
19. **(D)** If the justice system is working correctly, guilt leads to conviction and innocence leads to vindication.
20. **(C)** Overindulgence in liquor may lead to alcoholism; overindulgence in food may lead to obesity.
21. **(B)** Taxation without representation was one of the causes of the American Revolution; disagreement over slavery was one of the causes of the Civil War.
22. **(A)** A fire very often causes smoke; profligacy, extravagant spending, very often leads one into debt. *Prodigality* is a synonym for *profligacy*.
23. **(D)** Work creates income; food promotes growth.
24. **(D)** In this case, either cause may have either effect, but maintaining the analogy, inexperience may lead to an error, while carelessness may lead to an accident.
25. **(B)** C : A :: D: B. Tyranny can lead to oppression just as crime can lead to prison.
26. **(B)** A flame may burn you; an insult may anger you.

TEST 4: PART TO WHOLE

1. C	8. B	15. B	22. C
2. A	9. B	16. D	23. B
3. B	10. D	17. C	24. C
4. C	11. C	18. C	25. C
5. D	12. B	19. B	26. B
6. B	13. C	20. D	
7. C	14. C	21. B	

EXPLANATORY ANSWERS

1. **(C)** Versailles is part of the class of buildings called palace; the Bastille is a part of the class of buildings called prison.

2. **(A)** The prologue is the first part of a play; the preamble is the first part of our Constitution. Articles and amendments are also parts of our constitution, but the fact that the prologue is the *first* part governs the analogy and the answer.

3. **(B)** Read this analogy as D : C :: B : A. A sentence is part of a paragraph; a word is part of a sentence.

4. **(C)** A : C :: B : D. A bead is a component part of a necklace; a link is a component part of a chain.

5. **(D)** A pit is at the center of a peach; the sun is at the center of our solar system. While this is definitely a part-to-whole analogy, you would be equally correct classifying it as a relationship based on location.

6. **(B)** A slice is a member of a group of slices that form a loaf; an island is a member of a group of islands that form an archipelago.

7. **(C)** The peak is the high point of a mountain; the crest is the high point of a wave.

8. **(B)** Meat is one of the items that make up the wares of a market; a steer is one of the animals that make up the livestock on a ranch. Again, you could legitimately classify this as a relationship based upon location or place.

9. **(B)** Ingredients make up a recipe; colors make up the spectrum.

10. **(D)** A stone is part of the quarry; wood is part of the forest. Once more, place serves well as a rationale. This analogy reads as D : B :: C : A.

11. **(C)** Granite is a rock of the quartz family; marble is a rock of the limestone family. You could equally say that granite is composed of quartz, and marble is composed of limestone.

12. **(B)** Steel is one of many alloys; iron is one of many elements.

13. **(C)** His fist is part of a man; its stinger is part of a bee. You could easily interpret this as a purposeful relationship. The purpose of the stinger is for the bee's self-defense. The purpose of the fist is for the man's self-defense. A shield is also used for defense, but it is not part of a man.

14. **(C)** Be careful. Part is to whole; Ontario is part of Canada. You were probably tempted to choose North America, but that would be a reversal of the relationship which can also be stated: The whole is Canada; its part is Ontario.

15. **(B)** Cadet and plebe are generally interchangeable terms, both referring to a student at a military academy. Thus, the position of a cadet as part of the student body at West Point is analogous to this position of a plebe as a member of the student body at Annapolis.

16. **(D)** The preface is the entry to a book; the lobby is the entry to a hotel. Of course, a room is also part of a hotel, but your analogy must be as specific as possible.
17. **(C)** The conductor is the leader of an orchestra; a chairman leads an assembly.
18. **(C)** Poetry is the larger class of which a sonnet is a kind or a part; music is the larger class of which a concert is a variety or part. Symphony, song, and etude are all other examples of the larger class called music.
19. **(B)** A petal is part of a flower; fur is part of a rabbit.
20. **(D)** Elements are part of the subject of chemistry; parts of speech are part of the subject of grammar. Grammar also concerns itself with subjects and predicates, but because *subject* may have more than one definition, you must choose the most certainly correct completion.
21. **(B)** Pine is a kind of tree; poinsettia is a kind of flower. Beware of associations that do not constitute true analogies.
22. **(C)** A carrot is a plant; a cow is an animal. In order for *meat* to be the correct answer, the analogy would have to read "carrot : cow :: vegetable : meat."
23. **(B)** A president is part of a corporation—in fact, its head. The governor is part of the state government—in fact, he or she is its head.
24. **(C)** A player is part of a team; an ear is part of a head. Be careful: The ear usually is behind the face.
25. **(C)** A clarinet is part of the woodwind instruments; a trombone is part of the brass instruments.
26. **(B)** The worthless part of the wine is the dregs; the worthless part of the wheat is the chaff.

TEST 5: PART TO PART

1. D	8. C	15. A	22. C
2. B	9. D	16. B	23. B
3. C	10. A	17. C	24. C
4. B	11. D	18. A	25. C
5. A	12. B	19. A	26. A
6. C	13. D	20. B	
7. B	14. D	21. D	

EXPLANATORY ANSWERS

1. **(D)** This is a difficult analogy to verbalize, although it is an easy one to answer. Basically nephew and niece are related to any one individual in the same way as uncle and aunt are to any one individual. In addition, nephew and niece are of the opposite sex, so uncle and aunt parallel that aspect of the relationship as well.
2. **(B)** A hand and elbow are both parts of the arm; a foot and knee are both parts of the leg. In addition, the relationship of the end of the appendage to the middle joint is the same. While a toe is also part of a leg, it is more immediately part of the foot, and the initial pair does not constitute a part-to-whole relationship.
3. **(C)** Sneaker and shoe are both footwear; mitten and glove are both handwear.
4. **(B)** Contralto and soprano are both female voices; baritone and tenor are both male voices.
5. **(A)** Cardinal and blue jay are both birds; St. Bernard and spaniel are both dogs.

Answer Key—Analogy Tests by Category

6. **(C)** Heart and lungs are both vital organs; brain and liver are also vital organs. In this case, the relationship is not only parallel but identical. The appendix is an internal organ, but it is not a vital organ.
7. **(B)** Lawnmower and rake are both lawn-care tools; mop and bucket are both floor-cleaning tools.
8. **(C)** High jump and long jump are both track-and-field events; hockey and soccer are both team sports that involve a goal net.
9. **(D)** Pen and chalk are both writing implements; a sheet of paper and a board are both surfaces upon which one can write.
10. **(A)** Nicotine and alcohol are both harmful, addictive substances; milk and orange juice are both healthful, nonaddictive substances.
11. **(D)** Perch and trout are both kinds of fish; puppy and kitten are both young animals. There is absolutely no relationship between the terms on the two sides of the proportion, but on each side the relationship of the terms is part to part, and that is sufficient to create an analogy.
12. **(B)** Carrot and potato are both root vegetables; lettuce and cabbage are both leaf vegetables that grow above ground. Beware of choosing a fourth term that is related to two related terms instead of a fourth term bearing the same relationship to the third term as the two related terms bear to one another. Both radish and onion are distracters of this type.
13. **(D)** The forward and guard both play basketball; the quarterback and punter both play football.
14. **(D)** A triangle and a square are both plane figures; a pyramid and a cube are both solid figures. In addition, the pyramid is the solid figure based upon a triangle, and the cube is the solid figure based upon a square.
15. **(A)** A goose and gander are female and male, but they are both geese. A cow and bull are female and male, but they are both cows or cattle.
16. **(B)** Senegal and Tunisia are both part of Africa and are both former French colonies. Bolivia and Colombia are both part of South America and are both former Spanish colonies. All four choices are in South America, so the analogy must be based upon the fact that the related countries are both part of a group of former Spanish colonies.
17. **(C)** Foot, kilometer, inch, and centimeter are all measures of length or distance.
18. **(A)** Ophelia and Hamlet are both characters in Shakespeare's play *Hamlet*. Portia and Shylock are both characters in Shakespeare's play *The Merchant of Venice*.
19. **(A)** Ewe and doe are females; cock and cob are males.
20. **(B)** Clam and oyster are mollusks; cow and sheep are ruminants.
21. **(D)** Bus and train are both forms of ground transportation; airplane and helicopter are both forms of air transportation.
22. **(C)** All four terms of this analogy represent parts of the same class. A gelding is a castrated horse; a capon is a castrated chicken; a steer is a castrated bull; a eunuch is a castrated human male.
23. **(B)** Eye and ear are both sensory organs; shirt and pants are both articles of clothing.
24. **(C)** Finger and palm are both parts of the hand; sole and heel are both parts of the foot. The relationship of the parts from one side of the equation to the other is not analogous, but because no other part-to-part choices are offered, a more precise relationship is not required.
25. **(C)** Button and sea are both parts of an article of clothing; headlight and bumper are both parts of a car.
26. **(A)** Wing and beak are both parts of a bird; paw and tail are both parts of an animal. *Foot* is not the correct answer because *paw* and *foot* are two names for the same part.

TEST 6: PURPOSE, USE, OR FUNCTION

1. B	8. A	15. A	22. A
2. A	9. B	16. D	23. C
3. D	10. C	17. B	24. D
4. B	11. B	18. B	25. B
5. D	12. A	19. A	26. C
6. D	13. C	20. D	
7. B	14. C	21. D	

EXPLANATORY ANSWERS

1. **(B)** A hitching post serves as a place to tie up a horse; a moorage serves as a place to tie up a craft. The distracter, vessel, which is a synonym of craft, is very tempting.

2. **(A)** The purpose of the bat is to hit the ball; the purpose of the battledore is to hit the shuttlecock. Even if the word *battledore* is unfamiliar to you, you should be able to choose the correct answer because no other choice could possibly bear the same relationship to *shuttlecock* as *bat* does to *ball*.

3. **(D)** The function of the airplane is to provide transportation; the function of the wireless is to provide communication. A wireless transmits a message, a functional relationship to be sure, but the relationship is not the same as that of airplane to transportation.

4. **(B)** The skin of the calf is tanned to make leather from which a shoe is made; the feathers of a goose are plucked to stuff a pillow.

5. **(D)** A cloth serves as a table dressing in the same way that a curtain serves as a window dressing.

6. **(D)** A gymnasium serves as a place in which one can enjoy exercise; a theater serves as a place in which one can enjoy a performance. If you wanted to classify this analogy as one of place, you would not be wrong. Classification is personal, and the category you assign is irrelevant; you just need to create a correct analogy.

7. **(B)** A crater serves as the opening through which smoke and gases escape from a volcano; a chimney serves as the conduit through which smoke and gases escape from a house. The flue is the effective portion of the chimney, but the chimney-to-flue relationship is the reverse of the crater-to-volcano relationship.

8. **(A)** A siphon serves to transfer gasoline; a shovel serves to transfer coal.

9. **(B)** The purpose of an archaeologist is to study antiquity; the purpose of an ichthyologist is to study marine life.

10. **(C)** The function of a meter is to measure; the function of a scope is to see. A telescope is used to see things that are far away, whereas a microscope is used to see things that are tiny.

11. **(B)** One purpose for raising a pig is to provide pork; one purpose for raising a cow is to provide beef.

12. **(A)** The role of the press is to print; the role of the eraser is to efface.

13. **(C)** Agar serves as a host medium for the growing of a culture; bread serves as a host medium for growing mold.

14. **(C)** A menu serves as a guide to the meal; a map serves as a guide to a trip.

15. **(A)** One's purpose in using an ax is to hew; one's purpose in using an awl is to punch holes, usually in leather.

16. **(D)** A cone serves as the seed pod, as the means of propagation of a pine tree; an acorn serves exactly the same role for an oak tree.

17. **(B)** A holster serves as a protective carrying case for a gun; a scabbard serves as a protective carrying case for a sword.

18. **(B)** A letter carrier carries the mail; a porter carries baggage.
19. **(A)** The function of a bandage is to cover and protect a wound; the function of a roof is to cover and protect a house.
20. **(D)** A siphon serves as a conduit for liquid; a flue serves as a conduit for smoke.
21. **(D)** The purpose of bread is to sustain man; the purpose of hay is to sustain a horse.
22. **(A)** On both sides of the analogy we have effective manners of execution. The gallows is used to hang the victim; the guillotine is used to behead.
23. **(C)** A barrel serves to store wine; a silo serves to store grain.
24. **(D)** Feathers serve as the outside covering of an ostrich; hair serves as the outside covering of an orangutan.
25. **(B)** A mask serves as protection for the face; a helmet serves as protection for the head.
26. **(C)** The wing is the bird's means of locomotion; the fin is the fish's means of locomotion. The wing and the fin serve analogous purposes for the bird and the fish.

TEST 7: ACTION TO OBJECT

1. C	8. B	15. C	22. B
2. B	9. B	16. B	23. D
3. D	10. C	17. B	24. B
4. A	11. B	18. B	25. C
5. B	12. C	19. B	26. D
6. D	13. D	20. C	
7. B	14. C	21. B	

EXPLANATORY ANSWERS

1. **(C)** You can hear a sound; you can see a picture.
2. **(B)** You mop the floor; you vacuum the carpet.
3. **(D)** To reach the edible portion, you peel a banana and shuck an oyster.
4. **(A)** When making changes, you make an alteration to a garment and make a revision to a book.
5. **(B)** You view a scene; you hear a concert.
6. **(D)** When you study, the object is to learn; when you try, the object is to succeed.
7. **(B)** You dredge silt; you scoop ice cream. The action of dragging and lifting is identical.
8. **(B)** You eat bread; you wear a coat.
9. **(B)** *Whet* and *hone* both mean sharpen. In common usage, you whet an appetite and hone a knife.
10. **(C)** The king reigns; the judge presides.
11. **(B)** A charitable person will overlook a mistake; a dedicated person will advocate a cause.
12. **(C)** One may profess or express love; one may assuage or calm fear. Reassurance is a means for assuaging a fear.
13. **(D)** You assimilate knowledge; you assume a debt.
14. **(C)** You thwart the aspirations of another; you stifle your own anger. Both have the effect of stopping a potential action.

15. **(C)** You hate your enemy but love your friend.
16. **(B)** A check can be the object of a forgery; a copyright can be the object of infringement. Both are illegal activities.
17. **(B)** Wood decays; iron rusts.
18. **(B)** Analysis of a misfunction or disease hopefully leads to diagnosis; research on almost any topic often results in a thesis, a theory or a dissertation.
19. **(B)** Mutiny, rebellion, or resistance to authority on a ship is analogous to desertion, absenting oneself without authorization, from the army.
20. **(C)** Irrigation brings in water as ventilation brings in air.
21. **(B)** Dishes break; clothing tears; accidents happen.
22. **(B)** The object of hearing is a tone; the object of sight is color.
23. **(D)** By way of repairing, you grind a knife and darn a stocking.
24. **(B)** In a quest for perfection, the cast will rehearse the play; the team will practice the game.
25. **(C)** If things go well, selling leads to a profit; bravery brings one fame.
26. **(D)** One mines salt; one quarries marble. This might just as well be an analogy of place. Salt comes from a mine; marble comes from a quarry.

TEST 8: ACTOR TO OBJECT

1. D	8. A	15. B	22. C
2. D	9. B	16. B	23. B
3. A	10. B	17. B	24. D
4. A	11. A	18. D	25. A
5. A	12. B	19. C	26. C
6. D	13. D	20. C	
7. B	14. A	21. D	

EXPLANATORY ANSWERS

1. **(D)** A salesman promotes a product; a teacher promotes a subject. While the action of a teacher directly impacts pupils, the analogous object of the salesman's activity would have to be customers.
2. **(D)** The moon travels around the Earth; the Earth travels around the sun.
3. **(A)** The pupil is guided by the teacher; the child is guided by its parent.
4. **(A)** A dog barks; a lion roars.
5. **(A)** An actress acts; a vocalist sings.
6. **(D)** The coach guides the player; the counselor guides the student.
7. **(B)** A composer writes music; an author writes a book.
8. **(A)** A bloom (blossom) withers; time passes.
9. **(B)** A mistake is changed by the action of an eraser; the Constitution is changed by the action of an amendment.
10. **(B)** The activity of the doctor is to treat a disease; the activity of the psychiatrist (a specific type of doctor) is to treat a disorder.

11. **(A)** A manicurist polishes nails; a barber trims hair.
12. **(B)** Parents command; children obey, usually.
13. **(D)** A woodsman uses an ax; a cobbler uses an awl.
14. **(A)** A fish swims; a man walks.
15. **(B)** A surgeon uses a scalpel to cut; a butcher uses a cleaver to cut. The butcher also uses a mallet in his work, but the implement for cutting is the cleaver.
16. **(B)** The activity of the physician is healing; the activity of the banker is lending. The bank also lends, but the analogy is better stated person to person.
17. **(B)** The man makes a speech; the bird sings a song.
18. **(D)** A carpenter uses a saw in his work; the mason uses a trowel.
19. **(C)** A tailor creates a pattern before any cloth is cut; an architect draws up a plan before building begins.
20. **(C)** An egg hatches; a seed germinates; there is rebirth.
21. **(D)** Vibration of sound waves creates tone; refraction of light rays creates color.
22. **(C)** The referee enforces the rules; one's conscience enforces one's morals.
23. **(B)** Freon is used in refrigeration; formaldehyde is used for preservation, often for biological specimens.
24. **(D)** A corral holds livestock; a cell holds prisoners.
25. **(A)** A mute softens the sound of a horn; a cushion softens the seat of a chair.
26. **(C)** Cork floats on water; oil floats on water.

TEST 9: PLACE

1. D	8. B	15. B	22. B
2. D	9. C	16. C	23. A
3. A	10. B	17. D	24. D
4. C	11. B	18. A	25. B
5. D	12. A	19. B	26. A
6. D	13. C	20. A	
7. C	14. D	21. C	

EXPLANATORY ANSWERS

1. **(D)** A thimble belongs on a finger; a sock belongs on a foot.
2. **(D)** The peasant lives in a hovel; the king lives in a palace.
3. **(A)** Railroads carry sustenance from one part of the country to another; arteries carry blood from one part of the body to another. Place alone is not enough categorization for solving this analogy. Three of the four choices are located in the body. The answer involves a combination of place and function.
4. **(C)** Money may be found in a bank; knowledge may be found in books.
5. **(D)** You race at the track; you swim at the pool.
6. **(D)** A general is a military leader on land; an admiral is a military leader at sea.
7. **(C)** A melon is a fruit that grows on a vine; a pear is a fruit that grows on a tree. Again, note the refinement beyond place in order to form the most complete analogy.

8. **(B)** Submarines and fish are found in the water; airplanes and birds are found in the sky. Note that in this analogy, the related terms share a location.

9. **(C)** Blood is carried in a vein just as water is carried by an aqueduct.

10. **(B)** The *franc* is the unit of currency used in France; the *peso* is the unit of currency used in Mexico.

11. **(B)** A fjord is a narrow arm of water that juts into the mainland; a peninsula is a narrow arm of land that juts into the sea.

12. **(A)** Chicago is a city in Illinois; Boston is a city in Massachusetts.

13. **(C)** Xanadu is a place in Samuel Taylor Coleridge's poem *Kubla Khan;* Shangri-La is a place in James Hilton's novel *Lost Horizon*. In the novel, Shangri-La is located in Tibet, but the location of the analogy is literary.

14. **(D)** A boat may be found on water; the location of a plane is the air.

15. **(B)** Look for the baby in the carriage; the man may be found in an automobile.

16. **(C)** Thailand and Cambodia are adjoining countries in Eastern Asia; France and Spain are adjoining countries in Europe. All the choices are countries in Europe, but only Spain adjoins France as Cambodia adjoins Thailand.

17. **(D)** A nurse works in a hospital; a teacher works in a school. A student also works in school, but the student's work is not nearly as analogous to the nurse's work as is the teacher's.

18. **(A)** The chauffeur drives the automobile; the engineer drives the train.

19. **(B)** The bagpipe is an instrument associated with Scotland; the guitar is the instrument of Spain.

20. **(A)** A cape is a promontory of a continent; a gulf is a promontory of an ocean. Categories do overlap; you may call this part to whole if you wish.

21. **(C)** The Globe Theater is in London; La Scala opera house is in Milan.

22. **(B)** Steppes are large, level, treeless plains of the Ukraine; pampas are large, level, grass-covered plains of Argentina.

23. **(A)** A manager works in an office; a scientist works in a laboratory.

24. **(D)** The faculty is a major functional unit of the university; the staff serves the same function in the hospital. An intern is a member of the staff.

25. **(B)** An eagle lives in an aerie, its nest high in the treetops; a rabbit lives in a burrow.

26. **(A)** The train pulls into the station; the steamer pulls in at the wharf. Resist the temptation to choose *pier,* the synonym of *wharf*.

TEST 10: ASSOCIATION

1. A	8. D	15. C	22. B
2. C	9. B	16. C	23. D
3. A	10. D	17. B	24. D
4. D	11. C	18. D	25. C
5. C	12. C	19. D	26. A
6. A	13. B	20. A	
7. A	14. A	21. D	

Answer Key—Analogy Tests by Category

EXPLANATORY ANSWERS

1. **(A)** Rayon is artificial silk; margarine is artificial butter. This analogy is as much one of definition as it is simple association.
2. **(C)** A parachute is rescue equipment associated with an airplane; a life preserver is rescue equipment associated with a boat.
3. **(A)** Food is associated with nutrition; light is associated with vision. This is not a cause-and-effect relationship because light does not cause vision. Of course, light is associated with all four choices, but its relationship to vision most closely parallels the relationship of food to nutrition.
4. **(D)** A service deserves a fee; a favor deserves thanks.
5. **(C)** Rubber protects against electrocution; likewise, a vaccine protects against disease.
6. **(A)** A foot soldier is in the infantry; a horse-mounted soldier is in the cavalry.
7. **(A)** You can get a present for your birthday; you may get a reward for an accomplishment.
8. **(D)** Terpsichore is the muse connected with ballet; Erato is the muse of poetry.
9. **(B)** The lawbreaker gets out of jail on bail; the release of a hostage is obtained by paying ransom.
10. **(D)** The gymnasium is associated with health; the library is associated with knowledge. The library is also commonly associated with books, but books in the library would be analogous to equipment in the gymnasium.
11. **(C)** The analogy is based upon association in common. Peas and carrots go together as do meat and potatoes.
12. **(C)** The king rules in the monarchy; the people rule in a democracy.
13. **(B)** Apartheid was the state policy of South Africa; collectivism was the state policy of the Soviet Union.
14. **(A)** Tears are associated with sorrow as laughter is associated with joy.
15. **(C)** A robin is often thought of as the first sign of spring; similarly, frost is often thought of as the first sign of winter.
16. **(C)** A bibliophile loves books; a philatelist collects stamps.
17. **(B)** A naiad is a water nymph; a dryad is a tree nymph.
18. **(D)** Famine is caused by lack of food; drought is caused by lack of water.
19. **(D)** The color purple is associated with royalty; the color blue is associated with sadness.
20. **(A)** All four terms of this analogy are associated with bad luck. A rabbit's foot is associated with good luck. The other two choices have nothing to do with luck.
21. **(D)** The flag at half-mast is a symbol of mourning; an elegy is a funeral dirge. The flag being flown upside down is a signal of distress and a call for help.
22. **(B)** This analogy is based on words that often appear in conjunction. Spring fever and autumn leaves simply go together.
23. **(D)** A wet suit is the garb associated with scuba diving; a tutu is clothing associated with ballet.
24. **(D)** Ecumenical has to do with the church; culinary has to do with the kitchen or with cooking.
25. **(C)** A team wins a pennant; an actor wins an Oscar™.
26. **(A)** King Midas had a touch of gold; William Jennings Bryan, as an orator, had a silver tongue. Bryan is further associated with silver in that he advocated replacing the gold standard with a silver standard.

TEST 11: SEQUENCE

1. A	8. C	15. B	22. B
2. A	9. C	16. D	23. B
3. B	10. B	17. C	24. B
4. D	11. D	18. C	25. B
5. B	12. B	19. D	26. D
6. D	13. C	20. B	
7. C	14. B	21. C	

EXPLANATORY ANSWERS

1. **(A)** May follows February with two months intervening (February, March, April, May); November follows August with two months intervening (August, September, October, November).

2. **(A)** Jefferson was the third president; Washington was the first.

3. **(B)** The letter Q follows the letter M with three letters intervening (M nop Q); the letter G follows the letter C with three letters intervening (C def G).

4. **(D)** All the terms of this analogy bear the same internal relationships. EFgH : ABcD :: MNoP : IJkL.

5. **(B)** By now, you should have a system for solving letters of the alphabet, days of the week, and months of the year sequence questions. TUESDAY (Wednesday) THURSDAY :: SATURDAY (Sunday) MONDAY.

6. **(D)** The Renaissance followed the Middle Ages; the only choice that followed 1700 is the 20th century.

7. **(C)** Silents preceded talkies on the movie screen; radio preceded television over the airwaves.

8. **(C)** A lamb develops into a sheep; a pup develops into a dog.

9. **(C)** Yesterday preceded today; the past preceded the present. Yesterday also preceded the present. When offered two choices that maintain the relationship, you must choose the best answer on some other basis. In this case, look for parallelisms in the word forms. This particular question poses especially distracting distracters. The relationship of *present* to *tomorrow* is a reversal of the initial relationship; *now* is a synonym of *present*.

10. **(B)** A colt is an incipient stallion; a stream may grow into a river. *Stream* and *brook* are synonyms.

11. **(D)** The mother is female parent to the female child, the daughter; the father is the male parent to the male child, the son.

12. **(B)** Dawn is the beginning of the day, and dusk is the end; infancy is the beginning of a lifetime, and elderliness is near its end.

13. **(C)** As in the previous analogy, we deal here with beginning and end. Spring is associated with rebirth; it is the beginning of the growing season. Winter is associated with the end of the year and the absence of new growth. The analogous relationship of birth to death should be clear.

14. **(B)** APRIL (May) JUNE :: JANUARY (February) MARCH.

15. **(B)** Maturity follows adolescence; childhood follows infancy.

16. **(D)** An intern, after a period of supervised experience, becomes a physician; an apprentice, after a period of supervised experience, becomes a craftsman.

17. **(C)** Great oaks grow from little acorns; an infant grows into an adult.

18. **(C)** The handplow preceded the tractor as the implement for preparing the fields for planting; the stairs preceded the elevator as a means for reaching higher floors of a building. The analogy is based upon sequence of technological development. This is a commonly used analogy form.

19. **(D)** TOMORROW (today) YESTERDAY :: FUTURE (present) PAST.

20. **(B)** Technology again: The horse is a less sophisticated means of transportation than the automobile; the letter is a less technologically sophisticated means of communication than is the telegram.

21. **(C)** Coke is a byproduct that follows coal; bread is the product that follows dough. The relationship is strictly sequential. The dough and coal are related only insofar as they precede bread and coke.

22. **(B)** The infant proceeds to the very next stage and becomes a toddler; an adolescent proceeds to the very next stage and becomes an adult. Proximity of stages as well as sequence enters into your correct choice.

23. **(B)** A club, as a weapon, long preceded the gun. In fact, the club is from the same prehistoric era as the cave, which preceded the house.

24. **(B)** A filly grows up to become a mare; a prince grows up to become a king.

25. **(B)** A bud develops and becomes a flower; a twig develops and becomes a branch.

26. **(D)** A motorcycle is a technologically sophisticated bicycle; an automobile is similarly related to a wagon.

TEST 12: CHARACTERISTIC

1. A	8. C	15. B	22. D
2. C	9. B	16. B	23. B
3. C	10. B	17. A	24. D
4. D	11. C	18. A	25. A
5. D	12. D	19. D	26. D
6. A	13. A	20. C	
7. D	14. B	21. C	

EXPLANATORY ANSWERS

1. **(A)** If you are rich, you own; if you are wise, you know.

2. **(C)** Man is omnivorous—he eats both animal and vegetable matter; a lion is carnivorous, eating only meat.

3. **(C)** The characteristic way in which a swallow deals with cold weather is by migration to warmer climates; a bear characteristically chooses hibernation.

4. **(D)** Iron is commonly found; diamonds are rare.

5. **(D)** The characteristic associated with a miser is stinginess; the characteristic associated with a hermit is solitude.

6. **(A)** Noise is audible; a picture is visible.

7. **(D)** A pilot must be alert; a marksman must be steady.

8. **(C)** Thunder is loud; a whale is large.

9. **(B)** The characteristic associated with an owl is wisdom; the characteristic associated with a beaver is industry—thus, "wise as an owl" and "busy as a beaver."

10. **(B)** Sugar is sweet; quinine is bitter.

11. **(C)** Fever is characteristic of sickness; clouds are characteristic of a storm.
12. **(D)** Noise is distracting; harmony is pleasing.
13. **(A)** The gourmet chooses to enjoy only the finest food; his characteristic behavior is discrimination. The glutton enjoys food in large quantities; his characteristic behavior is excess. Obesity is likely to be a characteristic of the glutton, but not necessarily. Some gluttons remain slim.
14. **(B)** Characteristically, a stream does not travel in a straight line; it tends to be meandering. A highway tends to be a direct route from one place to the next.
15. **(B)** As snow is to winter, so rain is to summer. Some analogies are so simple as to be disconcerting.
16. **(B)** Insecurity is characteristic of the novice as confidence is characteristic of the expert.
17. **(A)** Iron rusts; bread gets moldy.
18. **(A)** A rock sinks; a feather floats.
19. **(D)** A fox is known for its cunning; a sage is known for his or her wisdom.
20. **(C)** A cork is buoyant; a diamond is brilliant.
21. **(C)** You shiver with cold; you tremble with fear. With happiness, you quiver.
22. **(D)** The desert is dry; the tundra is frozen.
23. **(B)** A characteristic of the ingenue is her naiveté; a characteristic of the knave is chicanery, trickery, or artful deception.
24. **(D)** The seer is known for prescience; the philanthropist is known for charity.
25. **(A)** The hero's stock in trade is valor; the heretic makes a mark by dissent or nonconformity.
26. **(D)** A ball is resilient; an echo is resonant. Both bounce.

TEST 13: DEGREE

1. A	8. B	15. A	22. C
2. B	9. B	16. C	23. C
3. D	10. B	17. C	24. D
4. B	11. B	18. C	25. D
5. D	12. C	19. A	26. B
6. A	13. B	20. C	
7. D	14. D	21. B	

EXPLANATORY ANSWERS

1. **(A)** Probably is more likely than possible; expect connotes a greater degree of certainty than hope.
2. **(B)** Black is more intense than gray; pain is greater than discomfort.
3. **(D)** An oration is longer and more formal than a chat; a banquet is longer, larger, and more formal than a snack.
4. **(B)** A mile is very much longer than an inch; a skyscraper is very much taller than a hut.
5. **(D)** A shower represents a gentle rain, whereas a cloudburst is a very heavy rainfall. A breeze is a gentle wind, whereas a cyclone is a heavy windstorm.
6. **(A)** A month is longer than a week; a week is longer than a day. A week is also longer than an hour, but because *week* is the next smallest unit to *month,* your best choice in completing the analogy is to choose the next smallest unit to *week,* which is *day.*

7. **(D)** An eagle is larger than a hummingbird; a tree is larger than a shrub.
8. **(B)** A horsefly is an insect that is larger than another insect, a flea; a whale is a sea creature that is larger than another sea creature, a minnow.
9. **(B)** A century is ten times longer than a decade; a dime is ten times more valuable than a cent.
10. **(B)** An inch times an inch equals a square inch; a square inch times an inch equals a cubic inch. Anyway, a square inch is larger than an inch; a cubic inch is larger than a square inch.
11. **(B)** Sleet is a much more intensive form of precipitation than is mist; a gulp is a much more intensive intake of fluid than is a sip.
12. **(C)** To beg is on a smaller scale and less intensive than to plead; alms is generally on a small-change scale, while charity is generally associated with larger-scale giving. Philanthropy is the highest degree of giving, but *philanthropist* is the wrong answer because the person does not parallel another term.
13. **(B)** A limp is a flawed walk; a stammer is a flawed talk.
14. **(D)** Little is more than none, although not much more; seldom is more often than never, although not much more often.
15. **(A)** Bad is to worse as worse is to worst. Think carefully. Beginning with the initial pair: worst, worse, bad, good, better, best.
16. **(C)** This analogy has to do with the action of heat upon water: from ice to water to steam.
17. **(C)** One who is demonic is fiendish, much worse than naughty; rage is much more intense than simple anger.
18. **(C)** An hour is longer than a minute; a minute is longer than a second. The fact that there are 60 minutes in an hour and 60 seconds in a minute is irrelevant to this analogy.
19. **(A)** To laugh is more intensive than to smile; to bathe is more intensive than merely to wash.
20. **(C)** Run is greater than walk; to multiply makes the total grow much more quickly than to add.
21. **(B)** A gush is a much heavier, quicker flow than a trickle; torrid is much hotter than tepid.
22. **(C)** A week is longer than a day; a day is longer than an hour.
23. **(C)** To recommend is stronger and more compelling than to suggest; to calculate is much more accurate and specific than to estimate.
24. **(D)** To drone is to speak languidly in a monotone; to declaim is to make a fiery oration. To praise is to say something nice; to extol is to glorify.
25. **(D)** A quart is more than a pint; a gallon is more than a quart. A gallon is also more than a liter, but because the initial pair represents nonmetric measures, it is best to maintain the analogy in nonmetric terms.
26. **(B)** Grief is intensive and all-encompassing distress; to covet is to want inordinately.

TEST 14: GRAMMATICAL

1. B	8. D	15. B	22. D
2. C	9. A	16. B	23. B
3. C	10. B	17. C	24. D
4. A	11. D	18. B	25. A
5. B	12. C	19. C	26. D
6. A	13. C	20. A	
7. B	14. C	21. B	

EXPLANATORY ANSWERS

1. **(B)** SPRING : SPRUNG :: LIE : LAIN :: present : participle.
2. **(C)** ROSE : RISE :: WENT : GO :: past : present.
3. **(C)** SHABBILY : HARMONIOUSLY :: SHABBY : HARMONIOUS :: adverb : adjective.
4. **(A)** INFAMY : INFAMOUS :: PLAUSIBILITY : PLAUSIBLE :: noun : adjective.
5. **(B)** YOUR : THEIR :: BABIES' : ITS. All are possessives.
6. **(A)** SHEEP : ALUMNUS :: EWE : ALUMNA :: male : female.
7. **(B)** RAT : RATS :: MOUSE : MICE :: singular : plural.
8. **(D)** I : WE :: MOOSE : MOOSE :: singular : plural.
9. **(A)** LIES : DRINKS :: LAIN : DRUNK :: present : participle.
10. **(B)** HIM : US :: HE : WE :: objective : subjective.
11. **(D)** FIRST : ONE :: THIRD : THREE :: ordinal : cardinal.
12. **(C)** SPOKE : SPEAK :: TOLD : TELL :: past : present.
13. **(C)** REVERT : REVERSION :: SYMPATHIZE : SYMPATHY :: verb : noun.
14. **(C)** LB. : CAPT. :: POUND : CAPTAIN :: abbreviation : word. The abbreviation for lawyer is LLB.
15. **(B)** DOWN : DOWNY :: HISTORY : HISTORIC :: noun : verb.
16. **(B)** REGRESS : STERILIZE :: REGRESSIVE : STERILE :: verb : adjective.
17. **(C)** MAN'S : MINE :: MAN : I :: possessive : subjective.
18. **(B)** LAY : ATE :: LIES : EATS :: past : present. In order to determine the tense of the word *lay*, it is imperative to look at it in conjunction with the term in the C position.
19. **(C)** WE'RE : THEY'RE :: NE'ER : E'ER :: we are : they are :: never : ever. On each side of the analogy there are parallel contractions.
20. **(A)** HIS : ITS :: MINE : YOURS. All four terms are possessives. A pronoun does not take an apostrophe in the possessive.
21. **(B)** RELIEF : BELIEVE :: RECEIVE : DECEIT :: ie : ie : ei : ei. All seven terms correctly follow the rule, "I before E except after C," so this interpretation is the only one possible.
22. **(D)** LEAF : LEAVES :: MEDIUM : MEDIA :: singular : plural.
23. **(B)** LIVES : LIFE :: BROTHERS-IN-LAW : BROTHER-IN-LAW :: plural : singular.
24. **(D)** BRING : BROUGHT :: WRITE : WROTE :: present : past. Avoid the temptation to choose a relationship based only upon sound before looking for meaningful relationships.
25. **(A)** RADII : ANALYSES :: RADIUS : ANALYSIS :: plural : singular.
26. **(D)** SIMPLEST : MOST :: SIMPLE : MANY :: superlative : positive.

TEST 15: MISCELLANEOUS

1. D	8. A	15. B	22. D
2. A	9. C	16. A	23. C
3. C	10. D	17. D	24. A
4. B	11. B	18. C	25. D
5. A	12. A	19. D	26. D
6. C	13. C	20. A	
7. D	14. D	21. C	

EXPLANATORY ANSWERS

1. **(D)** The analogy has to do with people's middle names. You might call this a completion analogy. Thomas Alva Edison; Franklin Delano Roosevelt.

2. **(A)** The basis for this analogy is euphemisms. People who back certain rebel groups prefer to call those groups freedom fighters. Similarly, some people today prefer not to use the term died, substituting passed away in its place.

3. **(C)** The analogy is based on definition. A haiku is a poem of three lines; a sonnet is a poem of fourteen lines.

4. **(B)** Jenny Lind and Tom Thumb were both introduced and promoted by P. T. Barnum; *The Greatest Show on Earth* and *The Ten Commandments* were both produced by Cecil B. DeMille. *Gone with the Wind* was produced by David O. Selznick. The other two distracters are related to all three capitalized terms, but they do not serve to complete the analogy.

5. **(A)** Franklin W. Dixon and Carolyn Keene are pseudonyms used by the committee that authored both the Hardy Boys series and the Nancy Drew series of young people's mysteries. Ellery Queen, Jr., and Ellery Queen are both pseudonyms under which the same person, Manfred Lepofsky, wrote many adult mysteries.

6. **(C)** LAX and JFK are official designations of airports: Los Angeles and Kennedy, in New York. The FBI and CIA are both United States intelligence organizations, the first domestic and the second international. None of the other choices bears any meaningful relationship to the FBI.

7. **(D)** Rachel Carson's *Silent Spring* helped the nation to take notice of environmental exploitation. Harriet Beecher Stowe's *Uncle Tom's Cabin* caused people to consider more seriously the situation of black exploitation.

8. **(A)** If you stretch, you may call this an analogy of degree. Boiling uses more water than steaming. Similarly, frying uses more oil than sautéing.

9. **(C)** You would have to call this an analogy based on identity, or perhaps sequence. Muhammad Ali is Cassius Clay. Cassius Clay became Muhammad Ali when he converted to the Black Muslim faith. Kareem Abdul-Jabbar is Lew Alcindor. Lew Alcindor became Kareem Abdul-Jabbar when he converted to the Black Muslim faith.

10. **(D)** πr^2 is the formula for the area of a circle; $\frac{bh}{2}$ is the formula for calculating the area of a triangle.

11. **(B)** Achilles' downfall was the arrow that entered the unprotected area of his heel; Samson's downfall was the cutting of his hair. Delilah betrayed Samson by telling of his weakness, but Samson's hair, as a body part, is analogous to Achilles' heel.

12. **(A)** This is an analogy of identity. In Britain, a lorry is a truck, and braces are suspenders.

13. **(C)** England and Denmark are both constitutional monarchies; France and Israel both have republican forms of government. The like forms of government on each side of the equation create this analogy. Sweden and Thailand are both constitutional monarchies; China is a Communist dictatorship.

14. **(D)** Sometimes the trademark name of the earliest and most widely used entry into a field comes to be used by the public as the common name of the product itself. Thus, once it finds its way into the dessert dish, all gelatin dessert tends to be called Jello™; most office photocopiers tend to be called the Xerox™. This also can be read as Jello™ is a type of gelatin, and Xerox™ is a type of photocopier.

15. **(B)** AK and MN are correct postal service abbreviations for Alaska and Minnesota; AZ and PA are correct postal service abbreviations for Arizona and Pennsylvania. The other choices are not correct postal service abbreviations.

16. **(A)** It is hard to get away from definition, or at least association. Etymology is the study of words; hagiology is the study of saints.

17. **(D)** Zeus and Hera are husband and wife, king and queen of the Greek gods; Jupiter and Juno are husband and wife, the Roman counterparts of Zeus and Hera.

18. **(C)** Look for relationships without considering meanings whenever you encounter foreign words. You can always focus on meanings later if you find no simpler relationship. In this analogy, the first two terms are totally unrelated except that each comes from a different foreign language and that each has been incorporated into the English language without translation. On the other side of the analogy, it is possible to choose two more such words that come from two additional foreign languages and that have been incorporated into English. *Gesundheit* is German and means "good health"; *al dente* is Italian and means chewy, literally, "to the teeth"; *caveat emptor* is Latin and means "buyer beware"; *savoir faire* is French and means "social polish." *Amicus curiae* is also Latin, so it does not suit the requirement of the analogy.

19. **(D)** This analogy is based on the homophonic relationship between each pair. Blew and blue are pronounced the same yet have different meanings and spellings. The same is also true for hew and hue.

20. **(A)** The *Pastorale* and *Eroica* are both symphonies (the first by Tchaikovsky and the second by Beethoven), although composers are irrelevant to this analogy. The *Emperor* and the *Brandenburg* are concerti, the first by Beethoven and the second by Bach. You could legitimately categorize this as a part-to-part analogy. The *Egmont* is an overture, and *The Nutcracker* is a suite.

21. **(C)** The tactile sense is to the finger as the olfactory sense is to the nose.

22. **(D)** Koestler wrote *Darkness at Noon;* Beethoven wrote the *Moonlight Sonata*. The analogy moves from literature into music, but the relationship is clear.

23. **(C)** The relationship hinges upon the relationship between grandparent and grandchild. George V was Elizabeth II's grandfather; Isaac was grandfather of Joseph. The Biblical family progression is Abraham : Isaac :: Jacob : Joseph.

24. **(A)** Tofu and broccoli are considered to be among the most nutritious and healthful foods; potato chips and jelly beans fall into the category of junk foods.

25. **(D)** The first two countries, Tanzania and the United Arab Emirates, have in common that they came into being through the voluntary alliance of two or more independent countries. Estonia and Armenia also have histories in common. Both were once independent nations that were subsumed by the Soviet Union. Upon dissolution of the Soviet Union, they became independent nations again.

26. **(D)** This analogy is based upon unselfish sacrifice. In Dickens' novel *A Tale of Two Cities,* Sidney Carton goes to the guillotine in place of Charles Darnay. According to legend, in ancient Syracuse Pythias was sentenced to die, but his friend Damon volunteered to serve as hostage so that Pythias could return home to say goodbye. Theoretically, if Pythias had not returned, Damon would have died in his place, so the analogy is complete and accurate. Actually, Pythias did return, and the king, Dionysus, was so impressed that he pardoned him rather than proceeding with the execution.

7 Sample MATS

PART 3

PREVIEW

CHAPTER 5	*Sample Test 1*
CHAPTER 6	*Sample Test 2*
CHAPTER 7	*Sample Test 3*
CHAPTER 8	*Sample Test 4*
CHAPTER 9	*Sample Test 5*
CHAPTER 10	*Sample Test 6*
CHAPTER 11	*Sample Test 7*

SAMPLE TEST 1

Answer Sheet

1 ⓐ ⓑ ⓒ ⓓ	26 ⓐ ⓑ ⓒ ⓓ	51 ⓐ ⓑ ⓒ ⓓ	76 ⓐ ⓑ ⓒ ⓓ
2 ⓐ ⓑ ⓒ ⓓ	27 ⓐ ⓑ ⓒ ⓓ	52 ⓐ ⓑ ⓒ ⓓ	77 ⓐ ⓑ ⓒ ⓓ
3 ⓐ ⓑ ⓒ ⓓ	28 ⓐ ⓑ ⓒ ⓓ	53 ⓐ ⓑ ⓒ ⓓ	78 ⓐ ⓑ ⓒ ⓓ
4 ⓐ ⓑ ⓒ ⓓ	29 ⓐ ⓑ ⓒ ⓓ	54 ⓐ ⓑ ⓒ ⓓ	79 ⓐ ⓑ ⓒ ⓓ
5 ⓐ ⓑ ⓒ ⓓ	30 ⓐ ⓑ ⓒ ⓓ	55 ⓐ ⓑ ⓒ ⓓ	80 ⓐ ⓑ ⓒ ⓓ
6 ⓐ ⓑ ⓒ ⓓ	31 ⓐ ⓑ ⓒ ⓓ	56 ⓐ ⓑ ⓒ ⓓ	81 ⓐ ⓑ ⓒ ⓓ
7 ⓐ ⓑ ⓒ ⓓ	32 ⓐ ⓑ ⓒ ⓓ	57 ⓐ ⓑ ⓒ ⓓ	82 ⓐ ⓑ ⓒ ⓓ
8 ⓐ ⓑ ⓒ ⓓ	33 ⓐ ⓑ ⓒ ⓓ	58 ⓐ ⓑ ⓒ ⓓ	83 ⓐ ⓑ ⓒ ⓓ
9 ⓐ ⓑ ⓒ ⓓ	34 ⓐ ⓑ ⓒ ⓓ	59 ⓐ ⓑ ⓒ ⓓ	84 ⓐ ⓑ ⓒ ⓓ
10 ⓐ ⓑ ⓒ ⓓ	35 ⓐ ⓑ ⓒ ⓓ	60 ⓐ ⓑ ⓒ ⓓ	85 ⓐ ⓑ ⓒ ⓓ
11 ⓐ ⓑ ⓒ ⓓ	36 ⓐ ⓑ ⓒ ⓓ	61 ⓐ ⓑ ⓒ ⓓ	86 ⓐ ⓑ ⓒ ⓓ
12 ⓐ ⓑ ⓒ ⓓ	37 ⓐ ⓑ ⓒ ⓓ	62 ⓐ ⓑ ⓒ ⓓ	87 ⓐ ⓑ ⓒ ⓓ
13 ⓐ ⓑ ⓒ ⓓ	38 ⓐ ⓑ ⓒ ⓓ	63 ⓐ ⓑ ⓒ ⓓ	88 ⓐ ⓑ ⓒ ⓓ
14 ⓐ ⓑ ⓒ ⓓ	39 ⓐ ⓑ ⓒ ⓓ	64 ⓐ ⓑ ⓒ ⓓ	89 ⓐ ⓑ ⓒ ⓓ
15 ⓐ ⓑ ⓒ ⓓ	40 ⓐ ⓑ ⓒ ⓓ	65 ⓐ ⓑ ⓒ ⓓ	90 ⓐ ⓑ ⓒ ⓓ
16 ⓐ ⓑ ⓒ ⓓ	41 ⓐ ⓑ ⓒ ⓓ	66 ⓐ ⓑ ⓒ ⓓ	91 ⓐ ⓑ ⓒ ⓓ
17 ⓐ ⓑ ⓒ ⓓ	42 ⓐ ⓑ ⓒ ⓓ	67 ⓐ ⓑ ⓒ ⓓ	92 ⓐ ⓑ ⓒ ⓓ
18 ⓐ ⓑ ⓒ ⓓ	43 ⓐ ⓑ ⓒ ⓓ	68 ⓐ ⓑ ⓒ ⓓ	93 ⓐ ⓑ ⓒ ⓓ
19 ⓐ ⓑ ⓒ ⓓ	44 ⓐ ⓑ ⓒ ⓓ	69 ⓐ ⓑ ⓒ ⓓ	94 ⓐ ⓑ ⓒ ⓓ
20 ⓐ ⓑ ⓒ ⓓ	45 ⓐ ⓑ ⓒ ⓓ	70 ⓐ ⓑ ⓒ ⓓ	95 ⓐ ⓑ ⓒ ⓓ
21 ⓐ ⓑ ⓒ ⓓ	46 ⓐ ⓑ ⓒ ⓓ	71 ⓐ ⓑ ⓒ ⓓ	96 ⓐ ⓑ ⓒ ⓓ
22 ⓐ ⓑ ⓒ ⓓ	47 ⓐ ⓑ ⓒ ⓓ	72 ⓐ ⓑ ⓒ ⓓ	97 ⓐ ⓑ ⓒ ⓓ
23 ⓐ ⓑ ⓒ ⓓ	48 ⓐ ⓑ ⓒ ⓓ	73 ⓐ ⓑ ⓒ ⓓ	98 ⓐ ⓑ ⓒ ⓓ
24 ⓐ ⓑ ⓒ ⓓ	49 ⓐ ⓑ ⓒ ⓓ	74 ⓐ ⓑ ⓒ ⓓ	99 ⓐ ⓑ ⓒ ⓓ
25 ⓐ ⓑ ⓒ ⓓ	50 ⓐ ⓑ ⓒ ⓓ	75 ⓐ ⓑ ⓒ ⓓ	100 ⓐ ⓑ ⓒ ⓓ

TEAR HERE

Chapter 5

Sample Test 1

100 Questions • 50 Minutes

Directions: Each of these test questions consists of three capitalized words and four lettered words enclosed in parentheses. Two of the capitalized words are related in some way. Find the related words, and establish the nature of the relationship. Then study the four words lettered A, B, C, and D. Select the one lettered word that is related to the remaining capitalized word in the same way that the first two capitalized words are related. Mark the answer sheet for the letter preceding the word you select.

1. BALMY : MILD :: FAITHFUL : (A. explosive, B. docile, C. talkative, D. staunch)

2. BOLD : TIMID :: SQUANDER : (A. disperse, B. hoard, C. query, D. extinguish)

3. SEA : (A. fish, B. ocean, C. island, D. net) :: LAND : LAKE

4. GLASS : RUBBER :: BRITTLE : (A. elastic, B. scarce, C. tempered, D. spheroid)

5. DIAMETER : RADIUS :: (A. 3, B. 8, C. 5, D. 6) : 4

6. GLABROUS : FACTITIOUS :: HIRSUTE : (A. authentic, B. fictional, C. fluent, D. replete)

7. PARANOIA : SCHIZOPHRENIA :: MEGALOMANIA : (A. melancholia, B. carcinoma, C. hepatitis, D. glaucoma)

8. (A. sales, B. investment, C. management, D. interest) : PROFIT :: LABOR : WAGES

9. STUDENT : (A. backpack, B. briefcase, C. college, D. teacher) :: TRAVELER : SUITCASE

10. DENIGRATE : DEFAMER :: MEDIATE : (A. mathematician, B. arbitrator, C. employer, D. laborer)

ROAD MAP

- *Answer Key*
- *Explanatory Answers*

Master the Miller Analogies Test

11. LAKE WOBEGON : (A. Minneapolis, B. Winesburg, C. Canterbury, D. Minnesota) :: MUDVILLE : CASTERBRIDGE

12. CORNET : OBOE :: (A. cello, B. drum, C. harpsichord, D. xylophone) : GUITAR

13. JANUARY : WEDNESDAY :: JANUS : (A. Thor, B. Apollo, C. Odin, D. Diana)

14. HORSE : (A. equestrian, B. hoofed, C. cabriolet, D. herbivorous) :: TIGER : CARNIVOROUS

15. GOOD : BETTER :: (A. terrible, B. worse, C. improvement, D. bad) : WORST

16. CLAN : FEUD :: NATION : (A. war, B. politics, C. armaments, D. retaliation)

17. ABUNDANCE : ABROGATE :: DEARTH : (A. deny, B. establish, C. abstain, D. absolve)

18. ONOMATOPOEIA : METAPHOR :: SOUND : (A. hiss, B. rhyme, C. saying, D. comparison)

19. SACRAMENTO : HELENA :: ALBANY : (A. New York, B. Little Rock, C. Houston, D. San Francisco)

20. (A. scan, B. feel, C. dear, D. seen) : READ :: REAP : PEAR

21. CAUTIOUS : CIRCUMSPECT :: PRECIPITOUS : (A. premonitory, B. profound, C. stealthy, D. steep)

22. SEISMOGRAPH : GEOLOGY :: ELECTROENCEPHALOGRAPH : (A. bacteriology, B. biology, C. neurology, D. cardiology)

23. ACUTE : VENERATE :: CHRONIC : (A. revere, B. actuate, C. flout, D. repent)

24. (A. toad, B. lion, C. shark, D. alligator) : TURTLE :: TIGER : MAN

25. INSTINCT : PLAN :: UNCONSCIOUS : (A. involuntary, B. intentional, C. spontaneous, D. imaginary)

26. INDIA : (A. Sri Lanka, B. Greece, C. Afghanistan, D. Pakistan) :: ITALY : SWITZERLAND

27. SWIM : SWAM :: BURST : (A. busted, B. bursted, C. burst, D. bust)

28. RAISIN : GRAPE :: PRUNE : (A. apricot, B. currant, C. plum, D. berry)

29. GRAM : OUNCE :: LITER : (A. deciliter, B. quart, C. kilogram, D. pound)

30. BEAKER : CHEMIST :: STETHOSCOPE : (A. teacher, B. author, C. doctor, D. dentist)

31. LIMPID : LUCID :: TURBID : (A. torpid, B. muddy, C. truculent, D. serene)

32. MANGO : (A. coconut, B. tomato, C. cabbage, D. apple) :: PAPAYA : PASSIONFRUIT

33. .02 : .0004 :: .001 : (A. .000001, B. .0001, C. .0002, D. .000002)

34. SADNESS : PAIN :: FAILURE : (A. medication, B. palliation, C. pleasure, D. injury)

35. AMELIA EARHART : NELLIE BLY :: AVIATION : (A. medicine, B. journalism, C. law, D. prohibition)

36. ROMAN : MANOR :: (A. cleric, B. names, C. patrimony, D. estates) : MANSE

37. LACONIC : FLACCID :: REDUNDANT : (A. succinct, B. firm, C. flimsy, D. swollen)

38. PNEUMATICS : (A. medicine, B. disease, C. physics, D. cars) :: ESKER : GEOLOGY

39. NECKLACE : MEDAL :: ADORNMENT : (A. jewel, B. metal, C. decoration, D. bronze)

40. RIVER : STREAM :: MOUNTAIN : (A. cliff, B. hill, C. canyon, D. peak)

41. HECKLE : NEEDLE :: (A. stock, B. deplete, C. book, D. stylus) : REPLENISH

42. (A. guerrilla, B. terrorist, C. quash, D. mediate) : REBELLION :: NEGOTIATE : TREATY

43. BOTANIST : PLANTS :: GEOLOGIST : (A. trees, B. rocks, C. geography, D. gems)

44. CAT : FELINE :: OX : (A. equine, B. saturnine, C. bovine, D. canine)

45. WOLF : (A. wool, B. sheep, C. ewe, D. ram) :: DOG : CAT

46. (A. $\frac{5}{16}$, B. $\frac{3}{8}$, C. $\frac{2}{6}$, D. $\frac{5}{12}$) : $\frac{9}{24}$ :: $\frac{4}{11}$: $\frac{12}{33}$

47. FISHES : BIRDS :: (A. horses, B. cattle, C. wheat, D. mosses) : CEREALS

48. ROOM : CABIN :: HOUSE : (A. camp, B. cottage, C. hotel, D. ship)

49. BRASS : COPPER :: PEWTER : (A. lead, B. zinc, C. silver, D. bronze)

50. COWCATCHER : LOCOMOTIVE :: (A. coda, B. climax, C. epilogue, D. finale) : DENOUEMENT

51. PARIAH : OUTCAST :: ARCHON : (A. archivist, B. magistrate, C. martine, D. constable)

52. (A. cappuccino, B. shamrock, C. wine, D. palm trees) : VODKA :: DEVALERA : STALIN

53. LANCET : CUT :: CHAMOIS : (A. polish, B. pliant, C. smooth, D. sheep)

54. (A. utter, B. elapse, C. exude, D. time) : EMIT :: STEP : PETS

55. SAFE : NECKLACE :: COMBINATION : (A. torque, B. bangle, C. circlet, D. clasp)

56. EXPERIMENT : (A. science, B. elucidation, C. hypothesis, D. investigation) :: EXAMINATION : ACHIEVEMENT

57. BOY : BULLET :: MAN : (A. gun, B. artillery shell, C. holster, D. trigger)

58. ENERVATE : (A. eradicate, B. invigorate, C. disconcert, D. propagate) :: MALICE : BENEVOLENCE

59. EVIDENCE : CONVICTION :: (A. oxygen, B. carbon dioxide, C. match, D. light) : COMBUSTION

60. EDIFICATION : AWARENESS :: AGGRAVATION : (A. distress, B. excitement, C. reduction, D. deliberation)

GO ON TO THE NEXT PAGE

61. NEWTON : COPERNICUS :: SHAKESPEARE : (A. Fielding, B. Jonson, C. Dickens, D. Defoe)

62. ST. AUGUSTINE : (A. Florida, B. Virginia, C. France, D. Spain) :: JAMESTOWN : ENGLAND

63. SNOW : DRIFT :: (A. hill, B. rain, C. sand, D. desert) : DUNE

64. CATAMARAN : TERMAGANT :: RAFT : (A. grisette, B. spinnaker, C. spinster, D. shrew)

65. $3^2 : 2^3 :: 9 :$ (A. 1, B. 6, C. 4, D. 8)

66. FICTION : NOVELIST :: FACTS : (A. legend, B. story, C. historian, D. research)

67. HARVARD : YALE :: BROWN : (A. Princeton, B. Purdue, C. Emory, D. Dartmouth)

68. CAT : WOLF :: (A. lion, B. dog, C. man, D. tiger) : DUCK

69. WHO : I :: WHOM : (A. we, B. me, C. whose, D. mine)

70. (A. obsequious, B. obstreperous, C. complacent, D. contumelious) : SYCOPHANT :: CONTUMACIOUS : RENEGADE

71. DOWSER : ROD :: GEOMANCER : (A. stones, B. maps, C. plants, D. configurations)

72. MINERVA : ATHENA :: (A. Jupiter, B. Juno, C. Poseidon, D. Apollo) : ZEUS

73. (A. loss, B. victory, C. game, D. team) : WIN :: MEDICINE : CURE

74. SAFARI : SWAHILI :: SALAAM : (A. Arabic, B. shalom, C. peace, D. Africa)

75. ACID : ALKALI :: 6 : (A. 1, B. 4, C. 7, D. 8)

76. PEDESTAL : (A. column, B. sculpture, C. chandelier, D. stone) :: STALAGMITE : STALACTITE

77. BONA FIDE : IN TOTO :: CARTE BLANCHE : (A. eureka, B. status quo, C. avant-garde, D. ersatz)

78. SEA : COAST :: RIVER : (A. inlet, B. delta, C. stream, D. bank)

79. AMOUNT : NUMBER :: (A. lessen, B. augment, C. less, D. enumerate) : FEWER

80. VOLUME : CUBIC METER :: (A. area, B. length, C. capacity, D. mass) : LITER

81. (A. refrain, B. precede, C. sustain, D. foray) : FORBEAR :: ADUMBRATE : FORESHADOW

82. CHAMPION : CAUSE :: (A. signature, B. introduction, C. draft, D. ink) : LETTER

83. SHADOWS : CLOUDS :: SUN : (A. water, B. dark, C. rain, D. thunder)

84. WINTER : SUMMER :: BOSTON : (A. Miami, B. Madrid, C. Sao Paulo, D. San Diego)

85. CIRCLE : SPHERE :: (A. ice, B. angle, C. oval, D. square) : CUBE

86. KINETIC : MOTION :: PISCATORIAL : (A. pizza, B. painting, C. fish, D. picturesque)

87. RESPIRATION : CO_2 :: (A. hydrolysis, B. transpiration, C. oxidation, D. photosynthesis) : O_2

88. SAND : CLAY :: GLASS : (A. stone, B. hay, C. brick, D. dirt)

89. LOUISIANA PURCHASE : (A. Mexico, B. Spain, C. Great Britain, D. France) :: ALASKA : RUSSIA

90. X : M :: (A. V, B. X, C. L, D. I) : C

91. PUCCINI : OPERA :: (A. Pavlova, B. Verdi, C. "Giselle," D. Balanchine) : BALLET

92. POLTROON : TERROR :: PARANOIAC : (A. courage, B. shyness, C. persecution, D. paralysis)

93. DOOR : BOLT :: LETTER : (A. envelope, B. mail, C. seal, D. write)

94. AUTHOR : (A. royalties, B. charges, C. fees, D. contributions) :: AGENT : COMMISSIONS

95. OLD BAILEY : OLD VIC :: (A. Versailles, B. Bastille, C. Westminster, D. London) : LA SCALA

96. TRUDEAU : (A. Durant, B. De Toqueville, C. Malthus, D. Nast) :: ORWELL : HUXLEY

97. ORAL : AURAL :: SPEAK : (A. smell, B. see, C. sense, D. hear)

98. ACID : (A. $NaHCO_3$, B. H_2SO_4, C. NaCl, D. NaOH) :: ENZYME : AMYLASE

99. (A. sow, B. doe, C. vixen, D. bitch) : FOX :: DAM : SIRE

100. SALIVA : OIL :: MOUTH : (A. friction, B. comb, C. motor, D. cogwheel)

ANSWER KEY

1. D	21. D	41. A	61. B	81. A
2. B	22. C	42. C	62. D	82. C
3. C	23. C	43. B	63. C	83. A
4. A	24. D	44. C	64. D	84. C
5. B	25. B	45. B	65. D	85. D
6. A	26. D	46. B	66. C	86. C
7. A	27. C	47. D	67. D	87. D
8. C	28. C	48. D	68. C	88. C
9. A	29. B	49. A	69. B	89. D
10. B	30. C	50. B	70. A	90. D
11. B	31. B	51. B	71. D	91. D
12. A	32. A	52. B	72. A	92. C
13. C	33. A	53. A	73. C	93. C
14. D	34. D	54. D	74. A	94. A
15. B	35. B	55. D	75. D	95. B
16. A	36. B	56. C	76. C	96. D
17. B	37. B	57. B	77. C	97. D
18. D	38. C	58. B	78. D	98. B
19. B	39. C	59. A	79. C	99. C
20. C	40. B	60. A	80. C	100. C

EXPLANATORY ANSWERS

1. BALMY : MILD :: FAITHFUL : (A. explosive, B. docile, C. talkative, D. staunch)

(D) *Balmy* and *mild* are synonyms; therefore, the task is to look for a synonym for *faithful,* which in this case is *staunch.*

2. BOLD : TIMID :: SQUANDER : (A. disperse, B. hoard, C. query, D. extinguish)

(B) *Bold* and *timid* are related as antonyms. *Squander,* meaning to spend extravagantly, is the opposite of *hoard,* meaning to gather or accumulate.

3. SEA : (A. fish, B. ocean, C. island, D. net) :: LAND : LAKE

(C) *Land* and *lake* are related geographically in the same way as *sea* and *island;* as land surrounds a lake, so does sea surround an island.

4. GLASS : RUBBER :: BRITTLE : (A. elastic, B. scarce, C. tempered, D. spheroid)

(A) A specific characteristic of glass is that it is brittle. Similarly, a specific characteristic of rubber is that it is elastic.

5. DIAMETER : RADIUS :: (A. 3, B. 8, C. 5, D. 6) : 4

(B) This is a mathematical relationship. A diameter is twice the length of a radius in a given circle; therefore, the missing term must be a number that is twice as great as 4. That, of course, is 8. In your own mind, you might say simply, "2 : 1 :: 2 : 1."

6. GLABROUS : FACTITIOUS :: HIRSUTE : (A. authentic, B. fictional, C. fluent, D. replete)

(A) *Glabrous* (hairless) and *hirsute* (hairy) are antonyms. The only antonym for *factitious* (artificial) is *authentic.*

7. PARANOIA : SCHIZOPHRENIA :: MEGALOMANIA : (A. melancholia, B. carcinoma, C. hepatitis, D. glaucoma)

(A) Every term in this analogy is a form of mental illness. Paranoia, a psychosis characterized by delusions of persecution, and schizophrenia, a psychosis characterized by disintegration of the personality, are related by the fact that each is a form of mental illness. Megalomania, a psychosis characterized by infantile feelings of personal omnipotence, is also a form of mental illness. Therefore, the missing term must be melancholia, a psychosis characterized by extreme depression. All other choices name physical illnesses.

8. (A. sales, B. investment, C. management, D. interest) : PROFIT :: LABOR : WAGES

(C) Labor is associated with wages in the same way that management is associated with profit. In both cases, the association is of people working for a reward. Sales, investment, and interest may each be said to yield a profit, but these do not parallel the relationship of people to their reward as established by the given word pair. In solving this analogy, you must have the mental flexibility to think of *labor* and *management* as groups of people rather than as activities. If you think of *labor* as an activity, there are too many possible correct answers.

9. STUDENT : (A. backpack, B. briefcase, C. college, D. teacher) :: TRAVELER : SUITCASE

(A) This is an analogy of purpose and association. A traveler uses a suitcase; similarly, a student uses a backpack.

10. DENIGRATE : DEFAMER :: MEDIATE : (A. mathematician, B. arbitrator, C. employer, D. laborer)

(B) The relationship is one of action to actor. Denigrate (to belittle or to malign) is the action taken by the defamer (one who injures by giving misleading or false reports) in the same way that mediate (to act as an intermediary agent) is the action taken by the arbitrator (one chosen to settle differences between parties in dispute).

11. LAKE WOBEGON : (A. Minneapolis, B. Winesburg, C. Canterbury, D. Minnesota) :: MUDVILLE : CASTERBRIDGE

(B) Mudville, the town in the poem "Casey at the Bat," and Casterbridge, the town in the Hardy novel *The Mayor of Casterbridge,* are fictional places. Likewise, Lake Wobegon, of Keillor's book *Lake Wobegon Days,* and Winesburg, of Anderson's *Winesburg, Ohio,* are fictional places.

12. CORNET : OBOE :: (A. cello, B. drum, C. harpsichord, D. xylophone) : GUITAR

(A) This is a part-to-part analogy. A cornet and an oboe are each part of the larger category of wind instruments in the same way that a guitar and a cello are each part of the larger category of string instruments. A harpsichord, too, belongs to the category of string instruments; however, because it has internal rather than external strings, it is not as closely related to guitar as is cello.

13. JANUARY : WEDNESDAY :: JANUS : (A. Thor, B. Apollo, C. Odin, D. Diana)

(C) January was named for Janus, the guardian deity of gates in Roman mythology, as Wednesday was named for Odin, chief of the Scandinavian gods. The Anglo-Saxon version of Odin was Woden; hence, Woden's Day became Wednesday.

14. HORSE : (A. equestrian, B. hoofed, C. cabriolet, D. herbivorous) :: TIGER : CARNIVOROUS

(D) This is a characteristic relationship. A specific characteristic of a tiger is that it is carnivorous (meat-eating), as a specific characteristic of a horse is that it is herbivorous (plant-eating).

15. GOOD : BETTER :: (A. terrible, B. worse, C. improvement, D. bad) : WORST

(B) This is an analogy of degree. Adjectives such as *good* and *bad* have three degrees of comparison: positive, comparative, and superlative. In this question, *good,* which is the positive degree, is less good than *better,* the comparative degree, to the same extent that *worse,* the comparative, is less bad than *worst,* the superlative degree.

16. CLAN : FEUD :: NATION : (A. war, B. politics, C. armaments, D. retaliation)

(A) The relationship is one of object to action. Just as a clan may become involved in a feud, so may a nation become involved in a war. If you solve this analogy via an A : C :: B : D model, the relationship becomes one of degree. A clan is smaller than a nation; thus, its conflict, a feud, is smaller than a war.

17. ABUNDANCE : ABROGATE :: DEARTH : (A. deny, B. establish, C. abstain, D. absolve)

(B) *Abundance* and *dearth* are antonyms. The opposite of *abrogate* (to nullify or cancel) is *establish*.

18. ONOMATOPOEIA : METAPHOR :: SOUND : (A. hiss, B. rhyme, C. saying, D. comparison)

(**D**) Onomatopoeia (a word whose sound suggests its sense) is a figure of speech that makes a sound relationship. Metaphor (an implied comparison between unlike things) is a figure of speech that makes a comparison.

19. SACRAMENTO : HELENA :: ALBANY : (A. New York, B. Little Rock, C. Houston, D. San Francisco)

(**B**) Sacramento and Helena are related because each is a capital city: Sacramento is the capital of California, and Helena is the capital of Montana. Because Albany is also a state capital, it must be paired with Little Rock, the capital of Arkansas, to complete the analogy.

20. (A. scan, B. feel, C. dear, D. seen) : READ :: REAP : PEAR

(**C**) This is a nonsemantic analogy. Transposing the first and last letters of *reap* forms the word *pear*, just as transposing the first and last letters of *read* forms the word *dear*.

21. CAUTIOUS : CIRCUMSPECT :: PRECIPITOUS : (A. premonitory, B. profound, C. stealthy, D. steep)

(**D**) *Cautious* and *circumspect* are related as synonyms. The only synonym offered for *precipitous* is *steep*.

22. SEISMOGRAPH : GEOLOGY :: ELECTROENCEPHALOGRAPH : (A. bacteriology, B. biology, C. neurology, D. cardiology)

(**C**) This is an analogy of purpose. A seismograph, an instrument for recording vibrations within the earth, is used in geology (the study of the earth), just as an electroencephalograph, an instrument for recording brain waves, is used in neurology (the scientific study of the nervous system).

23. ACUTE : VENERATE :: CHRONIC : (A. revere, B. actuate, C. flout, D. repent)

(**C**) *Acute* and *chronic* are related as antonyms. *Acute* means having a sudden onset, a sharp rise, and a short course; *chronic* means marked by long duration or frequent recurrence. *Venerate,* which means to honor, must therefore be paired with its opposite, *flout,* meaning to scoff or to treat with contemptuous disregard.

24. (A. toad, B. lion, C. shark, D. alligator) : TURTLE :: TIGER : MAN

(**D**) This is a part-to-part analogy. Tiger and man are each part of the larger category of mammals. Turtle, which is part of the larger category of reptiles, must therefore be paired with alligator, the only reptile among the answer choices. A toad is an amphibian.

25. INSTINCT : PLAN :: UNCONSCIOUS : (A. involuntary, B. intentional, C. spontaneous, D. imaginary)

(**B**) An instinct is an unreasoned or unconscious response to a stimulus. A plan is a reasoned or intentional response to a stimulus.

26. INDIA : (A. Sri Lanka, B. Greece, C. Afghanistan, D. Pakistan) :: ITALY : SWITZERLAND

(**D**) The relationship between Italy and Switzerland is that they share a common border, as do India and Pakistan.

27. SWIM : SWAM :: BURST : (A. busted, B. bursted, C. burst, D. bust)

(**C**) The grammatical relationship between *swim* and *swam* is one of present tense to past tense; therefore, the task is to find the past tense of *burst,* which is also *burst*.

82 Master the Miller Analogies Test

28. RAISIN : GRAPE :: PRUNE : (A. apricot, B. currant, C. plum, D. berry)

(C) The relationship is one of origin or sequence. A raisin is a dried grape, just as a prune is a dried plum.

29. GRAM : OUNCE :: LITER : (A. deciliter, B. quart, C. kilogram, D. pound)

(B) A gram is a metric measure of weight. It is paired with an ounce, which is an American measure of weight. A liter is a metric measure of volume that must be paired with its near equivalent, an American quart. In the American system of weights and measures, an ounce may also be a measure of volume, but it would be impossible to create an analogy with the necessary parallels with any interpretation other than that ounce is a measure of weight.

30. BEAKER : CHEMIST :: STETHOSCOPE : (A. teacher, B. author, C. doctor, D. dentist)

(C) This is an analogy of tool to its user or object to actor. A beaker is used by a chemist in the course of his or her work, as a stethoscope is used by a doctor in the performance of his or her work.

31. LIMPID : LUCID :: TURBID : (A. torpid, B. muddy, C. truculent, D. serene)

(B) *Limpid* and *lucid* are synonyms meaning clear. A synonym for *turbid* is *muddy*.

32. MANGO : (A. coconut, B. tomato, C. cabbage, D. apple) :: PAPAYA : PASSIONFRUIT

(A) The mango, coconut, papaya, and passionfruit are all juicy fruits that are grown primarily in tropical climates.

33. .02 : .0004 :: .001 : (A. .000001, B. .0001, C. .0002, D. .000002)

(A) $(.02)^2 = .0004$; $(.001)^2 = .000001$.

34. SADNESS : PAIN :: FAILURE : (A. medication, B. palliation, C. pleasure, D. injury)

(D) The relationship of the given word pair is one of cause and effect. Sadness may be caused by failure in the same way that pain may be caused by an injury.

35. AMELIA EARHART : NELLIE BLY :: AVIATION : (A. medicine, B. journalism, C. law, D. prohibition)

(B) This is an analogy of the association of famous women to the field in which they pioneered. Amelia Earhart achieved fame as one of the first women in aviation; Nellie Bly was one of the first women in journalism.

36. ROMAN : MANOR :: (A. cleric, B. names, C. patrimony, D. estates) : MANSE

(B) *Roman* and *manor* are anagrams. So, too, are *names* and *manse*.

37. LACONIC : FLACCID :: REDUNDANT : (A. succinct, B. firm, C. flimsy, D. swollen)

(B) *Laconic* (concise) and *redundant* (excessively wordy) are antonyms. Among the answer choices, the only antonym for *flaccid* (flabby or limp) is *firm*.

38. PNEUMATICS : (A. medicine, B. disease, C. physics, D. cars) :: ESKER : GEOLOGY

(C) An esker (a ridge formed by a glacial stream) is part of the field of geology, as pneumatics (the use of gas or air pressure) is part of the field of physics.

Sample Test 1   83

39. NECKLACE : MEDAL :: ADORNMENT : (A. jewel, B. metal, C. decoration, D. bronze)

(C) A necklace is used for adornment as a medal is used for decoration.

40. RIVER : STREAM :: MOUNTAIN : (A. cliff, B. hill, C. canyon, D. peak)

(B) This is an analogy of degree. A river is larger than a stream, as a mountain is larger than a hill.

41. HECKLE : NEEDLE :: (A. stock, B. deplete, C. book, D. stylus) : REPLENISH

(A) *Heckle* and *needle* are synonyms meaning to harass or badger. The only synonym offered for *replenish* is *stock*.

42. (A. guerrilla, B. terrorist, C. quash, D. mediate) : REBELLION :: NEGOTIATE : TREATY

(C) The relationship of the given word pair is action to object. One may negotiate (bring about by mutual agreement) a treaty just as one may quash (crush) a rebellion.

43. BOTANIST : PLANTS :: GEOLOGIST : (A. trees, B. rocks, C. geography, D. gems)

(B) The first word pair is related by the association of a scientist to the object of study. Of the choices offered, only the study of rocks is related to the geologist as the study of plants is related to the botanist. To the extent that gemstones occur naturally among the rocks, the geologist will study them as well, but the primary concern of a geologist is rocks, their composition, and their history.

44. CAT : FELINE :: OX : (A. equine, B. saturnine, C. bovine, D. canine)

(C) *Feline* means of or relating to the cat family, as *bovine* means of or relating to the ox or cow family.

45. WOLF : (A. wool, B. sheep, C. ewe, D. ram) :: DOG : CAT

(B) A dog and cat are simply two different kinds of animal. A wolf and sheep are likewise two different kinds of animal. Gender is not a factor in the relationship of dog to cat, so it must not enter the analogy in relationship to the wolf.

46. (A. $\frac{5}{16}$, B. $\frac{3}{8}$, C. $\frac{2}{6}$, D. $\frac{5}{12}$) : $\frac{9}{24}$ :: $\frac{4}{11}$: $\frac{12}{33}$

(B) Dividing the numerator and denominator by 3, $\frac{12}{33}$ can be reduced to $\frac{4}{11}$. Similarly, dividing the numerator and denominator by 3, $\frac{9}{24}$ can be reduced to $\frac{3}{8}$.

47. FISHES : BIRDS :: (A. horses, B. cattle, C. wheat, D. mosses) : CEREALS

(D) This is an analogy of sequence. On the evolutionary scale, fishes appeared long before birds in the animal world; mosses appeared long before cereals in the plant world.

48. ROOM : CABIN :: HOUSE : (A. camp, B. cottage, C. hotel, D. ship)

(D) A room is a division of a house—specifically, a living unit of a house. A cabin is a living unit of a ship.

49. BRASS : COPPER :: PEWTER : (A. lead, B. zinc, C. silver, D. bronze)

(A) Brass is an alloy consisting essentially of copper and zinc. Pewter is an alloy consisting of tin and lead.

84   Master the Miller Analogies Test

50. COWCATCHER : LOCOMOTIVE :: (A. coda, B. climax, C. epilogue, D. finale) : DENOUEMENT

(**B**) A cowcatcher immediately precedes a locomotive as a climax (the point of highest dramatic tension) immediately precedes the denouement (the unraveling or outcome of a sequence of events) in a story or a play.

51. PARIAH : OUTCAST :: ARCHON : (A. archivist, B. magistrate, C. martine, D. constable)

(**B**) *Pariah* and *outcast* are synonyms. The only synonym offered for *archon* is *magistrate*.

52. (A. cappuccino, B. shamrock, C. wine, D. palm trees) : VODKA :: DEVALERA : STALIN

(**B**) Joseph Stalin was the leader of the Soviet Union, which is intimately associated with vodka. Eamon Devalera was the leader of Ireland, which is intimately associated with the shamrock.

53. LANCET : CUT :: CHAMOIS : (A. polish, B. pliant, C. smooth, D. sheep)

(**A**) This is an analogy of purpose. A lancet is a sharp surgical instrument used to cut; a chamois is a soft, pliant leather prepared from the skin of the chamois or from sheepskin used to polish.

54. (A. utter, B. elapse, C. exude, D. time) : EMIT :: STEP : PETS

(**D**) This is a nonsemantic analogy. *Time* spelled backward is *emit,* as *step* spelled backward is *pets*.

55. SAFE : NECKLACE :: COMBINATION : (A. torque, B. bangle, C. circlet, D. clasp)

(**D**) A safe is opened by a combination; a necklace is opened by a clasp.

56. EXPERIMENT : (A. science, B. elucidation, C. hypothesis, D. investigation) :: EXAMINATION : ACHIEVEMENT

(**C**) An experiment tests a hypothesis as an examination tests achievement.

57. BOY : BULLET :: MAN : (A. gun, B. artillery shell, C. holster, D. trigger)

(**B**) The relationship is one of degree. A man is larger than a boy; an artillery shell is larger and more effective than a bullet.

58. ENERVATE : (A. eradicate, B. invigorate, C. disconcert, D. propagate) :: MALICE : BENEVOLENCE

(**B**) *Malice* and *benevolence* are antonyms. The only antonym offered for *enervate* (to drain of strength) is *invigorate*.

59. EVIDENCE : CONVICTION :: (A. oxygen, B. carbon dioxide, C. match, D. light) : COMBUSTION

(**A**) Evidence is necessary for conviction in the judicial process, just as oxygen is necessary for the chemical process of combustion. Heat is also necessary for combustion, but the source of heat may be other than a match.

60. EDIFICATION : AWARENESS :: AGGRAVATION : (A. distress, B. excitement, C. reduction, D. deliberation)

(**A**) The relationship of the given word pair is one of cause and effect because edification (enlightenment) results in awareness. Similarly, aggravation results in distress.

61. NEWTON : COPERNICUS :: SHAKESPEARE : (A. Fielding, B. Jonson, C. Dickens, D. Defoe)

(**B**) Newton and Copernicus are noted for their contributions to the field of science. Both Shakespeare and Jonson are well known for both drama and poetry. Notice that each of the alternatives names a figure from the field of literature; therefore, it is necessary to narrow the relationship to a particular area or areas of literature in order to answer this question correctly.

62. ST. AUGUSTINE : (A. Florida, B. Virginia, C. France, D. Spain) :: JAMESTOWN : ENGLAND

(**D**) Jamestown was England's first permanent settlement in the New World, just as St. Augustine was Spain's first permanent settlement.

63. SNOW : DRIFT :: (A. hill, B. rain, C. sand, D. desert) : DUNE

(**C**) When blown by the wind, snow forms a drift, and sand forms a dune.

64. CATAMARAN : TERMAGANT :: RAFT : (A. grisette, B. spinnaker, C. spinster, D. shrew)

(**D**) *Catamaran* and *raft* are synonyms, as are *termagant* and *shrew*.

65. $3^2 : 2^3 :: 9 :$ (A. 1, B. 6, C. 4, D. 8)

(**D**) $3^2 = 3 \times 3 = 9$
$2^3 = 2 \times 2 \times 2 = 8$

66. FICTION : NOVELIST :: FACTS : (A. legend, B. story, C. historian, D. research)

(**C**) Fiction is the province of the novelist, as facts are the province of the historian.

67. HARVARD : YALE :: BROWN : (A. Princeton, B. Purdue, C. Emory, D. Dartmouth)

(**D**) The relationship between the terms of the given word pair is one of place. Harvard and Yale are both located in New England, as are Brown and Dartmouth.

68. CAT : WOLF :: (A. lion, B. dog, C. man, D. tiger) : DUCK

(**C**) A cat and wolf are related in that they are each members of the larger category of four-legged creatures. A duck, which is a two-legged creature, must therefore be paired with the only other two-legged creature, which is man.

69. WHO : I :: WHOM : (A. we, B. me, C. whose, D. mine)

(**B**) This is a grammatical analogy. *Who* is nominative, and *whom* is objective. Likewise, *I* is nominative, and *me* is objective.

70. (A. obsequious, B. obstreperous, C. complacent, D. contumelious) : SYCOPHANT :: CONTUMACIOUS : RENEGADE

(**A**) The relationship between the words of the given pair is one of characteristic. *Contumacious* (an adjective meaning rebellious) describes a renegade (a noun meaning one who rejects lawful or conventional behavior). Similarly, *obsequious* (an adjective meaning subservient) describes a sycophant (a noun meaning servile flatterer or parasite).

71. DOWSER : ROD :: GEOMANCER : (A. stones, B. maps, C. plants, D. configurations)

(**D**) A dowser divines the presence of water or minerals by means of a rod, as a geomancer divines by means of geographical features or configurations.

72. MINERVA : ATHENA :: (A. Jupiter, B. Juno, C. Poseidon, D. Apollo) : ZEUS

(A) The relationship is that of father to daughter. Athena was the daughter of Zeus in Greek mythology; Minerva was the daughter of Jupiter in Roman mythology.

73. (A. loss, B. victory, C. game, D. team) : WIN :: MEDICINE : CURE

(C) The objective of a game is to win, as the objective of medicine is to cure. The relationship is that of objective to action.

74. SAFARI : SWAHILI :: SALAAM : (A. Arabic, B. shalom, C. peace, D. Africa)

(A) *Safari* means journey in the Swahili language. *Salaam* is an Arabic greeting. This is an answer you should be able to get by elimination. Swahili is a language, and Arabic is the only language offered among the choices.

75. ACID : ALKALI :: 6 : (A. 1, B. 4, C. 7, D. 8)

(D) Acidity and alkalinity are expressed on a pH scale whose values run from 0 to 14, with 7 representing neutrality. Numbers less than 7 indicate increasing acidity, and numbers greater than 7 represent increasing alkalinity. Therefore, ACID : ALKALI :: 6 (a pH indicating mild acidity) : 8 (a pH indicating mild alkalinity).

76. PEDESTAL : (A. column, B. sculpture, C. chandelier, D. stone) :: STALAGMITE : STALACTITE

(C) Stalagmites and stalactites are deposits of calcium carbonate formed by the dripping of calcareous water in a cave. A stalagmite grows up from the floor of the cave, while a stalactite hangs down from the ceiling of the cave. Similarly, a pedestal is an architectural support or base that raises something up from the ground, and a chandelier is a lighting fixture that hangs down from the ceiling.

77. *BONA FIDE* : *IN TOTO* :: *CARTE BLANCHE* : (A. *eureka*, B. *status quo*, C. *avant-garde*, D. *ersatz*)

(C) *Bona fide* (meaning in good faith) and *in toto* (meaning in full) are Latin words that have been borrowed intact for use in English. *Avant-garde* (meaning pioneer) and *carte blanche* (meaning blanket permission) are French words that have been borrowed intact for use in English. *Eureka* is borrowed from the Greek; *status quo* comes from Latin; and *ersatz* comes from German.

78. SEA : COAST :: RIVER : (A. inlet, B. delta, C. stream, D. bank)

(D) This is an analogy of place or of whole to part. The land bordering the sea is the coast, as the land bordering a river is a bank.

79. AMOUNT : NUMBER :: (A. lessen, B. augment, C. less, D. enumerate) : FEWER

(C) In this grammatical analogy, *amount* refers to quantity or bulk, while *number* refers to items that can be counted one by one. Similarly, *less* refers to quantity, and *fewer* refers to items that can be counted.

80. VOLUME : CUBIC METER :: (A. area, B. length, C. capacity, D. mass) : LITER

(C) The relationship expressed by the given word pair is one of measurement. Volume may be measured in cubic meters, as capacity may be measured in liters.

81. (A. refrain, B. precede, C. sustain, D. foray) : FORBEAR :: ADUMBRATE : FORESHADOW

(**A**) *Adumbrate* and *foreshadow* are synonyms. The only synonym offered for *forbear* (meaning to hold back or abstain) is *refrain*.

82. CHAMPION : CAUSE :: (A. signature, B. introduction, C. draft, D. ink) : LETTER

(**C**) This is an analogy of action to object. One may champion a cause, as one may draft a letter. This is another of those analogy questions that requires mental flexibility. If you insist upon thinking of *champion* as a noun—for indeed a champion may have a cause—you cannot find a parallel noun on the other side of the analogy. Once you switch your thinking and recognize that *champion* is being used as a verb, it is easy to find a parallel activity the object of which is a letter.

83. SHADOWS : CLOUDS :: SUN : (A. water, B. dark, C. rain, D. thunder)

(**A**) Sun is necessary to the formation of shadows, as water is necessary to the formation of clouds. C : A :: D : B.

84. WINTER : SUMMER :: BOSTON : (A. Miami, B. Madrid, C. Sao Paulo, D. San Diego)

(**C**) When it is winter in Boston, it is summer in Sao Paulo because the seasons are reversed in the northern and southern hemispheres.

85. CIRCLE : SPHERE :: (A. ice, B. angle, C. oval, D. square) : CUBE

(**D**) A circle is a plane figure; a sphere is the corresponding solid figure. A square is a plane figure, and a cube is the corresponding solid figure.

86. KINETIC : MOTION :: PISCATORIAL : (A. pizza, B. painting, C. fish, D. picturesque)

(**C**) *Kinetic* is an adjective meaning of or relating to motion, as *piscatorial* is an adjective meaning of or relating to fish.

87. RESPIRATION : CO_2 :: (A. hydrolysis, B. transpiration, C. oxidation, D. photosynthesis) : O_2

(**D**) During the process of respiration, living things take in oxygen and give off CO_2 and water. During the process of photosynthesis, green plants take in carbon dioxide and water and give off O_2.

88. SAND : CLAY :: GLASS : (A. stone, B. hay, C. brick, D. dirt)

(**C**) The relationship existing between the terms of the given word pair is one of purpose because sand is used to make glass. Similarly, clay is used to make brick.

89. LOUISIANA PURCHASE : (a. Mexico, b. Spain, c. Great Britain, d. France) :: ALASKA : RUSSIA

(**D**) Alaska was purchased from Russia (in 1867), as the area known as the Louisiana Purchase was purchased from France (in 1803).

90. X : M :: (A. V, B. X, C. L, D. I) : C

(**D**) The relationship between Roman numerals X (10) and M (1000) is 1 to 100. The same relationship exists between the Roman numerals I (1) and C (100).

91. PUCCINI : OPERA :: (A. Pavlova, B. Verdi, C. *Giselle,* D. Balanchine) : BALLET

(D) Puccini created operas, as Balanchine created ballets. Although Pavlova was a famous ballerina and *Giselle* is the name of a well-known ballet, only Balanchine (as a choreographer) stands in the same relationship to the ballet as Puccini (as a composer) stands in relationship to opera.

92. POLTROON : TERROR :: PARANOIAC : (A. courage, B. shyness, C. persecution, D. paralysis)

(C) A characteristic of a poltroon (coward) is a feeling of terror, as a characteristic of a paranoiac is a feeling of persecution.

93. DOOR : BOLT :: LETTER : (A. envelope, B. mail, C. seal, D. write)

(C) The relationship between the terms of the given word pair is one of object to action. However, three of the choices offered are actions one may take on the object letter. Therefore, it is necessary to narrow the relationship to the specific action of closing or securing. A door is secured by a bolt, and a letter is secured by a seal.

94. AUTHOR : (A. royalties, B. charges, C. fees, D. contributions) :: AGENT : COMMISSIONS

(A) The relationship is one of an individual to his or her means of payment. An agent receives commissions (a percentage of the total fees paid) for his or her part in a business transaction. An author receives royalties (a percentage of the total payment made for a work) for his or her part in creating the work sold.

95. OLD BAILEY : OLD VIC :: (A. Versailles, B. Bastille, C. Westminster, D. London) : LA SCALA

(B) The Old Vic is a theater is London; La Scala is the Milan opera house. Both are houses in which performances take place. Old Bailey is a London court with prison attached; the Bastille was a Paris prison.

96. TRUDEAU : (A. Durant, B. De Toqueville, C. Malthus, D. Nast) :: ORWELL : HUXLEY

(D) Both George Orwell and Aldous Huxley wrote novels with heavy political content set in the future. Both Garry Trudeau and Thomas Nast gained fame as political cartoonists.

97. ORAL : AURAL :: SPEAK : (A. smell, B. see, C. sense, D. hear)

(D) *Oral* means uttered by the mouth or spoken. *Aural* means of or relating to the ear or to the sense of hearing. Therefore, *oral* describes *speak* as *aural* describes *hear*.

98. ACID : (A. $NaHCO_3$, B. H_2SO_4, C. NaCl, D. NaOH) :: ENZYME : AMYLASE

(B) The formula for a specific acid is H_2SO_4 (sulfuric acid). The name for a specific enzyme is amylase.

99. (A. sow, B. doe, C. vixen, D. bitch) : FOX :: DAM : SIRE

(C) This analogy is one of female to male. A vixen is a female animal, and a fox is her male counterpart. A dam is a female animal parent, and a sire is the male counterpart.

100. SALIVA : OIL :: MOUTH : (A. friction, B. comb, C. motor, D. cogwheel)

(C) A characteristic of saliva is that it lubricates the mouth. A characteristic of oil is that it lubricates a motor.

SAMPLE TEST 2

Answer Sheet

1. ⓐ ⓑ ⓒ ⓓ
2. ⓐ ⓑ ⓒ ⓓ
3. ⓐ ⓑ ⓒ ⓓ
4. ⓐ ⓑ ⓒ ⓓ
5. ⓐ ⓑ ⓒ ⓓ
6. ⓐ ⓑ ⓒ ⓓ
7. ⓐ ⓑ ⓒ ⓓ
8. ⓐ ⓑ ⓒ ⓓ
9. ⓐ ⓑ ⓒ ⓓ
10. ⓐ ⓑ ⓒ ⓓ
11. ⓐ ⓑ ⓒ ⓓ
12. ⓐ ⓑ ⓒ ⓓ
13. ⓐ ⓑ ⓒ ⓓ
14. ⓐ ⓑ ⓒ ⓓ
15. ⓐ ⓑ ⓒ ⓓ
16. ⓐ ⓑ ⓒ ⓓ
17. ⓐ ⓑ ⓒ ⓓ
18. ⓐ ⓑ ⓒ ⓓ
19. ⓐ ⓑ ⓒ ⓓ
20. ⓐ ⓑ ⓒ ⓓ
21. ⓐ ⓑ ⓒ ⓓ
22. ⓐ ⓑ ⓒ ⓓ
23. ⓐ ⓑ ⓒ ⓓ
24. ⓐ ⓑ ⓒ ⓓ
25. ⓐ ⓑ ⓒ ⓓ
26. ⓐ ⓑ ⓒ ⓓ
27. ⓐ ⓑ ⓒ ⓓ
28. ⓐ ⓑ ⓒ ⓓ
29. ⓐ ⓑ ⓒ ⓓ
30. ⓐ ⓑ ⓒ ⓓ
31. ⓐ ⓑ ⓒ ⓓ
32. ⓐ ⓑ ⓒ ⓓ
33. ⓐ ⓑ ⓒ ⓓ
34. ⓐ ⓑ ⓒ ⓓ
35. ⓐ ⓑ ⓒ ⓓ
36. ⓐ ⓑ ⓒ ⓓ
37. ⓐ ⓑ ⓒ ⓓ
38. ⓐ ⓑ ⓒ ⓓ
39. ⓐ ⓑ ⓒ ⓓ
40. ⓐ ⓑ ⓒ ⓓ
41. ⓐ ⓑ ⓒ ⓓ
42. ⓐ ⓑ ⓒ ⓓ
43. ⓐ ⓑ ⓒ ⓓ
44. ⓐ ⓑ ⓒ ⓓ
45. ⓐ ⓑ ⓒ ⓓ
46. ⓐ ⓑ ⓒ ⓓ
47. ⓐ ⓑ ⓒ ⓓ
48. ⓐ ⓑ ⓒ ⓓ
49. ⓐ ⓑ ⓒ ⓓ
50. ⓐ ⓑ ⓒ ⓓ
51. ⓐ ⓑ ⓒ ⓓ
52. ⓐ ⓑ ⓒ ⓓ
53. ⓐ ⓑ ⓒ ⓓ
54. ⓐ ⓑ ⓒ ⓓ
55. ⓐ ⓑ ⓒ ⓓ
56. ⓐ ⓑ ⓒ ⓓ
57. ⓐ ⓑ ⓒ ⓓ
58. ⓐ ⓑ ⓒ ⓓ
59. ⓐ ⓑ ⓒ ⓓ
60. ⓐ ⓑ ⓒ ⓓ
61. ⓐ ⓑ ⓒ ⓓ
62. ⓐ ⓑ ⓒ ⓓ
63. ⓐ ⓑ ⓒ ⓓ
64. ⓐ ⓑ ⓒ ⓓ
65. ⓐ ⓑ ⓒ ⓓ
66. ⓐ ⓑ ⓒ ⓓ
67. ⓐ ⓑ ⓒ ⓓ
68. ⓐ ⓑ ⓒ ⓓ
69. ⓐ ⓑ ⓒ ⓓ
70. ⓐ ⓑ ⓒ ⓓ
71. ⓐ ⓑ ⓒ ⓓ
72. ⓐ ⓑ ⓒ ⓓ
73. ⓐ ⓑ ⓒ ⓓ
74. ⓐ ⓑ ⓒ ⓓ
75. ⓐ ⓑ ⓒ ⓓ
76. ⓐ ⓑ ⓒ ⓓ
77. ⓐ ⓑ ⓒ ⓓ
78. ⓐ ⓑ ⓒ ⓓ
79. ⓐ ⓑ ⓒ ⓓ
80. ⓐ ⓑ ⓒ ⓓ
81. ⓐ ⓑ ⓒ ⓓ
82. ⓐ ⓑ ⓒ ⓓ
83. ⓐ ⓑ ⓒ ⓓ
84. ⓐ ⓑ ⓒ ⓓ
85. ⓐ ⓑ ⓒ ⓓ
86. ⓐ ⓑ ⓒ ⓓ
87. ⓐ ⓑ ⓒ ⓓ
88. ⓐ ⓑ ⓒ ⓓ
89. ⓐ ⓑ ⓒ ⓓ
90. ⓐ ⓑ ⓒ ⓓ
91. ⓐ ⓑ ⓒ ⓓ
92. ⓐ ⓑ ⓒ ⓓ
93. ⓐ ⓑ ⓒ ⓓ
94. ⓐ ⓑ ⓒ ⓓ
95. ⓐ ⓑ ⓒ ⓓ
96. ⓐ ⓑ ⓒ ⓓ
97. ⓐ ⓑ ⓒ ⓓ
98. ⓐ ⓑ ⓒ ⓓ
99. ⓐ ⓑ ⓒ ⓓ
100. ⓐ ⓑ ⓒ ⓓ

TEAR HERE

Chapter 6

Sample Test 2

100 Questions • 50 Minutes

Directions: Each of these test questions consists of three capitalized words and four lettered words enclosed in parentheses. Two of the capitalized words are related in some way. Find the two related words, and establish the nature of the relationship. Then study the four words lettered A, B, C, and D. Select the one lettered word that is related to the remaining capitalized words in the same way that the first two capitalized words are related. Mark the answer sheet for the letter preceding the word you select.

ROAD MAP

- *Answer Key*
- *Explanatory Answers*

1. SURFEIT : (A. collect, B. empty, C. glut, D. spoil) :: ARROGATE : USURP

2. ROBBERY : INCARCERATION :: (A. marking, B. singing, C. sleeping, D. embezzlement) : APPLAUSE

3. ICHTHYOLOGY : (A. insects, B. mammals, C. fish, D. invertebrates) :: ORNITHOLOGY : BIRDS

4. FIRST : PENULTIMATE :: JANUARY : (A. December, B. November, C. February, D. June)

5. HOPE : PLEASURE :: DESPONDENCY : (A. frolic, B. gratification, C. joy, D. anguish)

6. DICHOTOMY : DISSEMBLE :: DIVISION : (A. feign, B. assemble, C. resemble, D. return)

7. LONGFELLOW : WHITMAN :: (A. Tagore, B. Keats, C. Heine, D. Dickens) : TENNYSON

8. MITER : BISHOP :: (A. stole, B. cleric, C. robe, D. biretta) : PRIEST

9. OK : PA :: KS : (A. CT, B. AZ, C. WV, D. NY)

10. SEED : BREED :: (A. origin, B. specimen, C. need, D. act) : DEED

11. (A. influence, B. compose, C. touch, D. infect) : RESULT :: AFFECT : EFFECT

12. SAUTÉING : COOKERY :: PAINTING : (A. juggling, B. forestry, C. art, D. medicine)

13. CAMPHOR : AROMATIC :: LILAC : (A. lavender, B. leaf, C. fragrant, D. rose)

14. (A. skiers, B. winter, C. athletes, D. blades) : SKATES :: RUNNERS : SLEDS

15. LOCARNO : SWITZERLAND :: ARGONNE : (A. France, B. Quebec, C. Germany, D. Belgium)

16. ARMY : FOOD :: DEFENSE : (A. digestion, B. vegetation, C. nutrition, D. supply)

17. LESSING : (A. Fitzgerald, B. Woolf, C. Orwell, D. Wolfe) :: JONG : WALKER

18. BENEFICENT : INIMICAL :: DELETERIOUS : (A. amicable, B. hostile, C. matchless, D. ordinary)

19. ANEMOMETER : (A. smell, B. texture, C. wind, D. pressure) :: ODOMETER : DISTANCE

20. WHIP : HORN :: CRACK : (A. blow, B. break, C. tattoo, D. march)

21. HILL : MOUNTAIN :: (A. depression, B. discomfort, C. headache, D. fear) : PAIN

22. (A. *The Merry Widow*, B. *Naughty Marietta*, C. *Iolanthe*, D. *Carmen*) : *MIKADO* :: *H.M.S. PINAFORE* : *GONDOLIERS*

23. BELL : HOLMES :: (A. Watson, B. Edison, C. Graham, D. Doyle) : WATSON

24. WHEEL : COG :: (A. heaven, B. ribbon, C. rim, D. bulb) : FILAMENT

25. POLICEMAN : (A. convict, B. justice, C. conduct, D. crime) :: DENTIST : CAVITY

26. ROUND : CHUCK :: (A. circle, B. flank, C. chipped, D. throw) : RIB

27. FRACTIOUS : SYSTEMATIC :: DEBILITATE : (A. invigorate, B. undermine, C. diverge, D. annul)

28. FOUR : TWENTY :: (A. two, B. five, C. three, D. seven) : FIFTEEN

29. GROUND CREW : SEMAPHORE :: PILOT : (A. radio, B. airplane, C. stewardess, D. copilot)

30. GLAND : ENDOCRINE :: MUSCLE : (A. hard, B. strong, C. desiccated, D. striated)

31. PROHIBITED : BANNED :: CANONICAL : (A. reputable, B. authoritative, C. referred, D. considered)

32. INTERMINABLE : ENDLESS :: APPARENT : (A. concise, B. ostensible, C. transparent, D. improbable)

33. ICE : STEAM :: BRICK : (A. straw, B. mortar, C. pole, D. stone)

34. BREATHING : (A. oxygen, B. lungs, C. carbon dioxide, D. nose) :: CRYING : TEARS

35. MARRY : REPENT :: HASTE : (A. contrition, B. delay, C. leisure, D. deliberate)

36. JAMES I : (A. James II, B. George I, C. Elizabeth I, D. Charles I) :: GEORGE V : EDWARD VIII

37. PLANS : ARCHITECT :: TREACHERY : (A. thief, B. traitor, C. cheater, D. killer)

38. LILY : ROSEMARY :: PURITY : (A. lamb, B. squalor, C. remembrance, D. thyme)

39. ANCHOR : KEY :: (A. dock, B. boat, C. prow, D. keel) : CHAIN

40. (A. Scopes, B. Darrow, C. Darwin, D. Jennings) : BRYAN :: SACCO : VANZETTI

41. (A. subterranean, B. subconscious, C. superb, D. advertised) : SUBLIMINAL :: PLETHORIC : SUPERFLUOUS

42. VICTORY : PYRRHIC :: FRUIT : (A. ripe, B. bitter, C. pie, D. tree)

43. TOUCH : DOWN :: (A. walk, B. river, C. home, D. stocking) : RUN

44. MITOSIS : DIVISION :: OSMOSIS : (A. diffusion, B. concentration, C. digestion, D. metamorphosis)

45. SUN : (A. summer, B. tan, C. sunscreen, D. beach) :: COLD : OVERCOAT

46. PHOEBUS : (A. Helius, B. Eos, C. Diana, D. Perseus) :: SUN : MOON

47. (A. equality, B. generous, C. wantonness, D. goodness) : LIBERTINE :: ADVOCACY : LAWYER

48. POUND : KILOGRAM :: WEIGHT : (A. weight, B. area, C. volume, D. capacity)

49. PRECARIOUS : ZEALOUS :: CERTAIN : (A. apathetic, B. ardent, C. indigent, D. sensitive)

50. PONDER : THOUGHT :: ARBITRATE : (A. endorscment, B. plan, C. fine, D. dispute)

51. OBSTRUCT : IMPENETRABLE :: IMPEDE : (A. forbearing, B. hidden, C. impervious, D. merciful)

52. OCTAVE : SESTET :: (A. scale, B. ending, C. quatrain, D. symphony) : COUPLET

53. NOVEL : (A. epic, B. drama, C. volume, D. story) :: *TOM SAWYER* : *AENEID*

54. PURSER : (A. bank, B. ship, C. race track, D. highway) :: BRAKEMAN : TRAIN

55. DRINK : SECURITY :: THIRST : (A. assuredness, B. stocks, C. fear, D. money)

56. CIRCLE : OVAL :: (A. figure, B. octagon, C. starfish, D. semicircle) : PARALLELOGRAM

57. RESILIENCY : RUBBER :: LAMBENCY : (A. oil, B. sheep, C. candlelight, D. lawn)

58. VIRTUOSO : (A. orchestra, B. home, C. prison, D. college) :: TEACHER : CLASSROOM

59. KEYBOARD : (A. small, B. office, C. mouse, D. radio) :: LIPSTICK : COMPACT

60. (A. 4, B. 7, C. 9, D. 14) : 28 :: 11 : 44

GO ON TO THE NEXT PAGE

94 Master the Miller Analogies Test

61. CAPE : WADI :: PROMONTORY : (A. gully, B. waterfall, C. meadow, D. fen)

62. BINDING : BOOK :: WELDING : (A. box, B. tank, C. chair, D. wire)

63. SERFDOM : FEUDALISM :: ENTREPRENEURSHIP : (A. laissez-faire, B. captain, C. radical, D. capitalism)

64. (A. bassos, B. dynamos, C. heroes, D. solos) : EMBARGOES :: VOLCANOES : TOMATOES

65. FOAL : HORSE :: CYGNET : (A. ring, B. fish, C. swan, D. constellation)

66. WARFARE : (A. ingenuity, B. commerce, C. separate, D. destruction) :: TYRANNY : DISSENT

67. HOUSE : BUILD :: TRENCH : (A. dig, B. trap, C. obliterate, D. dry)

68. CELL : WORKER :: ORGANISM : (A. occupation, B. proletariat, C. product, D. nation)

69. ANGLO-SAXON : ENGLISH :: LATIN : (A. Roman, B. Greek, C. Italian, D. Mediterranean)

70. SHERMAN : GEORGIA :: KITCHENER : (A. South Africa, B. Rome, C. Australia, D. Quebec)

71. CHARM : TALISMAN :: FEALTY : (A. allegiance, B. faith, C. payment, D. real estate)

72. ACCELERATOR : (A. cylinder, B. inertia, C. motion, D. exhaust) :: CATALYST : CHANGE

73. INTELLIGENCE : UNDERSTANDING :: CONFUSION : (A. unhappiness, B. pleasure, C. school, D. comprehension)

74. TALKING : YELLING :: GIGGLING : (A. rejoicing, B. laughing, C. chuckling, D. sneering)

75. 49 : 7 :: (A. 98, B. 103, C. 94, D. 144) : 12

76. (A. Chrysler, B. mink, C. chauffeur, D. Boeing) : CADILLAC :: BEAVER : CHEVROLET

77. BREAK : BROKEN :: FLY : (A. flied, B. flew, C. flown, D. flying)

78. DEFALCATE : EXCULPATE :: EMBEZZLEMENT : (A. blame, B. uncover, C. exoneration, D. divulge)

79. SAW : (A. teeth, B. knife, C. board, D. blade) :: SCISSORS : CLOTH

80. PEDAL : PIANO :: BRIDGE : (A. case, B. tune, C. rosin, D. violin)

81. BUCOLIC : CIMMERIAN :: PEACEFUL : (A. warlike, B. tenebrous, C. doubtful, D. smirking)

82. FLATTERY : (A. unity, B. self-interest, C. honesty, D. openness) :: FLIGHT : SAFETY

83. PRAYER : (A. church, B. Bible, C. religion, D. fulfillment) :: RESEARCH : DISCOVERY

84. PAYMENT : PREMIUM :: DEBT : (A. cracker, B. prize, C. insurance, D. scarcity)

85. SACRIFICE : HIT :: STEAL : (A. leave, B. slay, C. walk, D. rob)

86. (A. clap, B. play, C. doom, D. fork) : MOOD :: SLEEK : KEELS

87. DEMOLISH : BUILDING :: (A. sail, B. raze, C. dock, D. scuttle) : SHIP

88. LOGGIA : JALOUSIE :: GALLERY : (A. lintel, B. dowel, C. jamb, D. shutter)

89. PAGE : CUB :: (A. book, B. paper, C. herald, D. knight) : REPORTER

90. VIRGO : TAURUS :: SEPTEMBER : (A. May, B. January, C. June, D. November)

91. FELICITY : CONGENIAL :: BLISS : (A. clever, B. compatible, C. fierce, D. unfriendly)

92. WHEEL : FENDER :: (A. dashboard, B. bow, C. caboose, D. pedal) : RUDDER

93. REQUEST : VISIT :: DEMAND : (A. return, B. welcome, C. invasion, D. house)

94. DENOUEMENT : (A. climax, B. outcome, C. complication, D. untying) :: DEBIT : CREDIT

95. STRAIGHT : POKER :: SMASH : (A. hit, B. tennis, C. ruin, D. bat)

96. (A. small, B. sandwich, C. surprise, D. tight) : SCROOGE :: LYNCH : GUILLOTINE

97. VALLEY : GORGE :: MOUNTAIN : (A. hill, B. cliff, C. acme, D. high)

98. ALPHA : OMEGA :: MERCURY : (A. Saturn, B. planet, C. Pluto, D. Venus)

99. CHIFFON : TWEED :: (A. synthetic, B. sheer, C. dark, D. textured) : ROUGH

100. SIDEREAL : (A. side, B. part, C. stars, D. planets) :: LUNAR : MOON

ANSWER KEY

1. C	21. B	41. B	61. A	81. B
2. B	22. C	42. B	62. B	82. B
3. C	23. A	43. C	63. D	83. D
4. B	24. D	44. A	64. C	84. C
5. D	25. D	45. C	65. C	85. C
6. A	26. B	46. C	66. D	86. C
7. B	27. A	47. C	67. A	87. D
8. D	28. C	48. A	68. B	88. D
9. D	29. A	49. A	69. C	89. D
10. C	30. D	50. D	70. A	90. A
11. A	31. B	51. C	71. A	91. B
12. C	32. B	52. C	72. C	92. B
13. C	33. A	53. A	73. A	93. C
14. D	34. C	54. B	74. B	94. C
15. A	35. C	55. C	75. D	95. B
16. C	36. D	56. B	76. B	96. B
17. B	37. B	57. C	77. C	97. B
18. A	38. C	58. A	78. C	98. C
19. C	39. B	59. C	79. C	99. B
20. A	40. B	60. B	80. D	100. C

EXPLANATORY ANSWERS

1. SURFEIT : (A. collect, B. empty, C. glut, D. spoil) :: ARROGATE : USURP

(**C**) *Arrogate* and *usurp*, which both mean to seize without justification, are related as synonyms; the only synonym for *surfeit*, meaning to satiate, is *glut*.

2. ROBBERY : INCARCERATION :: (A. marking, B. singing, C. sleeping, D. embezzlement) : APPLAUSE

(**B**) This is a cause-and-effect analogy. Robbery can result in incarceration, and singing can result in applause.

3. ICHTHYOLOGY : (A. insects, B. mammals, C. fish, D. invertebrates) :: ORNITHOLOGY : BIRDS

(**C**) The relationship is one of classification. Ichthyology is the study of fish, and ornithology is the study of birds.

4. FIRST : PENULTIMATE :: JANUARY : (A. December, B. November, C. February, D. June)

(**B**) This is a sequence relationship. January is the first month of a year, and November is the penultimate, or next to last, month of a year.

5. HOPE : PLEASURE :: DESPONDENCY : (A. frolic, B. gratification, C. joy, D. anguish)

(**D**) Hope and despondency are contrasting concepts. The concept that contrasts with pleasure is anguish.

6. DICHOTOMY : DISSEMBLE :: DIVISION : (A. feign, B. assemble, C. resemble, D. return)

(**A**) *Dichotomy* and *division* are synonyms; a synonym for *dissemble* (meaning to disguise) is *feign*.

7. LONGFELLOW : WHITMAN :: (A. Tagore, B. Keats, C. Heine, D. Dickens) : TENNYSON

(**B**) The relationship between Longfellow and Whitman is that both of them were American poets. Because Tennyson was an English poet, the task is to determine who is another English poet. Keats is the only choice. Dickens was an English novelist, Heine was a German poet and philosopher, and Tagore was a Hindu poet.

8. MITER : BISHOP :: (A. stole, B. cleric, C. robe, D. biretta) : PRIEST

(**D**) The analogy is one of association. A miter is a head ornament usually worn by a bishop; a biretta is a cap characteristically worn by a priest. A stole and a robe are also worn by a priest, but biretta more specifically completes the correspondence with miter as headgear.

9. OK : PA :: KS : (A. CT, B. AZ, C. WV, D. NY)

(**D**) OK and KS are both proper post office abbreviations for states (Oklahoma and Kansas). Oklahoma is also on the southern border of Kansas; PA (Pennsylvania in post office abbreviation) is on the southern border of NY (New York). WV (West Virginia) also borders upon PA, but its geographic relationship to PA is the reverse of that of KS to OK. KS is to the north of OK; WV is to the south of PA.

10. SEED : BREED :: (A. origin, B. specimen, C. need, D. act) : DEED

(C) This is a nonsemantic analogy. *Seed, breed, deed,* and *need* all rhyme.

11. (A. influence, B. compose, C. touch, D. infect) : RESULT :: AFFECT : EFFECT

(A) This is an analogy of synonyms. *Affect* is a verb meaning *to influence. Effect* as a noun means *result.* (The verb *effect* means *to bring about.*)

12. SAUTÉING : COOKERY :: PAINTING : (A. juggling, B. forestry, C. art, D. medicine)

(C) The relationship is one of action to object. Sautéing is one act or form of cookery; painting is one act or form of art.

13. CAMPHOR : AROMATIC :: LILAC : (A. lavender, B. leaf, C. fragrant, D. rose)

(C) *Aromatic* is a characteristic of camphor; a characteristic of lilac is *fragrant.*

14. (A. skiers, B. winter, C. athletes, D. blades) : SKATES :: RUNNERS : SLEDS

(D) This is a part-to-whole analogy. Blades are parts of skates; runners are parts of sleds.

15. LOCARNO : SWITZERLAND :: ARGONNE : (A. France, B. Quebec, C. Germany, D. Belgium)

(A) The relationship is one of place. Locarno is located in Switzerland; the Argonne, a region that saw fierce fighting during the First World War, is in France near the Belgian border.

16. ARMY : FOOD :: DEFENSE : (A. digestion, B. vegetation, C. nutrition, D. supply)

(C) This is a purpose analogy. A purpose of an army is to provide defense; a purpose of food is to provide nutrition.

17. LESSING : (A. Fitzgerald, B. Woolf, C. Orwell, D. Wolfe) :: JONG : WALKER

(B) Lessing, Woolf, Jong, and Walker are all female authors. All other answer choices refer to male authors.

18. BENEFICENT : INIMICAL :: DELETERIOUS : (A. amicable, B. hostile, C. matchless, D. ordinary)

(A) *Beneficent* (beneficial) and *deleterious* (harmful) are antonyms. The only available antonym for *inimical* (hostile) is *amicable* (friendly).

19. ANEMOMETER : (A. smell, B. texture, C. wind, D. pressure) :: ODOMETER : DISTANCE

(C) The analogy is one of function. An odometer measures distance; an anemometer measures the velocity of the wind.

20. WHIP : HORN :: CRACK : (A. blow, B. break, C. tattoo, D. march)

(A) The relationship is one of object to action. One may crack a whip; one may blow a horn.

21. HILL : MOUNTAIN :: (A. depression, B. discomfort, C. headache, D. fear) : PAIN

(B) In this analogy of degree, a hill is a smaller version of a mountain; discomfort is a lesser version of pain. Note that a headache and depression are specific types of pain or discomfort, not degrees.

22. (A. *The Merry Widow,* B. *Naughty Marietta,* C. *Iolanthe,* D. *Carmen*) : MIKADO :: H.M.S. PINAFORE : GONDOLIERS

(**C**) The relationship is one of classification or part to part. The *Mikado, H.M.S. Pinafore,* and *Gondoliers* are all operettas written by Gilbert and Sullivan. *Iolanthe* is the only other Gilbert and Sullivan operetta offered among the choices.

23. BELL : HOLMES :: (A. Watson, B. Edison, C. Graham, D. Doyle) : WATSON

(**A**) This analogy is based upon the relationship of an individual to his assistant. Sherlock Holmes' name is often paired with that of his loyal and admiring assistant, Watson. The first person to hear a message over the newly invented telephone was Alexander Graham Bell's assistant, Watson.

24. WHEEL : COG :: (A. heaven, B. ribbon, C. rim, D. bulb) : FILAMENT

(**D**) This is a part-to-whole relationship. A cog is part of a wheel, just as a filament is a part of a light bulb.

25. POLICEMAN : (A. convict, B. justice, C. conduct, D. crime) :: DENTIST : CAVITY

(**D**) One characteristic of a dentist is that he fights a cavity. Similarly, a characteristic of a policeman is that he fights crime.

26. ROUND : CHUCK :: (A. circle, B. flank, C. chipped, D. throw) : RIB

(**B**) Every term in this analogy—round, chuck, and rib—is a cut of beefsteak. Therefore, the missing term must be flank.

27. FRACTIOUS : SYSTEMATIC :: DEBILITATE : (A. invigorate, B. undermine, C. diverge, D. annul)

(**A**) The given pair are related as antonyms because *fractious* means wild or unruly, the opposite of *systematic. Debilitate,* which means to weaken, must be paired with its opposite, *invigorate,* which means to strengthen.

28. FOUR : TWENTY :: (A. two, B. five, C. three, D. seven) : FIFTEEN

(**C**) In this numerical analogy, the relationship between four and twenty is a one-to-five ratio; the number with the same ratio to fifteen is three. The sentence by which you solve this analogy question is: "Twenty divided by five equals four; fifteen divided by five equals three."

29. GROUND CREW : SEMAPHORE :: PILOT : (A. radio, B. airplane, C. stewardess, D. copilot)

(**A**) The analogy is based upon actor and object or, better still, worker and tool. The ground crew gives messages to the cockpit crew by way of semaphore flags or lights; the pilot transmits messages by way of radio.

30. GLAND : ENDOCRINE :: MUSCLE : (A. hard, B. strong, C. desiccated, D. striated)

(**D**) Endocrine is one type of gland; one type of muscle is striated.

31. PROHIBITED : BANNED :: CANONICAL : (A. reputable, B. authoritative, C. referred, D. considered)

(**B**) *Prohibited* and *banned* are related as synonyms; a synonym for *canonical* is *authoritative.*

32. INTERMINABLE : ENDLESS :: APPARENT : (A. concise, B. ostensible, C. transparent, D. improbable)

(B) *Interminable* and *endless* are synonyms, as are *apparent* and *ostensible*.

33. ICE : STEAM :: BRICK : (A. straw, B. mortar, C. pole, D. stone)

(A) This analogy has to do with characteristics. Ice is solid; steam has little substance. Brick is solid; by comparison with brick, straw has little substance.

34. BREATHING : (A. oxygen, B. lungs, C. carbon dioxide, D. nose) :: CRYING : TEARS

(C) The relationship is action to object because crying releases tears. The task, then, is to determine what breathing releases. The process of respiration involves the intake of oxygen and the release of carbon dioxide.

35. MARRY : REPENT :: HASTE : (A. contrition, B. delay, C. leisure, D. deliberate)

(C) In this adage analogy, the familiar saying is "Marry in haste; repent at leisure."

36. JAMES I : (A. James II, B. George I, C. Elizabeth I, D. Charles I) :: GEORGE V : EDWARD VIII

(D) The relationship is one of sequence. The English king Edward VIII followed George V. To complete the analogy, you must choose Charles I, successor to James I.

37. PLANS : ARCHITECT :: TREACHERY : (A. thief, B. traitor, C. cheater, D. killer)

(B) The analogy is based upon association. Plans are associated with an architect, as treachery is associated with a traitor.

38. LILY : ROSEMARY :: PURITY : (A. lamb, B. squalor, C. remembrance, D. thyme)

(C) This analogy is based on symbolism or simple association. The lily is a symbol of purity; rosemary is for remembrance.

39. ANCHOR : KEY :: (A. dock, B. boat, C. prow, D. keel) : CHAIN

(B) A key hangs from a chain; an anchor hangs from a boat.

40. (A. Scopes, B. Darrow, C. Darwin, D. Jennings) : BRYAN :: SACCO : VANZETTI

(B) Sacco and Vanzetti are associated as co-defendants in a famous trial. Bryan and Darrow are associated as opposing counsel in the famous trial of John Scopes, who was tried for teaching the theory of evolution in defiance of Tennessee law.

41. (A. subterranean, B. subconscious, C. superb, D. advertised) : SUBLIMINAL :: PLETHORIC : SUPERFLUOUS

(B) *Plethoric* and *superfluous* are synonyms for excess; a synonym for *subliminal* is *subconscious*, meaning outside the area of conscious awareness.

42. VICTORY : PYRRHIC :: FRUIT : (A. ripe, B. bitter, C. pie, D. tree)

(B) A Pyrrhic victory is a bitter one because it means a victory gained at ruinous loss; therefore, *Pyrrhic* is an undesirable characteristic of victory. A similar undesirable characteristic of fruit is *bitterness*.

43. TOUCH : DOWN :: (A. walk, B. river, C. home, D. stocking) : RUN

(C) The relationship between *touch* and *down* is grammatical because these words can be used by themselves and also as a common sports-oriented compound word; therefore, the task is to determine which word can be used by itself and also as part of a common sports-oriented compound word with *run*. *Home* is the correct choice.

44. MITOSIS : DIVISION :: OSMOSIS : (A. diffusion, B. concentration, C. digestion, D. metamorphosis)

(A) The relationship is one of part to whole. Mitosis is one kind of division—specifically, the series of processes that takes place in the nucleus of a dividing cell, which results in the formation of two new nuclei each having the same number of chromosomes as the parent nucleus. Osmosis is one kind of diffusion—specifically, diffusion through a semipermeable membrane separating a solution of lesser solute concentration from one of greater concentration to equalize the concentration of the two solutions.

45. SUN : (A. summer, B. tan, C. sunscreen, D. beach) :: COLD : OVERCOAT

(C) The purpose or function of an overcoat is to protect one from the cold; sunscreen protects one from the sun.

46. PHOEBUS : (A. Helius, B. Eos, C. Diana, D. Perseus) :: SUN : MOON

(C) This is a mythological analogy. Phoebus is the god of the sun; Diana is the goddess of the moon.

47. (A. equality, B. generous, C. wantonness, D. goodness) : LIBERTINE :: ADVOCACY : LAWYER

(C) The relationship is one of characteristic. One characteristic of a lawyer is his advocacy or support of his client; a characteristic of a libertine, or one who leads a dissolute life, is wantonness.

48. POUND : KILOGRAM :: WEIGHT : (A. weight, B. area, C. volume, D. capacity)

(A) This is a descriptive analogy. A pound is a measurement of weight; a kilogram is also a measure of weight.

49. PRECARIOUS : ZEALOUS :: CERTAIN : (A. apathetic, B. ardent, C. indigent, D. sensitive)

(A) *Precarious* and *certain* are antonyms; an antonym for *zealous* is *apathetic*.

50. PONDER : THOUGHT :: ARBITRATE : (A. endorsement, B. plan, C. fine, D. dispute)

(D) The correspondence is one of action to object. To ponder aids thought; to arbitrate aids a dispute.

51. OBSTRUCT : IMPENETRABLE :: IMPEDE : (A. forbearing, B. hidden, C. impervious, D. merciful)

(C) *Obstruct* and *impede* are synonyms; a synonym for *impenetrable* is *impervious*.

52. OCTAVE : SESTET :: (A. scale, B. ending, C. quatrain, D. symphony) : COUPLET

(C) This is an analogy of parts. *Octave, sestet,* and *couplet* are all parts of a sonnet. Only *quatrain* among the choices is also a part of a sonnet. If you know nothing about sonnets, you might notice that the three capitalized terms all have something to do with numbers—octave, 8; sestet, 6; couplet, 2—and so choose as the fourth term *quatrain*, 4.

53. NOVEL : (A. epic, B. drama, C. volume, D. story) :: TOM SAWYER : AENEID

(A) The relationship between *Tom Sawyer* and the *Aeneid* is one of classification. *Tom Sawyer* is a novel, and the *Aeneid* is an epic.

54. PURSER : (A. bank, B. ship, C. race track, D. highway) :: BRAKEMAN : TRAIN

(B) The correspondence is one of association or place. A brakeman is associated with a train; a purser is associated with a ship.

55. DRINK : SECURITY :: THIRST : (A. assuredness, B. stocks, C. fear, D. money)

(C) Drink serves the function of relieving thirst; security serves the function of relieving fear.

56. CIRCLE : OVAL :: (A. figure, B. octagon, C. starfish, D. semicircle) : PARALLELOGRAM

(B) A circle and an oval are both figures enclosed with one continuous curved side. Because a parallelogram is a figure enclosed with straight sides, the task is to find another straight-sided figure. Octagon is the only available choice.

57. RESILIENCY : RUBBER :: LAMBENCY : (A. oil, B. sheep, C. candlelight, D. lawn)

(C) *Resiliency* is a characteristic of rubber; *lambency*, which means *brightness* or *flickering*, is a characteristic of candlelight.

58. VIRTUOSO : (A. orchestra, B. home, C. prison, D. college) :: TEACHER : CLASSROOM

(A) A teacher works in a classroom; therefore, the task is to determine where a virtuoso works. Among the choices, an orchestra is the most likely place.

59. KEYBOARD : (A. small, B. office, C. mouse, D. radio) :: LIPSTICK : COMPACT

(C) In this part-to-part analogy, lipstick and a compact are usually parts of the contents of a purse; a keyboard and a mouse are usually parts of a computer.

60. (A. 4, B. 7, C. 9, D. 14) : 28 :: 11 : 44

(B) The numerical relationship between 11 and 44 is a ratio of 1 to 4; therefore, the task is to determine what number when paired with 28 is also in the ratio of 1 to 4. The answer is 7. The sentence is: "$44 \div 11 = 4$, just as $28 \div 7 = 4$."

61. CAPE : WADI :: PROMONTORY : (A. gully, B. waterfall, C. meadow, D. fen)

(A) *Cape* and *promontory* are synonyms meaning a point of land jutting into the sea; a synonym for *wadi* is *gully*.

62. BINDING : BOOK :: WELDING : (A. box, B. tank, C. chair, D. wire)

(B) Binding secures or holds together a book; welding secures or holds together a tank.

63. SERFDOM : FEUDALISM :: ENTREPRENEURSHIP : (A. laissez-faire, B. captain, C. radical, D. capitalism)

(D) *Serfdom* is a characteristic of feudalism; *entrepreneurship* is a characteristic of capitalism. Laissez-faire may be an aspect of both entrepreneurship and of capitalism, but in creating an analogy, *capitalism* forms a much better parallel with *feudalism*.

64. (A. bassos, B. dynamos, C. heroes, D. solos) : EMBARGOES :: VOLCANOES : TOMATOES

(C) The relationship between *volcanoes* and *tomatoes* is grammatical. Each is a plural formed by adding "es." Because *embargoes* is also a plural formed by adding "es," the task is to find another word that also forms its plural this way. *Heroes* is the correct choice.

65. FOAL : HORSE :: CYGNET : (A. ring, B. fish, C. swan, D. constellation)

(C) A foal is a young horse; a cygnet is a young swan. The relationship is one of young to old, or sequence.

66. WARFARE : (A. ingenuity, B. commerce, C. separate, D. destruction) :: TYRANNY : DISSENT

(D) This analogy is one of cause and effect. Tyranny often leads to dissent; warfare often leads to destruction.

67. HOUSE : BUILD :: TRENCH : (A. dig, B. trap, C. obliterate, D. dry)

(A) The relationship is object to action. A house is something to build; a trench is something to dig.

68. CELL : WORKER :: ORGANISM : (A. occupation, B. proletariat, C. product, D. nation)

(B) The correspondence is one of part to whole. A cell is part of an organism; a worker is part of the proletariat. A worker may also be part of a nation, but *proletariat* is more specifically related to a worker.

69. ANGLO-SAXON : ENGLISH :: LATIN : (A. Roman, B. Greek, C. Italian, D. Mediterranean)

(C) This is a sequence relationship. Anglo-Saxon is an early form of English; Latin is an early form of Italian.

70. SHERMAN : GEORGIA :: KITCHENER : (A. South Africa, B. Rome, C. Australia, D. Quebec)

(A) General Sherman is remembered for his march through Georgia during the Civil War. He burned everything in his path as part of the Union's "scorched earth" policy. General Kitchener followed an identical policy in his conquest of South Africa during the Boer War.

71. CHARM : TALISMAN :: FEALTY : (A. allegiance, B. faith, C. payment, D. real estate)

(A) *Charm* and *talisman* are synonyms; a synonym for *fealty* is *allegiance*.

72. ACCELERATOR : (A. cylinder, B. inertia, C. motion, D. exhaust) :: CATALYST : CHANGE

(C) The relationship is that of cause and effect. A catalyst causes change, and an accelerator causes motion.

73. INTELLIGENCE : UNDERSTANDING :: CONFUSION : (A. unhappiness, B. pleasure, C. school, D. comprehension)

(A) *Understanding* is a characteristic of intelligence; a characteristic of confusion is *unhappiness*.

74. TALKING : YELLING :: GIGGLING : (A. rejoicing, B. laughing, C. chuckling, D. sneering)

(B) Yelling is a greater degree of talking; a greater degree of giggling is laughing. Chuckling, while not exactly a synonym for giggling, is of the same degree. Rejoicing is more inclusive than laughing; it adds a dimension not called for in an analogy that begins "talking : yelling" and which offers a more specific choice.

75. 49 : 7 :: (A. 98, B. 103, C. 94, D. 144) : 12

(D) The number 7 squared is 49; the number 12 squared is 144.

76. (A. Chrysler, B. mink, C. chauffeur, D. Boeing) : CADILLAC :: BEAVER : CHEVROLET

(B) The correspondence is one of part to part. Chevrolet and Cadillac are both types of automobiles. Because a beaver is a type of animal, to complete the analogy, another type of animal must be selected. Mink is the only available choice.

77. BREAK : BROKEN :: FLY : (A. flied, B. flew, C. flown, D. flying)

(C) In this grammatical analogy, the past participle of *break* is *broken;* the past participle of *fly* is *flown*.

78. DEFALCATE : EXCULPATE :: EMBEZZLEMENT : (A. blame, B. uncover, C. exoneration, D. divulge)

(C) This is an action-to-object analogy. To defalcate is an act of embezzlement; to exculpate is an act of exoneration.

79. SAW : (A. teeth, B. knife, C. board, D. blade) :: SCISSORS : CLOTH

(C) The relationship is one of purpose because the purpose of scissors is to cut cloth, just as the purpose of a saw is to cut a board.

80. PEDAL : PIANO :: BRIDGE : (A. case, B. tune, C. rosin, D. violin)

(D) A pedal is part of a piano; a bridge is part of a violin.

81. BUCOLIC : CIMMERIAN :: PEACEFUL : (A. warlike, B. tenebrous, C. doubtful, D. smirking)

(B) *Bucolic* and *peaceful* are synonyms because *bucolic* refers to pastoral and peaceful scenes; a synonym of *cimmerian,* meaning shrouded in gloom and darkness, is *tenebrous*.

82. FLATTERY : (A. unity, B. self-interest, C. honesty, D. openness) :: FLIGHT : SAFETY

(B) A purpose of flight is safety; a purpose of flattery is self-interest.

83. PRAYER : (A. church, B. Bible, C. religion, D. fulfillment) :: RESEARCH : DISCOVERY

(D) The relationship is one of purpose. The aim of research is discovery; the aim of prayer is fulfillment.

84. PAYMENT : PREMIUM :: DEBT : (A. cracker, B. prize, C. insurance, D. scarcity)

(C) The correspondence is one of association. *Payment* is the term applied to money expended to reduce a debt, just as *premium* is the term applied to money expended to obtain insurance.

85. SACRIFICE : HIT :: STEAL : (A. leave, B. slay, C. walk, D. rob)

(C) *Sacrifice, hit,* and *steal* are all plays in baseball games. Among the choices, only *walk* is another type of baseball play.

86. (A. clap, B. play, C. doom, D. fork) : MOOD :: SLEEK : KEELS

(C) The relationship is nonsemantic. *Sleek* spelled backward is *keels; mood* spelled backward is *doom*. Actually, once you have ascertained that there is no meaningful nor grammatical relationship among the three capitalized terms, you need only note that all three contain double letters and that only one choice has double letters.

87. DEMOLISH : BUILDING :: (A. sail, B. raze, C. dock, D. scuttle) : SHIP

(D) The relationship is action to object. To destroy a building, you can demolish it; to destroy a ship, you can scuttle it.

88. LOGGIA : JALOUSIE :: GALLERY : (A. lintel, B. dowel, C. jamb, D. shutter)

(D) Loggia and gallery are both types of porches; because jalousie is a type of blind, the task is to find another type of blind, and *shutter* is the correct choice.

89. PAGE : CUB :: (A. book, B. paper, C. herald, D. knight) : REPORTER

(D) The relationship is one of degree. A cub is a young reporter; a page is a young knight.

90. VIRGO : TAURUS :: SEPTEMBER : (A. May, B. January, C. June, D. November)

(A) The zodiac sign Virgo is associated with the month of September; Taurus is associated with May.

91. FELICITY : CONGENIAL :: BLISS : (A. clever, B. compatible, C. fierce, D. unfriendly)

(B) *Felicity* and *bliss* are synonyms; a synonym for *congenial* is *compatible*.

92. WHEEL : FENDER :: (A. dashboard, B. bow, C. caboose, D. pedal) : RUDDER

(B) Both a wheel and a fender are parts of a larger automotive unit; a rudder and a bow are both parts of a ship.

93. REQUEST : VISIT :: DEMAND : (A. return, B. welcome, C. invasion, D. house)

(C) The relationship is one of degree. *Request* is a polite term, and a demand can be an unpleasant request. *Visit* is a polite term, so the task is to find a word that denotes an unpleasant visit. *Invasion* is the correct choice.

94. DENOUEMENT : (A. climax, B. outcome, C. complication, D. untying) :: DEBIT : CREDIT

(C) *Debit* and *credit* are antonyms; an antonym for *denouement* is *complication*.

95. STRAIGHT : POKER :: SMASH : (A. hit, B. tennis, C. ruin, D. bat)

(B) A *straight* is a characteristic of a poker game; a *smash* is a characteristic stroke in a game of tennis.

96. (A. small, B. sandwich, C. surprise, D. tight) : SCROOGE :: LYNCH : GUILLOTINE

(B) Every term in this analogy is a word derived from a person's name. *Scrooge* comes from Dickens' Ebenezer Scrooge in *A Christmas Carol; lynch,* to put to death by mob action, comes from a Judge Lynch; and a guillotine takes its name from Dr. Joseph Guillotin. Among the choices, only *sandwich* describes both a thing and a person from which it takes its name. The Earl of Sandwich is said to have been the first to put meat between slices of bread.

97. VALLEY : GORGE :: MOUNTAIN : (A. hill, B. cliff, C. acme, D. high)

(B) A gorge is a steep part of a valley; a cliff is a steep part of a mountain.

98. ALPHA : OMEGA :: MERCURY : (A. Saturn, B. planet, C. Pluto, D. Venus)

(C) The relationship is one of sequence. Just as Alpha and Omega are the first and last letters in the Greek alphabet, Mercury and Pluto, respectively, are the planets closest to and farthest from the sun.

99. CHIFFON : TWEED :: (A. synthetic, B. sheer, C. dark. D. textured) : ROUGH

(B) This analogy is one of characteristic. A characteristic of tweed is that it is rough; a characteristic of chiffon is that it is sheer.

100. SIDEREAL : (A. side, B. part, C. stars, D. planets) :: LUNAR : MOON

(C) The relationship is one of association. *Lunar* is associated with the moon; *sidereal* is related to the stars.

SAMPLE TEST 3

Answer Sheet

1 ⓐⓑⓒⓓ	26 ⓐⓑⓒⓓ	51 ⓐⓑⓒⓓ	76 ⓐⓑⓒⓓ
2 ⓐⓑⓒⓓ	27 ⓐⓑⓒⓓ	52 ⓐⓑⓒⓓ	77 ⓐⓑⓒⓓ
3 ⓐⓑⓒⓓ	28 ⓐⓑⓒⓓ	53 ⓐⓑⓒⓓ	78 ⓐⓑⓒⓓ
4 ⓐⓑⓒⓓ	29 ⓐⓑⓒⓓ	54 ⓐⓑⓒⓓ	79 ⓐⓑⓒⓓ
5 ⓐⓑⓒⓓ	30 ⓐⓑⓒⓓ	55 ⓐⓑⓒⓓ	80 ⓐⓑⓒⓓ
6 ⓐⓑⓒⓓ	31 ⓐⓑⓒⓓ	56 ⓐⓑⓒⓓ	81 ⓐⓑⓒⓓ
7 ⓐⓑⓒⓓ	32 ⓐⓑⓒⓓ	57 ⓐⓑⓒⓓ	82 ⓐⓑⓒⓓ
8 ⓐⓑⓒⓓ	33 ⓐⓑⓒⓓ	58 ⓐⓑⓒⓓ	83 ⓐⓑⓒⓓ
9 ⓐⓑⓒⓓ	34 ⓐⓑⓒⓓ	59 ⓐⓑⓒⓓ	84 ⓐⓑⓒⓓ
10 ⓐⓑⓒⓓ	35 ⓐⓑⓒⓓ	60 ⓐⓑⓒⓓ	85 ⓐⓑⓒⓓ
11 ⓐⓑⓒⓓ	36 ⓐⓑⓒⓓ	61 ⓐⓑⓒⓓ	86 ⓐⓑⓒⓓ
12 ⓐⓑⓒⓓ	37 ⓐⓑⓒⓓ	62 ⓐⓑⓒⓓ	87 ⓐⓑⓒⓓ
13 ⓐⓑⓒⓓ	38 ⓐⓑⓒⓓ	63 ⓐⓑⓒⓓ	88 ⓐⓑⓒⓓ
14 ⓐⓑⓒⓓ	39 ⓐⓑⓒⓓ	64 ⓐⓑⓒⓓ	89 ⓐⓑⓒⓓ
15 ⓐⓑⓒⓓ	40 ⓐⓑⓒⓓ	65 ⓐⓑⓒⓓ	90 ⓐⓑⓒⓓ
16 ⓐⓑⓒⓓ	41 ⓐⓑⓒⓓ	66 ⓐⓑⓒⓓ	91 ⓐⓑⓒⓓ
17 ⓐⓑⓒⓓ	42 ⓐⓑⓒⓓ	67 ⓐⓑⓒⓓ	92 ⓐⓑⓒⓓ
18 ⓐⓑⓒⓓ	43 ⓐⓑⓒⓓ	68 ⓐⓑⓒⓓ	93 ⓐⓑⓒⓓ
19 ⓐⓑⓒⓓ	44 ⓐⓑⓒⓓ	69 ⓐⓑⓒⓓ	94 ⓐⓑⓒⓓ
20 ⓐⓑⓒⓓ	45 ⓐⓑⓒⓓ	70 ⓐⓑⓒⓓ	95 ⓐⓑⓒⓓ
21 ⓐⓑⓒⓓ	46 ⓐⓑⓒⓓ	71 ⓐⓑⓒⓓ	96 ⓐⓑⓒⓓ
22 ⓐⓑⓒⓓ	47 ⓐⓑⓒⓓ	72 ⓐⓑⓒⓓ	97 ⓐⓑⓒⓓ
23 ⓐⓑⓒⓓ	48 ⓐⓑⓒⓓ	73 ⓐⓑⓒⓓ	98 ⓐⓑⓒⓓ
24 ⓐⓑⓒⓓ	49 ⓐⓑⓒⓓ	74 ⓐⓑⓒⓓ	99 ⓐⓑⓒⓓ
25 ⓐⓑⓒⓓ	50 ⓐⓑⓒⓓ	75 ⓐⓑⓒⓓ	100 ⓐⓑⓒⓓ

TEAR HERE

Chapter 7

Sample Test 3

100 Questions • 50 Minutes

Directions: Each of these test questions consists of three capitalized words and four lettered words enclosed in parentheses. Two of the capitalized words are related in some way. Find the two related words, and establish the nature of the relationship. Then study the four words lettered A, B, C, and D. Select the one lettered word that is related to the remaining capitalized word in the same way that the first two capitalized words are related. Mark the answer sheet for the letter preceding the word you select.

ROAD MAP

- *Answer Key*
- *Explanatory Answers*

1. SCEPTER : AUTHORITY :: SCALES : (A. weight, B. justice, C. commerce, D. greed)

2. STONEHENGE : EASTER ISLAND :: (A. yeti, B. dodo, C. nene, D. rhea) : LOCH NESS MONSTER

3. WORM : MOUSE :: BIRD : (A. man, B. snake, C. rodent, D. cheese)

4. (A. artist, B. description, C. narration, D. personality) : CHARACTERIZATION :: PICTURE : PORTRAIT

5. (A. orate, B. sing, C. mumble, D. speak) : TALK :: SCRAWL : WRITE

6. LYNDON JOHNSON : JOHN F. KENNEDY :: ANDREW JOHNSON : (A. Ulysses S. Grant, B. Abraham Lincoln, C. Martin Van Buren, D. William Pierce)

7. 46 : 39 :: (A. 61, B. 42, C. 76, D. 39) : 54

8. STEAM : WATER :: (A. lake, B. cloud, C. salt, D. tide) : OCEAN

9. SODIUM : SALT :: OXYGEN : (A. acetylene, B. carbon tetrachloride, C. water, D. ammonia)

10. (A. theft, B. notoriety, C. police, D. jail) : CRIME :: CEMETERY : DEATH

11. GRASS : (A. cow, B. onion, C. lettuce, D. earth) :: SNOW : MILK

12. HAND : (A. girth, B. fingers, C. horse, D. glove) :: LIGHT-YEAR : SPACE

13. QUISLING : CHAMBERLAIN :: COLLABORATION : (A. appeasement, B. negotiation, C. rejection, D. diplomacy)

14. PICCOLO : (A. trumpet, B. trombone, C. horn, D. baritone saxophone) :: VIOLIN : BASS

15. DIVULGE : DISCLOSE :: APPRAISAL : (A. revision, B. respite, C. continuation, D. estimate)

16. WEALTH : TANGIBLE :: (A. price, B. gold, C. success, D. gifts) : INTANGIBLE

17. HEMOGLOBIN : COACHES :: BLOOD : (A. train, B. whip, C. fuel, D. road)

18. SHELTER : (A. refuge, B. cave, C. mansion, D. protection) :: BREAD : CAKE

19. AFFLUENT : (A. charity, B. diligence, C. misfortune, D. indifference) :: IMPOVERISHED : LAZINESS

20. INNING : BASEBALL :: (A. time, B. midnight, C. era, D. chronology) : HISTORY

21. E.M. : (A. A.C., B. L.G., C. P.D., D. P.G.) :: FORSTER : WODEHOUSE

22. (A. stifle, B. tell, C. joke, D. offer) : LAUGH :: THROW : JAVELIN

23. CHARLESTON : (A. Tucson, B. Jackson, C. Williamsburg, D. Chicago) :: BOSTON : PHILADELPHIA

24. VINTNER : MINER :: (A. vines, B. wine, C. liquid, D. bottle) : ORE

25. (A. jaguar, B. mink, C. lion, D. chinchilla) : GIRAFFE :: TIGER : ZEBRA

26. (A. Athena, B. Artemis, C. Hera, D. Medea) : FRIGGA :: ZEUS : ODIN

27. 5 : 8 :: 25 : (A. 29, B. 40, C. 60, D. 108)

28. LIMP : CANE :: (A. cell, B. muscle, C. heat, D. cold) : TISSUE

29. CONFESSOR : KINGMAKER :: EDWARD : (A. Warwick, B. Alfred, C. George, D. Gloucester)

30. (A. parchment, B. concrete, C. cardboard, D. timber) : ADOBE :: PAPER : PAPYRUS

31. HANDS : ARMS :: (A. Roman, B. crack, C. Diana, D. destiny) : MORPHEUS

32. HYMN : THEIR :: CELL : (A. score, B. peal, C. tree, D. mile)

33. DOG : SWAN :: (A. bark, B. noise, C. days, D. collie) : SONG

34. EINSTEIN : MALTHUS :: RELATIVITY : (A. population, B. religion, C. economy, D. democracy)

35. GALLEY : ROOKERY :: MEAL : (A. ship, B. seal, C. peal, D. chess)

36. PEACH : (A. apple, B. beet, C. grape, D. tomato) :: CHERRY : RADISH

37. LASSITUDE : (A. longitude, B. languor, C. purity, D. alacrity) :: PARSIMONY : BENEFACTION

38. THERMOSTAT : REGULATE :: (A. draft, B. windows, C. insulation, D. thermometer) : CONSERVE

39. MONGREL : PEDIGREE :: BOOR : (A. thoroughbred, B. manners, C. ancestry, D. lineage)

40. (A. earth, B. Venus, C. Sputnik, D. berry) : PLANET :: CANAL : RIVER

41. PIRAEUS : OSTIA :: (A. Athens, B. Florence, C. Milan, D. Crete) : ROME

42. (A. psychology, B. philology, C. philosophy, D. philately) : PHRENOLOGY :: ASTRONOMY : ASTROLOGY

43. ORACLE : LOGICIAN :: INTUITION : (A. guess, B. syllogism, C. faith, D. Venn)

44. PELEE : (A. France, B. soccer, C. Martinique, D. Brazil) :: ETNA : SICILY

45. GERONTOLOGY : GENEALOGY :: (A. families, B. aging, C. gerunds, D. birth) : LINEAGE

46. ROMAN : (A. Caesar, B. backward, C. gladiator, D. handlebar) :: NOSE : MUSTACHE

47. HYDROGEN : 1 :: (A. carbon, B. oxygen, C. nitrogen, D. potassium) : 16

48. (A. protein, B. nucleus, C. neutron, D. vacuole) : PROTON :: ARCH : HEEL

49. 19 : 23 :: (A. 7, B. 11, C. 13, D. 17) : 13

50. BOND : STOCK :: DEBT : (A. preferred, B. option, C. equality, D. equity)

51. (A. Laos, B. Indonesia, C. Afghanistan, D. Japan) : INDIA :: NEVADA : COLORADO

52. CONCISE : (A. refined, B. expanded, C. convex, D. blunt) :: REMOVE : OBLITERATE

53. TRAINING : ACUMEN :: (A. stupidity, B. experience, C. hunger, D. restlessness) : INANITION

54. BANTAM : (A. fly, B. chicken, C. fowl, D. small) :: WELTER : LIGHT

55. JACKET : (A. lapel, B. button, C. vest, D. dinner) :: PANTS : CUFF

56. (A. grave, B. aggravated, C. theft, D. first degree) : GRAND :: ASSAULT : LARCENY

57. (A. Athena, B. Ceres, C. Artemis, D. Aphrodite) : ZEUS :: EVE : ADAM

58. SERAPHIC : (A. Napoleonic, B. Mephistophelean, C. Alexandrine, D. euphoric) :: IMPROVIDENT : PRESCIENT

59. STRIPES : (A. bars, B. oak leaf, C. stars, D. general) :: SERGEANT : MAJOR

GO ON TO THE NEXT PAGE

60. (A. precarious, B. deleterious, C. deterred, D. immortal) : CELEBRATED :: DEADLY : LIONIZED

61. MANET : REMBRANDT :: (A. Picasso, B. Dali, C. Pollock, D. Cézanne) : VAN GOGH

62. (A. glove, B. stocking, C. weakness, D. mitt) : GAUNTLET :: HAT : HELMET

63. STAPES : COCHLEA :: BRIM : (A. hat, B. derby, C. crown, D. head)

64. (A. rococo, B. severe, C. Etruscan, D. stylish) : ORNAMENTED :: SOGGY : MOIST

65. BURSAR : (A. funds, B. semester, C. accounts, D. purse) :: SEMINAR : IVY

66. NEW YORK : RHODES :: LIBERTY : (A. Colossus, B. London, C. tyranny, D. freedom)

67. RUBY : EMERALD :: TOMATO : (A. rose, B. radish, C. pasta, D. lettuce)

68. SOLID : MELTING :: SOLUTION : (A. saturation, B. liquefaction, C. heating, D. mixing)

69. (A. royal, B. kingly, C. regal, D. princely) : LAGER :: TIME : EMIT

70. HENRY FIELDING : (A. Victorian, B. Romantic, C. Restoration, D. Augustan) :: BEN JONSON : ELIZABETHAN

71. ARKANSAS : FLORIDA :: NEW MEXICO : (A. Tennessee, B. Ohio, C. California, D. Illinois)

72. SIN : ATONEMENT :: (A. clemency, B. peace, C. war, D. virtue) : REPARATION

73. (A. solo, B. duet, C. trio, D. quartet) : QUINTET :: BOXING : BASKETBALL

74. JULIAN : GREGORIAN :: (A. pope, B. Mayan, C. American, D. Canadian) : AZTEC

75. (A. echo, B. elephant, C. page, D. blue) : MEMORY :: DENIM : BLOSSOM

76. (A. Jupiter, B. Hippocrates, C. Cadmus, D. Ptolemy) : HANNIBAL :: CADUCEUS : SWORD

77. STYX : RUBICON :: ANATHEMA : (A. curse, B. pariah, C. parsee, D. song)

78. EPISTEMOLOGY : (A. letters, B. weapons, C. knowledge, D. roots) :: PALEONTOLOGY : FOSSILS

79. (A. ear, B. foundry, C. corps, D. fife) : FLINT :: DRUM : STEEL

80. JAVELIN : (A. run, B. pass, C. mount, D. toss) :: EYE : BLINK

81. PLATO : (A. Socrates, B. Sophocles, C. Aristophanes, D. Aristotle) :: FREUD : JUNG

82. (A. law, B. book, C. band, D. wagon) : WAINWRIGHT :: DICTIONARY : LEXICOGRAPHER

83. 15 : 6 :: 23 : (A. 8, B. 7, C. 6, D. 5)

84. CONCERT : (A. andante, B. a cappella, C. opera, D. artistry) :: PERFORMANCE : PANTOMIME

85. (A. uniform, B. commander, C. platoon, D. sentry) : DOG :: GARRISON : FLOCK

86. PORTUGAL : IBERIA :: TOOTH : (A. dentist, B. cavity, C. nail, D. comb)

87. RADIUS : (A. circle, B. arc, C. chord, D. diameter) :: YARD : FATHOM

88. EMINENT : LOWLY :: FREQUENT : (A. often, B. frivolous, C. rare, D. soon)

89. FILIGREE : METAL :: (A. lace, B. linen, C. cotton, D. silk) : THREAD

90. INTAGLIO : (A. cameo, B. caviar, C. Machiavellian, D. harem) :: CONCAVE : CONVEX

91. MEZZANINE : (A. orchestra, B. stage, C. proscenium, D. second balcony) :: ABDOMEN : THORAX

92. ROTUND : GAUNT :: (A. unruly, B. onerous, C. tractable, D. strong) : CONTUMACIOUS

93. GLACIER : MOLASSES :: (A. dirge, B. moth, C. spring, D. mountain) : TORTOISE

94. FOLD : (A. fell, B. hand, C. falls, D. boat) :: FORD : STREAM

95. VERDI : (A. *La Traviata,* B. *Fidelio,* C. *Aida,* D. *Rigoletto*) :: CHOPIN : *PARSIFAL*

96. SUBSTITUTE : TEAM :: UNDERSTUDY : (A. school, B. congregation, C. actor, D. cast)

97. PORT : (A. vintage, B. harbor, C. starboard, D. left) :: HEADLIGHTS : TRUNK

98. YORKTOWN : VICKSBURG :: CONCORD : (A. Philadelphia, B. Providence, C. Antietam, D. Valley Forge)

99. (A. border, B. score, C. quart, D. quatrain) : LINE :: SQUARE : CORNER

100. ROOSTER : (A. crow, B. coop, C. egg, D. owl) :: EFFERVESCENT : EFFETE

ANSWER KEY

1. B	21. D	41. A	61. D	81. D
2. A	22. A	42. A	62. A	82. D
3. B	23. C	43. B	63. C	83. D
4. B	24. B	44. C	64. A	84. B
5. C	25. A	45. B	65. B	85. D
6. B	26. C	46. D	66. A	86. D
7. A	27. B	47. B	67. D	87. D
8. B	28. D	48. C	68. A	88. C
9. C	29. A	49. B	69. C	89. A
10. D	30. B	50. D	70. D	90. A
11. C	31. D	51. C	71. C	91. D
12. C	32. B	52. D	72. C	92. C
13. A	33. C	53. C	73. A	93. A
14. D	34. A	54. A	74. B	94. B
15. D	35. B	55. A	75. A	95. B
16. C	36. B	56. B	76. B	96. D
17. A	37. D	57. A	77. A	97. C
18. C	38. C	58. B	78. C	98. C
19. B	39. B	59. B	79. D	99. D
20. C	40. C	60. B	80. D	100. D

EXPLANATORY ANSWERS

1. SCEPTER : AUTHORITY :: SCALES : (A. weight, B. justice, C. commerce, D. greed)

(B) A scepter is a symbol of authority; scales are a symbol of justice.

2. STONEHENGE : EASTER ISLAND :: (A. yeti, B. dodo, C. nene, D. rhea) : LOCH NESS MONSTER

(A) The factor that all terms of this analogy have in common is that all concern mysteries. Stonehenge and the statues at Easter Island present mysteries as to their origin and purpose. The yeti, otherwise known as the Abominable Snowman, and the Loch Ness Monster present mysteries as to their existence and nature. The dodo is an extinct bird presenting no mystery. The nene is a Hawaiian goose, and the rhea is a South American bird somewhat akin to an ostrich.

3. WORM : MOUSE :: BIRD : (A. man, B. snake, C. rodent, D. cheese)

(B) The relationship is that of object to actor or eaten to eater. A bird eats a worm; a snake eats a mouse.

4. (A. artist, B. description, C. narration, D. personality) : CHARACTERIZATION :: PICTURE : PORTRAIT

(B) A portrait is a picture of a person; a characterization is a description of the qualities or traits of a person.

5. (A. orate, B. sing, C. mumble, D. speak) : TALK :: SCRAWL : WRITE

(C) To mumble is to talk carelessly, thus making it difficult to be understood; to scrawl is to write carelessly, thus making it difficult to be understood.

6. LYNDON JOHNSON : JOHN F. KENNEDY :: ANDREW JOHNSON : (A. Ulysses S. Grant, B. Abraham Lincoln, C. Martin Van Buren, D. William Pierce)

(B) Lyndon Johnson was the vice president who succeeded John F. Kennedy following Kennedy's assassination. Andrew Johnson was the vice president under Abraham Lincoln who became president after Lincoln's assassination.

7. 46 : 39 :: (A. 61, B. 42, C. 76, D. 39) : 54

(A) In a mathematical analogy, always look first for the simplest relationship between two terms. The difference between 46 and 39 is 7. Because the number in choice (A) is 7 greater than the fourth term, your analogy is all set. $46 - 39 = 7$; $61 - 54 = 7$. Choice (D) is incorrect because it reverses the order of the relationship.

8. STEAM : WATER :: (A. lake, B. cloud, C. salt, D. tide) : OCEAN

(B) This is an analogy of the gaseous to the liquid state of a substance. Steam is the vapor form into which water is converted by heat. A cloud is the vapor form into which ocean water is converted by condensation.

9. SODIUM : SALT :: OXYGEN : (A. acetylene, B. carbon tetrachloride, C. water, D. ammonia)

(C) Sodium is one of the elements of salt; oxygen is one of the elements of water.

10. (A. theft, B. notoriety, C. police, D. jail) : CRIME :: CEMETERY : DEATH

(D) In this analogy of cause and effect, a crime usually results in time spent in jail; death usually results in burial in a cemetery.

11. GRASS : (A. cow, B. onion, C. lettuce, D. earth) :: SNOW : MILK

(C) Snow and milk are related because they are both white; grass and lettuce are both green.

12. HAND : (A. girth, B. fingers, C. horse, D. glove) :: LIGHT-YEAR : SPACE

(C) This analogy is one of measurement. A light-year is a unit of measurement in space. A hand is a unit of measurement (equal to 4 inches) used to determine the height of a horse.

13. QUISLING : CHAMBERLAIN :: COLLABORATION : (A. appeasement, B. negotiation, C. rejection, D. diplomacy)

(A) This analogy comes straight out of World War II. Quisling was the Norwegian leader who quickly made common cause with the Nazis and became infamous for his collaboration. Chamberlain was the British Prime Minister who thought that appeasement, giving Czechoslovakia to Hitler, would satisfy the Nazi hunger for conquest and would avert the war.

14. PICCOLO : (A. trumpet, B. trombone, C. horn, D. baritone saxophone) :: VIOLIN : BASS

(D) A violin is a small, high-pitched string instrument; a bass is a large, low-pitched string instrument. Because a piccolo is a small, high-pitched woodwind instrument, then a large, low-pitched woodwind instrument must be selected to complete the analogy. A baritone saxophone is the correct choice. Trumpet and trombone are brass, not woodwind instruments. An English horn is classified as a woodwind, but an unspecified horn is considered brass.

15. DIVULGE : DISCLOSE :: APPRAISAL : (A. revision, B. respite, C. continuation, D. estimate)

(D) *Divulge* and *disclose* are synonyms; a synonym for *appraisal* is *estimate*.

16. WEALTH : TANGIBLE :: (A. price, B. gold, C. success, D. gifts) : INTANGIBLE

(C) The correspondence is one of characteristic. Wealth is usually measured in tangible units; success is often measured in intangible units.

17. HEMOGLOBIN : COACHES :: BLOOD : (A. train, B. whip, C. fuel, D. road)

(A) In this analogy of a part to a whole, hemoglobin is part of blood; coaches constitute parts of a train.

18. SHELTER : (A. refuge, B. cave, C. mansion, D. protection) :: BREAD : CAKE

(C) Bread and cake are related because the former is a necessity and the latter is a luxury; similarly, a shelter is a necessity, and a mansion is a luxury. It's a matter of degree.

19. AFFLUENT : (A. charity, B. diligence, C. misfortune, D. indifference) :: IMPOVERISHED : LAZINESS

(B) In this cause-and-effect analogy, diligence may contribute to making one affluent; laziness may contribute to making one impoverished.

20. INNING : BASEBALL :: (A. time, B. midnight, C. era, D. chronology) : HISTORY

(**C**) The relationship is one of measurement. A division of a baseball game is an inning; a phase of history is called an era.

21. E.M. : (A. A.C., B. L.G., C. P.D., D. P.G.) :: FORSTER : WODEHOUSE

(**D**) The analogy depends upon matching the initials to the last names of two British authors: E.M. Forster and P.G. Wodehouse.

22. (A. stifle, B. tell, C. joke, D. offer) : LAUGH :: THROW : JAVELIN

(**A**) This is an action-to-object analogy. One may throw a javelin, and one may stifle, or repress, a laugh. This question may prove puzzling because there is absolutely no meaningful relationship between throwing a javelin and stifling a laugh. However, the action-to-object relationship is real and legitimate.

23. CHARLESTON : (A. Tucson, B. Jackson, C. Williamsburg, D. Chicago) :: BOSTON : PHILADELPHIA

(**C**) In this place analogy, Charleston, Boston, and Philadelphia are related because they were important colonial cities. Among the available choices, only Williamsburg was another colonial city.

24. VINTNER : MINER :: (A. vines, B. wine, C. liquid, D. bottle) : ORE

(**B**) The relationship here is that of actor to the object of his or her actions. The miner works to extract ore from the earth; the vintner works to produce and to sell wine.

25. (A. jaguar, B. mink, C. lion, D. chinchilla) : GIRAFFE :: TIGER : ZEBRA

(**A**) A jaguar and a giraffe are related because both have spots; a tiger and a zebra are both striped.

26. (A. Athena, B. Artemis, C. Hera, D. Medea) : FRIGGA :: ZEUS : ODIN

(**C**) Zeus was king of the gods in Greek mythology; Hera was his wife. Odin was the supreme god in Norse mythology; Frigga was his wife.

27. 5 : 8 :: 25 : (A. 29, B. 40, C. 60, D. 108)

(**B**) 25 is the square of 5, but 64, the square of 8, is not offered as a choice, so you must rethink, $5 \times 5 = 25$; $5 \times 8 = 40$.

28. LIMP : CANE :: (A. cell, B. muscle, C. heat, D. cold) : TISSUE

(**D**) A person with a limp is likely to use a cane; a person with a cold is likely to use a tissue.

29. CONFESSOR : KINGMAKER :: EDWARD : (A. Warwick, B. Alfred, C. George, D. Gloucester)

(**A**) The correspondence is one of association. Edward was known as the Confessor; Warwick was known as the Kingmaker.

30. (A. parchment, B. concrete, C. cardboard, D. timber) : ADOBE :: PAPER : PAPYRUS

(**B**) This is an analogy of sequence. Adobe was used before concrete as a building material; papyrus was used before paper as a writing material.

31. HANDS : ARMS :: (A. Roman, B. crack, C. Diana, D. destiny) : MORPHEUS

(D) Truly this is an analogy based upon association. In commonly used expressions, the linkage is, "in the arms of Morpheus" and "in the hands of destiny."

32. HYMN : THEIR :: CELL : (A. score, B. peal, C. tree, D. mile)

(B) Each of the given terms in this analogy has a homophone, a word pronounced the same but spelled differently: *hymn* (*him*); *their* (*there*); and *cell* (*sell*). Among the choices, only *peal* has a homophone (*peel*).

33. DOG : SWAN :: (A. bark, B. noise, C. days, D. collie) : SONG

(C) The relationship is one of association. We speak of a swan song—that is, a farewell appearance or final act—and dog days, a period of hot, sultry weather or stagnation and inactivity. Swans do not sing; therefore, for purposes of this analogy, the barking of dogs is irrelevant.

34. EINSTEIN : MALTHUS :: RELATIVITY : (A. population, B. religion, C. economy, D. democracy)

(A) The correspondence is between a thinker and the theory with which he is associated. Einstein developed the theory of relativity; Malthus is famous for his theory of population. Although Malthus was an economist, it is not his field but his theory that successfully completes this analogy. The relationship of Malthus to the economy would be analogous to the relationship of Einstein to physics.

35. GALLEY : ROOKERY :: MEAL : (A. ship, B. seal, C. peal, D. chess)

(B) In this analogy of place, a galley is where a meal is produced, usually on board a ship; a rookery is the nesting place of a colony of seals, usually a rocky promontory or an isolated rock. It serves as the place where seals live and breed.

36. PEACH : (A. apple, B. beet, C. grape, D. tomato) :: CHERRY : RADISH

(B) A peach and a cherry are fruits that grow on trees; a radish and a beet are root vegetables.

37. LASSITUDE : (A. longitude, B. languor, C. purity, D. alacrity) :: PARSIMONY : BENEFACTION

(D) The opposite of *parsimony*, or *stinginess*, is *benefaction*, which means charitable donation; an antonym for *lassitude*, meaning *listlessness*, is *alacrity*, which means *promptness of response*.

38. THERMOSTAT : REGULATE :: (A. draft, B. windows, C. insulation, D. thermometer) : CONSERVE

(C) The purpose of a thermostat is to regulate room temperature; the purpose of insulation is to conserve energy.

39. MONGREL : PEDIGREE :: BOOR : (A. thoroughbred, B. manners, C. ancestry, D. lineage)

(B) A mongrel has no pedigree, just as a boor has no manners.

40. (A. earth, B. Venus, C. Sputnik, D. berry) : PLANET :: CANAL : RIVER

(C) The correspondence is between manmade and natural objects. Sputnik is a manmade object that orbits; a planet is a natural object that orbits. Similarly, a canal is a manmade waterway, and a river is a natural waterway.

41. PIRAEUS : OSTIA :: (A. Athens, B. Florence, C. Milan, D. Crete) : ROME

(A) In this place analogy, Piraeus is a port city near Athens; Ostia was a port city near Rome.

42. (A. psychology, B. philology, C. philosophy, D. philately) : PHRENOLOGY :: ASTRONOMY : ASTROLOGY

(A) Because astronomy and astrology both deal with the stars (with astronomy being the accepted science and astrology a disputed or questionable science), the task is to find an accepted science similar to the disputed science of phrenology (which deals with the head). Psychology is accepted and is the correct choice.

43. ORACLE : LOGICIAN :: INTUITION : (A. guess, B. syllogism, C. faith, D. Venn)

(B) The correspondence is one of thinker to tool. An oracle's prophecies can be based on intuition; a logician may reason by means of a syllogism, a formal scheme of deductive thinking.

44. PELEE : (A. France, B. soccer, C. Martinique, D. Brazil) :: ETNA : SICILY

(C) In this analogy of place or location, Etna is a volcano located on the island of Sicily. Pelee is a volcano located on the island of Martinique.

45. GERONTOLOGY : GENEALOGY :: (A. families, B. aging, C. gerunds, D. birth) : LINEAGE

(B) The relationship is one of classification. Gerontology is the study of aging; genealogy is the study of lineage.

46. ROMAN : (A. Caesar, B. backward, C. gladiator, D. handlebar) :: NOSE : MUSTACHE

(D) We speak of a Roman nose and a handlebar mustache. The correspondence is one of association.

47. HYDROGEN : 1 :: (A. carbon, B. oxygen, C. nitrogen, D. potassium) : 16

(B) Hydrogen, the lightest element, has an atomic weight of 1. Oxygen, with eight protons and eight neutrons in its nucleus, has an atomic weight of 16. Knowledge of chemistry is essential to this answer. Without such knowledge, you must guess.

48. (A. protein, B. nucleus, C. neutron, D. vacuole) : PROTON :: ARCH : HEEL

(C) The relationship is one of part to part. An arch and a heel are parts of a foot; protons and neutrons are parts of the nucleus of an atom.

49. 19 : 23 :: (A. 7, B. 11, C. 13, D. 17) : 13

(B) A prime number is a number that is divisible by no other numbers except 1 and itself. All the terms in question 49, the given terms and the choices, are prime numbers, so you must base your answer on another relationship. Numbers 19 and 23 are prime numbers in sequence. Completing the analogy, 11 and 13 are prime numbers in sequence.

50. BOND : STOCK :: DEBT : (A. preferred, B. option, C. equality, D. equity)

(D) A bond is certificate of debt issued by an institution. Stock is a certificate of equity, also issued by an institution.

120 Master the Miller Analogies Test

51. (A. Laos, B. Indonesia, C. Afghanistan, D. Japan) : INDIA :: NEVADA : COLORADO

(C) In this analogy of place, Nevada and Colorado are states separated by another state, Utah. India and Afghanistan are countries separated by another country, Pakistan.

52. CONCISE : (A. refined, B. expanded, C. convex, D. blunt) :: REMOVE : OBLITERATE

(D) *Remove* and *obliterate* are synonyms, both resulting in elimination, but varying in intensity. Therefore, you must find another word for *concise* that has the same result yet varies in intensity. *Concise* means *succinct* or *pithy; blunt* is a synonym but has the stronger connotation of *brusqueness* or *rudeness.*

53. TRAINING : ACUMEN :: (A. stupidity, B. experience, C. hunger, D. restlessness) : INANITION

(C) In this cause-and-effect analogy, training results in acumen or keenness of perception or discernment. Similarly, hunger results in inanition, a loss of vitality from absence of food and water.

54. BANTAM : (A. fly, B. chicken, C. fowl, D. small) :: WELTER : LIGHT

(A) Bantam, welter, light, and fly are all weight divisions in boxing.

55. JACKET : (A. lapel, B. button, C. vest, D. dinner) :: PANTS : CUFF

(A) A lapel is a folded-over part of a jacket; a cuff is a folded-over part of a pair of pants.

56. (A. grave, B. aggravated, C. theft, D. first degree) : GRAND :: ASSAULT : LARCENY

(B) *Assault* and *larceny* are both legal terms for crimes. *Grand* corresponds to *larceny,* describing the degree of the crime. The term that indicates the degree of assault is *aggravated.*

57. (A. Athena, B. Ceres, C. Artemis, D. Aphrodite) : ZEUS :: EVE : ADAM

(A) In this analogy of association of object to actor, Athena is said to have sprung from the head of Zeus; Eve is said to have been made from the rib of Adam.

58. SERAPHIC : (A. Napoleonic, B. Mephistophelean, C. Alexandrine, D. euphoric) :: IMPROVIDENT : PRESCIENT

(B) *Improvident* and *prescient* are related as antonyms. The former relates to the inability and the latter to the ability to foresee the future. Similarly, the opposite of *seraphic,* which means *angelic,* is *Mephistophelean,* which means *devilish.*

59. STRIPES : (A. bars, B. oak leaf, C. stars, D. general) :: SERGEANT : MAJOR

(B) In the army, stripes are associated with the rank of sergeant; an oak leaf is associated with the rank of major.

60. (A. precarious, B. deleterious, C. deterred, D. immortal) : CELEBRATED :: DEADLY : LIONIZED

(B) In this cause-and-effect analogy, something that is deleterious (exceedingly harmful) may prove deadly; a person who is celebrated (widely known) may be lionized.

61. MANET : REMBRANDT :: (A. Picasso, B. Dali, C. Pollock, D. Cézanne) : VAN GOGH

(D) Rembrandt and Van Gogh, the initial B : D related pair, were both Dutch painters. Manet and Cézanne were both French painters. The painter paired with the French Manet must be a French painter because the painter paired with the Dutch Rembrandt is a Dutch painter. Although Picasso spent most of his artistic life in France, he was Spanish.

62. (A. glove, B. stocking, C. weakness, D. mitt) : GAUNTLET :: HAT : HELMET

(A) A hat is a head covering worn in peace, and a helmet is a head covering worn in war; because a gauntlet is a hand covering worn in war, you must look for a hand covering that is worn in peace: a glove.

63. STAPES : COCHLEA :: BRIM : (A. hat, B. derby, C. crown, D. head)

(C) The stapes and the cochlea are parts of an ear; a brim and a crown are parts of a hat. This is a part-to-part analogy. Avoid the part-to-whole temptation.

64. (A. rococo, B. severe, C. Etruscan, D. stylish) : ORNAMENTED :: SOGGY : MOIST

(A) The relationship is one of degree. *Rococo* means excessively ornamented; *soggy* means excessively moist.

65. BURSAR : (A. funds, B. semester, C. accounts, D. purse) :: SEMINAR : IVY

(B) A bursar, a seminar, and ivy are all things associated with college. To complete the analogy, another term associated with college must be selected; that term is *semester*.

66. NEW YORK : RHODES :: LIBERTY : (A. Colossus, B. London, C. tyranny, D. freedom)

(A) The Statue of Liberty is set at the entrance to the harbor of New York; a bronze statue of Apollo, known as the Colossus, was set at the entrance to the harbor of ancient Rhodes. The analogy is one of place or location, but you do need some knowledge of ancient history in order to answer it.

67. RUBY : EMERALD :: TOMATO : (A. rose, B. radish, C. pasta, D. lettuce)

(D) A ruby is a red gem, and an emerald is a green gem; a tomato is red, and lettuce is green.

68. SOLID : MELTING :: SOLUTION : (A. saturation, B. liquefaction, C. heating, D. mixing)

(A) In this measurement analogy, the melting point is an important measure of a solid; the saturation point is an important measurement of a solution.

69. (A. royal, B. kingly, C. regal, D. princely) : LAGER :: TIME : EMIT

(C) In this nonsemantic analogy, *regal* spelled backward is *lager*; *time* spelled backward is *emit*.

70. HENRY FIELDING : (A. Victorian, B. Romantic, C. Restoration, D. Augustan) :: BEN JONSON : ELIZABETHAN

(D) The correspondence is one of association. Ben Jonson is associated with the Elizabethan period, the last part of the sixteenth century. Similarly, the novelist and playwright Henry Fielding is associated with the Augustan, or eighteenth-century, period.

122 Master the Miller Analogies Test

71. ARKANSAS : FLORIDA :: NEW MEXICO : (A. Tennessee, B. Ohio, C. California, D. Illinois)

(C) In this place analogy, Arkansas and New Mexico are interior states; Florida and California are related because they are coastal states.

72. SIN : ATONEMENT :: (A. clemency, B. peace, C. war, D. virtue) : REPARATION

(C) Atonement is compensation made for an offense against moral or religious law (a sin). Reparation is compensation made by a defeated nation for losses sustained by another nation as a result of war between the two nations.

73. (A. solo, B. duet, C. trio, D. quartet) : QUINTET :: BOXING : BASKETBALL

(A) A boxing match is fought by solo contestants, with one on each side; a basketball team is a quintet, with five players on each side.

74. JULIAN : GREGORIAN :: (A. pope, B. Mayan, C. American, D. Canadian) : AZTEC

(B) In this analogy, Julian, Gregorian, and Aztec are all types of calendars that were used at one time in the past. Among the available choices, only Mayan was another type of calendar.

75. (A. echo, B. elephant, C. page, D. blue) : MEMORY :: DENIM : BLOSSOM

(A) *Memory, denim,* and *blossom* are all related because of a common characteristic: They all tend to fade. An *echo* also fades.

76. (A. Jupiter, B. Hippocrates, C. Cadmus, D. Ptolemy) : HANNIBAL :: CADUCEUS : SWORD

(B) In this association analogy, a sword is a symbol of warfare, associated with Hannibal, a great soldier; a caduceus is a symbol for medicine and should be related to Hippocrates, a famous physician.

77. STYX : RUBICON :: ANATHEMA : (A. curse, B. pariah, C. parsee, D. song)

(A) This analogy is based on synonyms. Both the Styx and the Rubicon represent points of no return. The Styx is the river that the dead cross into Hades; the Rubicon is a line, which, once crossed, represents total commitment. An anathema is a curse.

78. EPISTEMOLOGY : (A. letters, B. weapons, C. knowledge, D. roots) :: PALEONTOLOGY : FOSSILS

(C) Paleontology is concerned with the study of fossils; epistemology is concerned with the study of knowledge.

79. (A. ear, B. foundry, C. corps, D. fife) : FLINT :: DRUM : STEEL

(D) In this part-to-part analogy, a fife is used with a drum to make up a marching corps; a flint is used with steel to produce a fire.

80. JAVELIN : (A. run, B. pass, C. mount, D. throw) :: EYE : BLINK

(D) The correspondence is one of object to action. One can blink an eye, and one can throw a javelin, a metal spear.

81. PLATO : (A. Socrates, B. Sophocles, C. Aristophanes, D. Aristotle) :: FREUD : JUNG

(D) Aristotle was a follower, albeit with modifications, of Plato; Jung was a follower, again with modifications, of Freud.

82. (A. law, B. book, C. band, D. wagon) : WAINWRIGHT :: DICTIONARY : LEXICOGRAPHER

(D) This analogy is one of worker to the article created. A lexicographer compiles a dictionary; a wainwright makes a wagon.

83. 15 : 6 :: 23 : (A. 8, B. 7, C. 6, D. 5)

(D) Think of this as a nonsemantic or configurational analogy utilizing numbers instead of words. 1 + 5 = 6; 2 + 3 = 5. In other words, the two digits of the first number added together create the next number.

84. CONCERT : (A. andante, B. a cappella, C. opera, D. artistry) :: PERFORMANCE : PANTOMIME

(B) A concert in which there is singing without musical accompaniment is a cappella; a dramatic performance in which there is no dialogue is a pantomime.

85. (A. uniform, B. commander, C. platoon, D. sentry) : DOG :: GARRISON : FLOCK

(D) A sentry guards a garrison; a sheep dog guards a flock.

86. PORTUGAL : IBERIA :: TOOTH : (A. dentist, B. cavity, C. nail, D. comb)

(D) Portugal is part of the peninsula of Iberia; a tooth is part of a comb. You must shift your thinking away from the mouth to arrive at the answer.

87. RADIUS : (A. circle, B. arc, C. chord, D. diameter) :: YARD : FATHOM

(D) A yard (3 feet) is half as long as a fathom (6 feet). In a given circle, the radius is half as long as the diameter.

88. EMINENT : LOWLY :: FREQUENT : (A. often, B. frivolous, C. rare, D. soon)

(C) *Eminent* and *lowly* are antonyms; an antonym for *frequent* is *rare*.

89. FILIGREE : METAL :: (A. lace, B. linen, C. cotton, D. silk) : THREAD

(A) In this definition analogy, filigree is delicate ornamental openwork made of metal; lace is delicate open-work fabric made from thread.

90. INTAGLIO : (A. cameo, B. caviar, C. Machiavellian, D. harem) :: CONCAVE : CONVEX

(A) *Concave* means curving inward, whereas *convex* means curving outward. Intaglio is incised carving. It relates, therefore, to *concave*. A cameo, which is carved in relief, corresponds to *convex*.

91. MEZZANINE : (A. orchestra, B. stage, C. proscenium, D. second balcony) :: ABDOMEN : THORAX

(D) The mezzanine is located directly below the second balcony, just as the abdomen is located below the thorax.

92. ROTUND : GAUNT :: (A. unruly, B. onerous, C. tractable, D. strong) : CONTUMACIOUS

(C) *Rotund,* which refers to something rounded in figure or plump, is the opposite of *gaunt,* which means *thin.* An antonym for *contumacious,* meaning *disobedient* or *rebellious,* is *tractable,* meaning *docile* or *yielding.*

93. GLACIER : MOLASSES :: (A. dirge, B. moth, C. spring, D. mountain) : TORTOISE

(A) A glacier, molasses, and a tortoise are all related because they move slowly. Among the choices given, only a dirge is also slow-moving.

94. FOLD : (A. fell, B. hand, C. falls, D. boat) :: FORD : STREAM

(B) In this action-to-object analogy, one may ford a stream, and one can fold a hand in cards. Mental flexibility is a must in answering Miller Analogy questions.

95. VERDI : (A. *La Traviata,* B. *Fidelio,* C. *Aida,* D. *Rigoletto*) :: CHOPIN : PARSIFAL

(B) Chopin did not compose *Parsifal.* To complete the analogy, you must select what Verdi did not compose. The correct choice is *Fidelio,* which was composed by Beethoven.

96. SUBSTITUTE : TEAM :: UNDERSTUDY : (A. school, B. congregation, C. actor, D. cast)

(D) A substitute is used to replace someone on a team; an understudy is used to replace someone in a cast.

97. PORT : (A. vintage, B. harbor, C. starboard, D. left) :: HEADLIGHTS : TRUNK

(C) Port and starboard are opposite sides of a ship; the headlights and the trunk are at opposite ends of an automobile.

98. YORKTOWN : VICKSBURG :: CONCORD : (A. Philadelphia, B. Providence, C. Antietam, D. Valley Forge)

(C) In this place analogy, Yorktown was the site of a major battle in the Revolutionary War; Vicksburg was the site of a major battle in the Civil War. Because Concord was also a site of a Revolutionary War battle, another Civil War battle site must be found to complete the analogy. Antietam is the correct choice.

99. (A. border, B. score, C. quart, D. quatrain) : LINE :: SQUARE : CORNER

(D) This analogy is based upon a four-in-one ratio. There are four lines in a quatrain and four corners to a square.

100. ROOSTER : (A. crow, B. coop, C. egg, D. owl.) :: EFFERVESCENT : EFFETE

(D) Because *effervescent,* meaning *exuberant,* and *effete,* meaning *exhausted,* are opposites, the task is to find a contrast for *rooster.* A rooster is associated with morning, whereas an owl is a night bird.

SAMPLE TEST 4

Answer Sheet

1 ⓐ ⓑ ⓒ ⓓ	26 ⓐ ⓑ ⓒ ⓓ	51 ⓐ ⓑ ⓒ ⓓ	76 ⓐ ⓑ ⓒ ⓓ
2 ⓐ ⓑ ⓒ ⓓ	27 ⓐ ⓑ ⓒ ⓓ	52 ⓐ ⓑ ⓒ ⓓ	77 ⓐ ⓑ ⓒ ⓓ
3 ⓐ ⓑ ⓒ ⓓ	28 ⓐ ⓑ ⓒ ⓓ	53 ⓐ ⓑ ⓒ ⓓ	78 ⓐ ⓑ ⓒ ⓓ
4 ⓐ ⓑ ⓒ ⓓ	29 ⓐ ⓑ ⓒ ⓓ	54 ⓐ ⓑ ⓒ ⓓ	79 ⓐ ⓑ ⓒ ⓓ
5 ⓐ ⓑ ⓒ ⓓ	30 ⓐ ⓑ ⓒ ⓓ	55 ⓐ ⓑ ⓒ ⓓ	80 ⓐ ⓑ ⓒ ⓓ
6 ⓐ ⓑ ⓒ ⓓ	31 ⓐ ⓑ ⓒ ⓓ	56 ⓐ ⓑ ⓒ ⓓ	81 ⓐ ⓑ ⓒ ⓓ
7 ⓐ ⓑ ⓒ ⓓ	32 ⓐ ⓑ ⓒ ⓓ	57 ⓐ ⓑ ⓒ ⓓ	82 ⓐ ⓑ ⓒ ⓓ
8 ⓐ ⓑ ⓒ ⓓ	33 ⓐ ⓑ ⓒ ⓓ	58 ⓐ ⓑ ⓒ ⓓ	83 ⓐ ⓑ ⓒ ⓓ
9 ⓐ ⓑ ⓒ ⓓ	34 ⓐ ⓑ ⓒ ⓓ	59 ⓐ ⓑ ⓒ ⓓ	84 ⓐ ⓑ ⓒ ⓓ
10 ⓐ ⓑ ⓒ ⓓ	35 ⓐ ⓑ ⓒ ⓓ	60 ⓐ ⓑ ⓒ ⓓ	85 ⓐ ⓑ ⓒ ⓓ
11 ⓐ ⓑ ⓒ ⓓ	36 ⓐ ⓑ ⓒ ⓓ	61 ⓐ ⓑ ⓒ ⓓ	86 ⓐ ⓑ ⓒ ⓓ
12 ⓐ ⓑ ⓒ ⓓ	37 ⓐ ⓑ ⓒ ⓓ	62 ⓐ ⓑ ⓒ ⓓ	87 ⓐ ⓑ ⓒ ⓓ
13 ⓐ ⓑ ⓒ ⓓ	38 ⓐ ⓑ ⓒ ⓓ	63 ⓐ ⓑ ⓒ ⓓ	88 ⓐ ⓑ ⓒ ⓓ
14 ⓐ ⓑ ⓒ ⓓ	39 ⓐ ⓑ ⓒ ⓓ	64 ⓐ ⓑ ⓒ ⓓ	89 ⓐ ⓑ ⓒ ⓓ
15 ⓐ ⓑ ⓒ ⓓ	40 ⓐ ⓑ ⓒ ⓓ	65 ⓐ ⓑ ⓒ ⓓ	90 ⓐ ⓑ ⓒ ⓓ
16 ⓐ ⓑ ⓒ ⓓ	41 ⓐ ⓑ ⓒ ⓓ	66 ⓐ ⓑ ⓒ ⓓ	91 ⓐ ⓑ ⓒ ⓓ
17 ⓐ ⓑ ⓒ ⓓ	42 ⓐ ⓑ ⓒ ⓓ	67 ⓐ ⓑ ⓒ ⓓ	92 ⓐ ⓑ ⓒ ⓓ
18 ⓐ ⓑ ⓒ ⓓ	43 ⓐ ⓑ ⓒ ⓓ	68 ⓐ ⓑ ⓒ ⓓ	93 ⓐ ⓑ ⓒ ⓓ
19 ⓐ ⓑ ⓒ ⓓ	44 ⓐ ⓑ ⓒ ⓓ	69 ⓐ ⓑ ⓒ ⓓ	94 ⓐ ⓑ ⓒ ⓓ
20 ⓐ ⓑ ⓒ ⓓ	45 ⓐ ⓑ ⓒ ⓓ	70 ⓐ ⓑ ⓒ ⓓ	95 ⓐ ⓑ ⓒ ⓓ
21 ⓐ ⓑ ⓒ ⓓ	46 ⓐ ⓑ ⓒ ⓓ	71 ⓐ ⓑ ⓒ ⓓ	96 ⓐ ⓑ ⓒ ⓓ
22 ⓐ ⓑ ⓒ ⓓ	47 ⓐ ⓑ ⓒ ⓓ	72 ⓐ ⓑ ⓒ ⓓ	97 ⓐ ⓑ ⓒ ⓓ
23 ⓐ ⓑ ⓒ ⓓ	48 ⓐ ⓑ ⓒ ⓓ	73 ⓐ ⓑ ⓒ ⓓ	98 ⓐ ⓑ ⓒ ⓓ
24 ⓐ ⓑ ⓒ ⓓ	49 ⓐ ⓑ ⓒ ⓓ	74 ⓐ ⓑ ⓒ ⓓ	99 ⓐ ⓑ ⓒ ⓓ
25 ⓐ ⓑ ⓒ ⓓ	50 ⓐ ⓑ ⓒ ⓓ	75 ⓐ ⓑ ⓒ ⓓ	100 ⓐ ⓑ ⓒ ⓓ

TEAR HERE

Chapter 8

Sample Test 4

100 Questions • 50 Minutes

Directions: Each of these test questions consists of three capitalized words and four lettered words enclosed in parentheses. Two of the capitalized words are related in some way. Find the two related words, and establish the nature of the relationship. Then study the four words lettered A, B, C, and D. Select the one lettered word that is related to the remaining capitalized word in the same way that the first two capitalized words are related. Mark the answer sheet for the letter preceding the word you select.

ROAD MAP

- *Answer Key*
- *Explanatory Answers*

1. NEEDLE : (A. thread, B. pen, C. eye, D. hole) :: GLOBE : ORANGE

2. ARCHIPELAGO : ISLAND :: GALAXY : (A. universe, B. space, C. star, D. Milky Way)

3. DUCTILE : (A. malleable, B. adamant, C. regal, D. channel) :: LATENT : COVERT

4. NEWSPRINT : (A. paper, B. linotype, C. newsstand, D. tree) :: STEEL : ORE

5. EXPERIMENTATION : MATRICULATION :: DISCOVERY : (A. mothering, B. molding, C. learning, D. wedding)

6. BUTTER : GUNS :: (A. plowshares, B. margarine, C. fig trees, D. pruning hooks) : SWORDS

7. *MAINE* : (A. Miami, B. Cuba, C. Puerto Rico, D. Quebec) :: *ARIZONA* : HAWAII

8. (A. *Plaza Suite*, B. *Manhattan*, C. *Brighton Beach Memoirs*, D. *Auntie Mame*) : *BILOXI BLUES* :: *ANNIE HALL* : *RADIO DAYS*

9. MANTISSA : LOGARITHM :: SINE : (A. cosine, B. ratio, C. exponent, D. trigonometry)

10. BOXER : BOER :: (A. England, B. China, C. India, D. Empress) : SOUTH AFRICA

11. (A. Bartók, B. Mozart, C. Fauré, D. Beethoven) : WAGNER :: TCHAIKOVSKY : PROKOFIEV

12. (A. grind, B. thresh, C. harvest, D. grow) : WHEAT :: DISTILL : WATER

13. BRAGGADOCIO : RETICENCE :: MISERLINESS : (A. profligacy, B. ecstasy, C. obloquy, D. falsity)

14. 625 : (A. 5^5, B. 6^4, C. 7^4, D. 12^3) :: 5^4 : 2,401

15. SANDHURST : ENGLAND :: (A. Harvard, B. Pittsburgh, C. West Point, D. MIT) : UNITED STATES

16. AURICLE : VENTRICLE :: (A. sinus, B. epiglottis, C. thalamus, D. esophagus) : CEREBELLUM

17. (A. trees, B. circus, C. merry-go-round, D. scooter) : STILTS :: BUS : AUDITORIUM

18. PARIS : (A. London, B. Priam, C. Achilles, D. Helen) :: ACHILLES : HECTOR

19. GENEROUS : LAVISH :: TIMOROUS : (A. tumid, B. craven, C. courageous, D. foolhardy)

20. MECCA : BENARES :: MOSLEM : (A. Islam, B. India, C. Hindu, D. Buddhist)

21. POLO : MALLET :: (A. hockey, B. football, C. baseball, D. basketball) : STICK

22. (A. barber, B. bristle, C. comb, D. stroke) : BRUSH :: CRUISER : FLEET

23. HUDSON : BUICK :: PACKARD : (A. Stutz, B. Locomobile, C. Maxwell, D. Oldsmobile)

24. IRREGULAR : SYMMETRY :: (A. dentures, B. savory, C. distasteful, D. cavernous) : TOOTHSOME

25. (A. Jenner, B. Magyar, C. Bede, D. Pericles) : KOOP :: SCHWEITZER : SALK

26. ASSAYER : ORE :: SPECTROMETER : (A. lens, B. refraction, C. mirror, D. eye)

27. BRAZIL : (A. Portugal, B. Spain, C. Venezuela, D. Suriname) :: GUYANA : FRENCH GUIANA

28. (A. lunch, B. meal, C. breakfast, D. brunch) : SUPPER :: SMOG : HAZE

29. APPRAISAL : REVENUE :: (A. defrosting, B. clear, C. hiding, D. sun) : VISIBILITY

30. F : X :: 1 : (A. 4, B. 8, C. 2, D. 6)

31. RUPEE : (A. shah, B. guilder, C. rial, D. krone) :: INDIA : NETHERLANDS

32. (A. servile, B. kowtow, C. unruly, D. inhibited) : OBSEQUIOUS :: IMPRECATORY : EULOGISTIC

33. BLUE : ORANGE :: (A. indigo, B. yellow, C. purple, D. red) : GREEN

34. CHEETAH : SPEED :: (A. blade, B. dullness, C. bird, D. incision) : KEENNESS

35. (A. hock, B. jockey, C. stable, D. hand) : HORSE :: TONGUE : BELL

36. EPILOGUE : NOVEL :: (A. cheers, B. curtain call, C. performance, D. introduction) : APPLAUSE

37. (A. Nantucket, B. Puerto Rico, C. Hawaii, D. Long Island) : UNITED STATES :: TASMANIA : AUSTRALIA

38. ANCHISES : (A. Troilus, B. Achilles, C. Ajax, D. Aeneas) :: JOCASTA : OEDIPUS

39. LEES : DREGS :: SYBARITIC : (A. sensual, B. moderate, C. cultish, D. servile)

40. ISRAEL : VIETNAM :: JORDAN : (A. Cambodia, B. Korea, C. Nepal, D. France)

41. MAP : (A. explorer, B. geography, C. legend, D. atlas) :: TEXT : FOOTNOTE

42. (A. clock, B. watch, C. time, D. hour) : TELL :: GUM : CHEW

43. BERET : DERBY :: PILLBOX : (A. fedora, B. shawl, C. cravat, D. stole)

44. COOPER : (A. lithographer, B. cartographer, C. photographer, D. biographer) :: BARREL : MAP

45. PUPA : (A. tadpole, B. larva, C. cocoon, D. insect) :: FETUS : CHILD

46. DEALING : STOCK EXCHANGE :: (A. preserving, B. selling, C. buying, D. copying) : LANDMARK

47. UPRISING : (A. revolution, B. settlement, C. quarrel, D. disquiet) :: FIB : LIE

48. (A. Crete, B. Malta, C. Sicily, D. Corsica) : SARDINIA :: BOLIVIA : ARGENTINA

49. EVIL : EXORCISE :: BREAD : (A. carbohydrate, B. break, C. sandwich, D. shred)

50. COWARD : (A. loser, B. lily-livered, C. hero, D. villain) :: YOLK : ALBUMEN

51. (A. humid, B. speedy, C. piquant, D. moist) : VAPID :: OBDURATE : COMPASSIONATE

52. CUCUMBER : WATERMELON :: CANTALOUPE : (A. squash, B. radish, C. cherry, D. plum)

53. (A. stick, B. percussion, C. cymbal, D. head) : DRUM :: STRINGS : VIOLIN

54. ILLNESS : (A. debility, B. hospital, C. doctor, D. panacea) :: VIBRATION : SOUND

55. VERDUN : DUNKIRK :: YPRES : (A. Belleau Woods, B. El Alamein, C. San Juan Hill, D. Marne)

56. (A. gain, B. reward, C. loot, D. profit) : ROBBERY :: REVENGE : VENDETTA

57. ANALYSIS : FREUD :: (A. manipulation, B. illness, C. sex, D. stimulation) : OSTEOPATHY

58. CLAUSTROPHOBIA : CLOSETS :: AGORAPHOBIA : (A. ships, B. sheep, C. plants, D. plains)

59. SEARCH : FIND :: FIGHT : (A. win, B. lose, C. seek, D. contend)

60. (A. affection, B. encouragement, C. blasphemy, D. oblivion) : FRACAS :: APHRODITE : MARS

61. H : S :: (A. M, B. L, C. I, D. P) : W

GO ON TO THE NEXT PAGE

62. HASTILY : DESPONDENTLY :: CIRCUMSPECTLY : (A. quick, B. circuit, C. rate, D. slowly)

63. BOXER : TABBY :: LABRADOR : (A. fighter, B. poodle, C. calico, D. nanny)

64. CROESUS : (A. boat, B. wealth, C. pleats, D. loyalty) :: ODYSSEUS : CRAFT

65. LUCERNE : MICHIGAN :: GENEVA : (A. United States, B. Victoria, C. Okeechobee, D. Switzerland)

66. (A. tally, B. game, C. concert, D. run) : SCORE :: PLAY : SCRIPT

67. FLAUBERT : (A. madame, B. field, C. knife, D. writer) :: JOYCE : PORTRAIT

68. DOG : INTRUDER :: (A. burglar, B. cat, C. knight, D. maiden) : DRAGON

69. MENDACIOUS : DECEITFUL :: AUSPICIOUS : (A. indifferent, B. submerged, C. propitious, D. bereft)

70. PARTRIDGE : RABBIT :: (A. quail, B. pen, C. birds, D. covey) : WARREN

71. LAPIDARY : (A. ruby, B. wood, C. lick, D. food) :: SCULPTOR : ALABASTER

72. BEES : FILE :: BIRDS : (A. grade, B. rank, C. fold, D. twist)

73. MANY : MUCH :: FEW : (A. minus, B. more, C. small, D. little)

74. FORSOOK : DRANK :: FROZEN : (A. swum, B. wrote, C. sang, D. chose)

75. SANDAL : BOOT :: (A. hammer, B. hatchet, C. shoemaker, D. blade) : AX

76. HORSE : (A. man, B. goat, C. archer, D. bull) :: CENTAUR : SATYR

77. (A. anode, B. bird, C. purchase, D. battery) : CELL :: ARROW : SHAFT

78. FELONY : MISDEMEANOR :: SIN : (A. piccalilli, B. picayune, C. peccadillo, D. picador)

79. NOVEMBER : APRIL :: (A. May, B. June, C. July, D. August) : SEPTEMBER

80. ALBANIA : POLAND :: CHINA : (A. Czechoslovakia, B. Russia, C. Sumatra, D. India)

81. WASTEFUL : (A. parsimonious, B. neglectful, C. vast, D. prodigal) :: DISINTERESTED : IMPARTIAL

82. SCHOONER : ZIGGURAT :: CRUISER : (A. cutter, B. campanile, C. viking, D. tug)

83. (A. pine, B. cedar, C. ash, D. willow) : OAK :: MOURNFUL : STURDY

84. ADVISE : EXHORT :: (A. force, B. tempt, C. prohibit, D. prevent) : ENTICE

85. STEEL : WELD :: LIPS : (A. frown, B. purse, C. fold, D. smirk)

86. TESTIMONY : (A. confession, B. judge, C. witness, D. trial) :: BIOGRAPHY : AUTOBIOGRAPHY

87. STRATUM : SYLLABUS :: (A. strati, B. stratums, C. stratus, D. strata) : SYLLABI

88. LAMB : DEER :: (A. rabbit, B. peacock, C. horse, D. pig) : LION

89. VELOCITY : (A. wind, B. earth, C. vibration, D. destruction) :: BEAUFORT : RICHTER

90. (A. distance, B. program, C. station, D. tube) : TELEVISION :: LEADER : ANARCHY

91. TAPS : VESPERS :: (A. painting, B. needle, C. revelry, D. reveille) : MATINS

92. PROSTRATE : (A. dazzling, B. stealing, C. submission, D. dehydrated) :: SUPINE : SLEEPING

93. MAHATMA GANDHI : WAR :: CARRY NATION : (A. suffrage, B. alcohol, C. temperance, D. employment)

94. $\frac{2}{7}$: (A. $\frac{1}{16}$, B. $\frac{3}{28}$, C. $\frac{3}{21}$, D. $\frac{1}{14}$) :: $\frac{4}{7}$: $\frac{1}{7}$

95. (A. roc, B. canary, C. albatross, D. condor) : VULTURE :: PHOENIX : EAGLE

96. TINE : FORK :: (A. car, B. gearshift, C. flange, D. wheelwright) : WHEEL

97. (A. tie, B. appearance, C. shoes, D. decoration) : ATTIRE :: WIT : COMMUNICATION

98. HUSK : (A. fish, B. chops, C. gristle, D. filet) :: GRAIN : MEAT

99. SURPRISED : (A. interested, B. astounded, C. expected, D. unknown) :: WORK : TOIL

100. INEBRIOUS : (A. intoxicated, B. dull, C. sincere, D. abstemious) :: SPARTAN : GARRULOUS

ANSWER KEY

1. B	21. A	41. C	61. B	81. D
2. C	22. B	42. C	62. D	82. B
3. A	23. D	43. A	63. C	83. D
4. D	24. C	44. B	64. B	84. B
5. C	25. A	45. D	65. C	85. B
6. A	26. B	46. A	66. C	86. A
7. B	27. D	47. A	67. A	87. D
8. C	28. D	48. D	68. C	88. B
9. D	29. A	49. B	69. C	89. C
10. B	30. A	50. C	70. D	90. A
11. D	31. B	51. C	71. A	91. D
12. B	32. C	52. A	72. B	92. C
13. A	33. D	53. D	73. D	93. B
14. C	34. A	54. A	74. A	94. D
15. C	35. A	55. B	75. B	95. A
16. C	36. B	56. C	76. B	96. C
17. D	37. C	57. A	77. D	97. D
18. C	38. D	58. D	78. C	98. C
19. B	39. A	59. A	79. B	99. B
20. C	40. A	60. A	80. A	100. D

EXPLANATORY ANSWERS

1. NEEDLE : (A. thread, B. pen, C. eye, D. hole) :: GLOBE : ORANGE

(**B**) A globe and an orange are related because they are both round; a needle and a pen are both pointed.

2. ARCHIPELAGO : ISLAND :: GALAXY : (A. universe, B. space, C. star, D. Milky Way)

(**C**) This is a whole-to-part analogy. An archipelago is made up of islands; a galaxy is made up of stars. A galaxy is part of the universe; the order of the relationship is the reverse of that between archipelago and island. The Milky Way is a galaxy.

3. DUCTILE : (A. malleable, B. adamant, C. regal, D. channel) :: LATENT : COVERT

(**A**) *Latent* and *covert* are synonyms meaning *hidden* or *concealed*. A synonym for *ductile,* which means something easily influenced or altered, is *malleable*.

4. NEWSPRINT : (A. paper, B. linotype, C. newsstand, D. tree) :: STEEL : ORE

(**D**) In this analogy, the relationship is one of source to product. An original source of steel is ore; an original source of newsprint is a tree.

5. EXPERIMENTATION : MATRICULATION :: DISCOVERY : (A. mothering, B. molding, C. learning, D. wedding)

(**C**) In this purpose analogy, a purpose of experimentation is discovery; a purpose of matriculation is learning.

6. BUTTER : GUNS :: (A. plowshares, B. margarine, C. fig trees, D. pruning hooks) : SWORDS

(**A**) The implication of the saying "Butter is better than guns" is that peace is better than war. The passage from Isaiah, "They shall bend their swords into plowshares ..." has the same implication. Pruning hooks are paired with spears.

7. *MAINE* : (A. Miami, B. Cuba, C. Puerto Rico, D. Quebec) :: *ARIZONA* : HAWAII

(**B**) The opening blow of Japan's involvement in the Second World War was the sinking of the battleship *Arizona* in Honolulu harbor in Hawaii. The Spanish American War began with the sinking of the battleship *Maine* in Havana harbor, Cuba.

8. (A. *Plaza Suite,* B. *Manhattan,* C. *Brighton Beach Memoirs,* D *Auntie Mame*) : *BILOXI BLUES* :: *ANNIE HALL* : *RADIO DAYS*

(**C**) *Annie Hall* and *Radio Days* are movies by Woody Allen in which he draws heavily upon his childhood experiences. *Brighton Beach Memoirs* and *Biloxi Blues* are autobiographical Neil Simon plays.

9. MANTISSA : LOGARITHM :: SINE : (A. cosine, B. ratio, C, exponent, D. trigonometry)

(**D**) This analogy from the language of mathematics is based on a part-to-whole relationship. A mantissa is the decimal part of a logarithm. Sine is a function in trigonometry.

10. BOXER : BOER :: (A. England, B. China, C. India, D. Empress) : SOUTH AFRICA

(B) This is an analogy involving history and place. The Boer War took place in South Africa; the Boxer Rebellion occurred in China.

11. (A. Bartók, B. Mozart, C. Fauré, D. Beethoven) : WAGNER :: TCHAIKOVSKY : PROKOFIEV

(D) Tchaikovsky and Prokofiev are related because they both are composers from Russia; therefore, to complete the analogy, Wagner, a composer from Germany, must be paired with Beethoven, another German composer.

12. (A. grind, B. thresh, C. harvest, D. grow) : WHEAT :: DISTILL : WATER

(B) In this action-to-object analogy, you distill water to remove unwanted substances from the refined water; similarly, you thresh wheat to separate the grains from the unwanted chaff.

13. BRAGGADOCIO : RETICENCE :: MISERLINESS : (A. profligacy, B. ecstasy, C. obloquy, D. falsity)

(A) *Braggadocio,* which means *boastfulness,* is opposite to *reticence;* an antonym for *miserliness,* which means *stinginess,* is *profligacy,* meaning *reckless wastefulness.*

14. 625 : (A. 5^5, B. 6^4, C. 7^4, D. 12^3) :: 5^4 : 2,401

(C) The nature of the relationship should be clear: synonyms. If need be, a bit of trial and error will yield the answer. $5^4 = 625 :: 7^4 = 2,401$.

15. SANDHURST : ENGLAND :: (A. Harvard, B. Pittsburgh, C. West Point, D. MIT) : UNITED STATES

(C) Sandhurst is a school in England that trains future military officers; West Point has the same function in the United States.

16. AURICLE : VENTRICLE :: (A. sinus, B. epiglottis, C. thalamus, D. esophagus) : CEREBELLUM

(C) In this part-to-part analogy, the auricle and ventricle are both parts of the heart; the cerebellum and thalamus are parts of the brain.

17. (A. trees, B. circus, C. merry-go-round, D. scooter) : STILTS :: BUS : AUDITORIUM

(D) A bus and an auditorium are related because they are intended to serve more than one person; stilts and a scooter are usually intended for one person alone.

18. PARIS : (A. London, B. Priam, C. Achilles, D. Helen) :: ACHILLES : HECTOR

(C) In Homer's *Iliad,* Achilles slew Hector, and later Paris slew Achilles.

19. GENEROUS : LAVISH :: TIMOROUS : (A. tumid, B. craven, C. courageous, D. foolhardy)

(B) A person who is extremely generous is lavish; a person who is extremely timorous is craven, or cowardly.

20. MECCA : BENARES :: MOSLEM : (A. Islam, B. India, C. Hindu, D. Buddhist)

(C) In this place analogy, Mecca is the sacred city of the Moslems; Benares is the sacred city of the Hindus.

21. POLO : MALLET :: (A. hockey, B. football, C. baseball, D. basketball) : STICK

(**A**) A mallet is a piece of equipment used by polo players. Similarly, a stick is a piece of equipment used by hockey players.

22. (A. barber, B. bristle, C. comb, D. stroke) : BRUSH :: CRUISER : FLEET

(**B**) In this analogy of a part to a whole, a bristle is part of a brush; a cruiser is part of a fleet.

23. HUDSON : BUICK :: PACKARD : (A. Stutz, B. Locomobile, C. Maxwell, D. Oldsmobile)

(**D**) Hudson and Packard are names of cars that are no longer made; Buick and Oldsmobile are names of currently produced cars.

24. IRREGULAR : SYMMETRY :: (A. dentures, B. savory, C. distasteful, D. cavernous) : TOOTHSOME

(**C**) *Irregular* is opposite in meaning to *symmetry*. An antonym for *toothsome*, which means *delicious*, is *distasteful*.

25. (A. Jenner, B. Magyar, C. Bede, D. Pericles) : KOOP :: SCHWEITZER : SALK

(**A**) Jenner, Koop, Schweitzer, and Salk are all related as physicians.

26. ASSAYER : ORE :: SPECTROMETER : (A. lens, B. refraction, C. mirror, D. eye)

(**B**) In this analogy of association, an assayer's job is to measure and analyze ore; a spectrometer measures and analyzes refraction.

27. BRAZIL : (A. Portugal, B. Spain, C. Venezuela, D. Suriname) :: GUYANA : FRENCH GUIANA

(**D**) Guyana, French Guiana, Brazil, and Suriname are all related in that they are the four South American countries in which Spanish is not the major language. Respectively, the languages spoken are English, French, Portuguese, and Dutch.

28. (A. lunch, B. meal, C. breakfast, D. brunch) : SUPPER :: SMOG : HAZE

(**D**) There is a two-to-one relationship in this analogy because smog is a combination of two atmospheric conditions, smoke and fog, while haze is one atmospheric condition. Similarly, brunch combines two meals, breakfast and lunch, while supper is just one meal.

29. APPRAISAL : REVENUE :: (A. defrosting, B. clear, C. hiding, D. sun) : VISIBILITY

(**A**) This is a purpose analogy. The purpose of the appraisal of a house is to gain tax revenue; the purpose of defrosting a windshield is to increase visibility. Note that the sun is a cause of visibility, not the purpose of it.

30. F : X :: 1 : (A. 4, B. 8, C. 2, D. 6)

(**A**) The correspondence is mathematical. F is the 6th letter of the alphabet, and X is the 24th. Their ratio is 1 : 4. Upon seeing the "X," you might have expected this analogy to be based upon Roman numerals, but you should have shifted gears very quickly upon the realization that "F" is not a Roman numeral.

31. RUPEE : (A. shah, B. guilder, C. rial, D. krone) :: INDIA : NETHERLANDS

(**B**) The rupee is the basic unit of currency in India. The basic unit of currency in the Netherlands is the guilder.

32. (A. servile, B. kowtow, C. unruly, D. inhibited) : OBSEQUIOUS :: IMPRECATORY : EULOGISTIC

(**C**) *Imprecatory,* which means *damning,* is opposite to *eulogistic,* meaning *full of praise.* Similarly, an antonym of *obsequious,* meaning *compliant,* is *unruly,* meaning *difficult to discipline.*

33. BLUE : ORANGE :: (A. indigo, B. yellow, C. purple, D. red) : GREEN

(**D**) Blue and orange are related as complementary colors; red and green are also complementary colors.

34. CHEETAH : SPEED :: (A. blade, B. dullness, C. bird, D. incision) : KEENNESS

(**A**) In this characteristic analogy, a cheetah is known for its speed; a blade is proverbially known for its keenness.

35. (A. hock, B. jockey, C. stable, D. hand) : HORSE :: TONGUE : BELL

(**A**) The correspondence is one of part to whole. A hock is part of a horse, the joint of the hind leg; a tongue is part of a bell.

36. EPILOGUE : NOVEL :: (A. cheers, B. curtain call, C. performance, D. introduction) : APPLAUSE

(**B**) In this sequence analogy, an epilogue follows the main action of a novel. A curtain call follows applause in a performance.

37. (A. Nantucket, B. Puerto Rico, C. Hawaii, D. Long Island) : UNITED STATES :: TASMANIA : AUSTRALIA

(**C**) Tasmania is an island state of Australia; Hawaii is an island state of the United States.

38. ANCHISES : (A. Troilus, B. Achilles, C. Ajax, D. Aeneas) :: JOCASTA : OEDIPUS

(**D**) Jocasta was the mother of Oedipus; Anchises was the father of Aeneas.

39. LEES : DREGS :: SYBARITIC : (A. sensual, B. moderate, C. cultish, D. servile)

(**A**) *Lees* is a synonym for *dregs.* Similarly, a synonym for *sybaritic,* devoted to pleasure or luxury, is *sensual.*

40. ISRAEL : VIETNAM :: JORDAN : (A. Cambodia, B. Korea, C. Nepal, D. France)

(**A**) Israel and Jordan are countries that were both once part of the land of Palestine. Vietnam and Cambodia were both once parts of French Indochina.

41. MAP : (A. explorer, B. geography, C. legend, D. atlas) :: TEXT : FOOTNOTE

(**C**) A footnote is an explanatory reference in a text; a legend is an explanatory list of symbols used on a map.

42. (A. clock, B. watch, C. time, D. hour) : TELL :: GUM : CHEW

(**C**) In this action-to-object analogy, one can tell time and one can chew gum.

43. BERET : DERBY :: PILLBOX : (A. fedora, B. shawl, C. cravat, D. stole)

(A) Beret, derby, pillbox, and fedora are types of hats.

44. COOPER : (A. lithographer, B. cartographer, C. photographer, D. biographer) :: BARREL : MAP

(B) The correspondence is one of worker to the thing created. A cooper makes a barrel; a cartographer makes a map.

45. PUPA : (A. tadpole, B. larva, C. cocoon, D. insect) :: FETUS : CHILD

(D) In this sequence analogy, the pupa is the last stage of development before the birth of an insect, just as the fetus is the last stage of development before the birth of a child.

46. DEALING : STOCK EXCHANGE :: (A. preserving, B. selling, C. buying, D. copying) : LANDMARK

(A) The correspondence is one of action to situation. Dealing is an activity related to the stock exchange. Preserving is a typical activity associated with a landmark.

47. UPRISING : (A. revolution, B. settlement, C. quarrel, D. disquiet) :: FIB : LIE

(A) In this analogy of degree, a fib is not quite telling a lie; an uprising may not quite be a revolution.

48. (A. Crete, B. Malta, C. Sicily, D. Corsica) : SARDINIA :: BOLIVIA : ARGENTINA

(D) The relationship is one of geographical location. Bolivia is a country directly north of Argentina. Corsica is an island located directly north of the island of Sardinia.

49. EVIL : EXORCISE : BREAD : (A. carbohydrate, B. break, C. sandwich, D. shred)

(B) The correspondence is one of object to action. One may exorcise evil; one may break bread.

50. COWARD : (A. loser, B. lily-livered, C. hero, D. villain) :: YOLK : ALBUMEN

(C) The yolk is the yellow part of an egg, and the albumen is part of the egg white. A coward is associated with the color yellow; a hero is associated with the color white.

51. (A. humid, B. speedy, C. piquant, D. moist) : VAPID :: OBDURATE : COMPASSIONATE

(C) *Obdurate*, meaning *hardened in feelings*, and *compassionate*, meaning *sympathetic to the distress of others*, are antonyms. *Piquant*, meaning *pungent* or *savory*, and *vapid*, meaning *insipid* or *flat*, are also antonyms.

52. CUCUMBER : WATERMELON :: CANTALOUPE : (A. squash, B. radish, C. cherry, D. plum)

(A) Cucumber, watermelon, cantaloupe, and squash are all related because they have many seeds and grow on vines.

53. (A. stick, B. percussion, C. cymbal, D. head) : DRUM :: STRINGS : VIOLIN

(D) In this part-to-whole analogy, a violin has strings and a drum has a head.

54. ILLNESS : (A. debility, B. hospital, C. doctor, D. panacea) :: VIBRATION : SOUND

(A) The correspondence is one of cause and effect. Vibration causes sound; illness causes debility.

55. VERDUN : DUNKIRK :: YPRES : (A. Belleau Woods, B. El Alamein, C. San Juan Hill, D. Marne)

(B) Verdun and Ypres were battles fought in World War I; Dunkirk and El Alamein were famous battles of World War II.

56. (A. gain, B. reward, C. loot, D. profit) : ROBBERY :: REVENGE : VENDETTA

(C) Revenge is the object of a vendetta; loot is the object of a robbery, Gain or profit might also be objects of robbery, but loot is a more specific and characteristic object.

57. ANALYSIS : FREUD :: (A. manipulation, B. illness, C. sex, D. stimulation) : OSTEOPATHY

(A) Freud attempted to relieve mental disorders through analysis; osteopath attempts to relieve physical disorders through manipulation of affected parts.

58. CLAUSTROPHOBIA : CLOSETS :: AGORAPHOBIA : (A. ships, B. sheep, C. plants, D. plains)

(D) A person suffering from claustrophobia (a fear of closed spaces) would fear closets; a person suffering from agoraphobia (fear of open spaces) would fear plains.

59. SEARCH : FIND :: FIGHT : (A. win, B. lose, C. seek, D. contend)

(A) A positive result of a search is to find what you are looking for; a positive result of a fight is to win.

60. (A. affection, B. encouragement, C. blasphemy, D. oblivion) : FRACAS :: APHRODITE : MARS

(A) In mythology, Mars, as the god of war, would encourage a fracas; as the goddess of love, Aphrodite would encourage affection.

61. H : S :: (A. M, B. L, C. I, D. P) : W

(B) In this sequence analogy, the difference between H, the eighth letter in the alphabet, and S, the nineteenth, is 11. The letter with the same relation to W, the 23rd letter, is L, the 12th letter in the alphabet.

62. HASTILY : DESPONDENTLY :: CIRCUMSPECTLY : (A. quick, B. circuit, C. rate, D. slowly)

(D) The correspondence here is grammatical. *Hastily, despondently,* and *circumspectly* are all related as adverbs. Among the choices given, only *slowly* is also an adverb.

63. BOXER : TABBY :: LABRADOR : (A. fighter, B. poodle, C. calico, D. nanny)

(C) Boxer and Labrador are both breeds of dog; tabby and calico are both descriptive terms applied to cat markings.

64. CROESUS : (A. boat, B. wealth, C. pleats, D. loyalty) :: ODYSSEUS : CRAFT

(B) In this characteristic analogy, Croesus was known for his great wealth; Odysseus was known for his great craft.

65. LUCERNE : MICHIGAN :: GENEVA : (A. United States, B. Victoria, C. Okeechobee, D. Switzerland)

(C) In this place analogy, Lake Lucerne and Lake Geneva are in Switzerland; Lake Michigan and Lake Okeechobee are in the United States.

66. (A. tally, B. game, C. concert, D. run) : SCORE :: PLAY : SCRIPT

(**C**) The script is the written text of a play; the score is the written version of the music to be played at a concert.

67. FLAUBERT : (A. madame, B. field, C. knife, D. writer) :: JOYCE : PORTRAIT

(**A**) James Joyce wrote a famous book with the word *portrait* in the title: *Portrait of the Artist as a Young Man*. Gustave Flaubert wrote a famous book with the word *madame* in the title: *Madame Bovary*.

68. DOG : INTRUDER :: (A. burglar, B. cat, C. knight, D. maiden) : DRAGON

(**C**) Call this one actor to object. The dog attacks the intruder; the knight attacks the dragon.

69. MENDACIOUS : DECEITFUL :: AUSPICIOUS : (A. indifferent, B. submerged, C. propitious, D. bereft)

(**C**) *Mendacious* and *deceitful* are synonyms, as are *auspicious* and *propitious*.

70. PARTRIDGE : RABBIT :: (A. quail, B. pen, C. birds, D. covey) : WARREN

(**D**) Rabbits congregate in a warren; partridges congregate in a covey.

71. LAPIDARY : (A. ruby, B. wood, C. lick, D. food) :: SCULPTOR : ALABASTER

(**A**) The relationship is one of worker to his material. A lapidary (an engraver of precious stones) may work with a ruby; a sculptor may work with alabaster.

72. BEES : FILE :: BIRDS : (A. grade, B. rank, C. fold, D. twist)

(**B**) The correspondence is one of association of words. We speak of birds and bees and also of rank and file.

73. MANY : MUCH :: FEW : (A. minus, B. more, C. small, D. little)

(**D**) The analogy is based upon the grammatical distinction between number and amount. Make up a parallel sentence to choose the best answer. "Many (in number) raindrops make much (in amount) water; few (in number) raindrops make little (in amount) water."

74. FORSOOK : DRANK :: FROZEN : (A. swum, B. wrote, C. sang, D. chose)

(**A**) In this grammatical analogy, *forsook* and *drank* are simple past tenses; *frozen* and *swum* are past participles.

75. SANDAL : BOOT :: (A. hammer, B. hatchet, C. shoemaker, D. blade) : AX

(**B**) This relationship is one of degree. A sandal is a lighter version of footwear than a boot; a hatchet is a smaller version of a sharp-edged instrument than an ax.

76. HORSE : (A. man, B. goat, C. archer, D. bull) :: CENTAUR : SATYR

(**B**) In this mythological analogy, a centaur is half horse, half man; a satyr is half goat, half man.

77. (A. anode, B. bird, C. purchase, D. battery) : CELL :: ARROW : SHAFT

(**D**) The correspondence is one of whole to part. A cell is part of a battery; a shaft is part of an arrow.

78. FELONY : MISDEMEANOR :: SIN : (A. piccalilli, B. picayune, C. peccadillo, D. picador)

(C) In this degree analogy, a felony is a more serious offense than a misdemeanor; similarly, a sin is a more serious offense than a peccadillo (a slight offense).

79. NOVEMBER : APRIL :: (A. May, B. June, C. July, D. August) : SEPTEMBER

(B) In the words of the well-known mnemonic rhyme, "Thirty days hath September, April, June, and November."

80. ALBANIA : POLAND :: CHINA : (A. Czechoslovakia, B. Russia, C. Sumatra, D. India)

(A) This analogy has to do with political alignments in the Communist world right up to the dissolution of the USSR. Albania and China had Communist governments that were entirely outside the sphere of influence of the Soviet Union. Poland and Czechoslovakia were very much under Soviet domination until their rebellions spurred the breakup of the union.

81. WASTEFUL : (A. parsimonious, B. neglectful, C. vast, D. prodigal) :: DISINTERESTED : IMPARTIAL

(D) *Disinterested* is a synonym for *impartial;* a synonym for *wasteful* is *prodigal.*

82. SCHOONER : ZIGGURAT :: CRUISER : (A. cutter, B. campanile, C. viking, D. tug)

(B) A schooner and a cruiser are both types of ships. A ziggurat and a campanile are both types of towers.

83. (A. pine, B. cedar, C. ash, D. willow) : OAK :: MOURNFUL : STURDY

(D) In this analogy of characteristics, we speak of the mighty (sturdy) oak and the weeping (mournful) willow.

84. ADVISE : EXHORT :: (A. force, B. tempt, C. prohibit, D. prevent) : ENTICE

(B) The relationship is one of degree. *Exhort* means to *urge on,* which is a stronger degree of *advise; entice* is a stronger degree of *tempt.*

85. STEEL : WELD :: LIPS : (A. frown, B. purse, C. fold, D. smirk)

(B) In this action-to-object analogy, you weld two pieces of steel to join or hold them together; you purse your lips by holding or pressing them together.

86. TESTIMONY : (A. confession, B. judge, C. witness, D. trial) :: BIOGRAPHY : AUTOBIOGRAPHY

(A) Testimony is a statement about someone else; a confession is a statement about oneself. A biography is the written history of another person's life; an autobiography is the written history of one's own life.

87. STRATUM : SYLLABUS :: (A. strati, B. stratums, C. stratus, D. strata) : SYLLABI

(D) The relationship in this analogy is grammatical. The plural of *syllabus* is *syllabi;* the plural of *stratum* is *strata.*

88. LAMB : DEER :: (A. rabbit, B. peacock, C. horse, D. pig) : LION

(B) A lamb and a deer are related because they are both considered mild-mannered; a peacock and a lion are related because they are both considered proud.

89. VELOCITY : (A. wind, B. earth, C. vibration, D. destruction) :: BEAUFORT : RICHTER

(**C**) The Beaufort Scale (invented by Sir Francis Beaufort) indicates velocity of the wind in numbers from 0 to 17. The Richter Scale (named after Charles Richter) indicates the magnitude of a seismic vibration or earthquake.

90. (A. distance, B. program, C. station, D. tube) : TELEVISION :: LEADER : ANARCHY

(**A**) The Greek root *tele* in *television* means *distance;* the Greek root *arch* in *anarchy* means *leader*.

91. TAPS : VESPERS :: (A. painting, B. needle, C. revelry, D. reveille) : MATINS

(**D**) Taps is an evening military signal, and vespers are evening prayers; reveille is a morning military signal, and matins are morning prayers.

92. PROSTRATE : (A. dazzling, B. stealing, C. submission, D. dehydrated) :: SUPINE : SLEEPING

(**C**) In this situation-to-action analogy, a person who is prostrate is in a position for submission; a person who is supine is in a position for sleeping.

93. MAHATMA GANDHI : WAR :: CARRY NATION : (A. suffrage, B. alcohol, C. temperance, D. employment)

(**B**) Mahatma Gandhi was opposed to all forms of violence, including war, as Carry Nation was opposed to the use of any kind of alcohol.

94. $\frac{2}{7}$: (A. $\frac{1}{16}$, B. $\frac{3}{28}$, C. $\frac{3}{21}$, D. $\frac{1}{14}$) :: $\frac{4}{7}$: $\frac{1}{7}$

(**D**) In this mathematical analogy, $\frac{1}{4}$ of $\frac{4}{7}$ is $\frac{1}{7}$; $\frac{1}{4}$ of $\frac{2}{7}$ is $\frac{1}{14}$.

95. (A. roc, B. canary, C. albatross, D. condor) : VULTURE :: PHOENIX : EAGLE

(**A**) The relationship is one of real to imaginary. A phoenix is an imaginary bird, and an eagle is an actual bird. Similarly, a roc is imaginary and a vulture is real.

96. TINE : FORK :: (A. car, B. gearshift, C. flange, D. wheelwright) : WHEEL

(**C**) A tine is part of a fork; a flange is part of a wheel.

97. (A. tie, B. appearance, C. shoes, D. decoration) : ATTIRE :: WIT : COMMUNICATION

(**D**) One's attire is brightened with some decoration; one's communication is brightened with wit.

98. HUSK : (A. fish, B. chops, C. gristle, D. filet) :: GRAIN : MEAT

(**C**) In this analogy, the relationship is one of discardable to usable. The husk is the discardable part of grain; gristle is the discardable part of meat.

99. SURPRISED : (A. interested, B. astounded, C. expected, D. unknown) :: WORK : TOIL

(**B**) The correspondence is one of degree. *Work* is a milder form of *toil; surprised* is a milder form of *astounded*.

100. INEBRIOUS : (A. intoxicated, B. dull, C. sincere, D. abstemious) :: SPARTAN : GARRULOUS

(**D**) *Spartan,* meaning *terse in speech,* is the opposite of *garrulous. Inebrious,* which means *drunken,* is the opposite of *abstemious,* or *temperate*.

SAMPLE TEST 5

Answer Sheet

1 ⓐ ⓑ ⓒ ⓓ	26 ⓐ ⓑ ⓒ ⓓ	51 ⓐ ⓑ ⓒ ⓓ	76 ⓐ ⓑ ⓒ ⓓ
2 ⓐ ⓑ ⓒ ⓓ	27 ⓐ ⓑ ⓒ ⓓ	52 ⓐ ⓑ ⓒ ⓓ	77 ⓐ ⓑ ⓒ ⓓ
3 ⓐ ⓑ ⓒ ⓓ	28 ⓐ ⓑ ⓒ ⓓ	53 ⓐ ⓑ ⓒ ⓓ	78 ⓐ ⓑ ⓒ ⓓ
4 ⓐ ⓑ ⓒ ⓓ	29 ⓐ ⓑ ⓒ ⓓ	54 ⓐ ⓑ ⓒ ⓓ	79 ⓐ ⓑ ⓒ ⓓ
5 ⓐ ⓑ ⓒ ⓓ	30 ⓐ ⓑ ⓒ ⓓ	55 ⓐ ⓑ ⓒ ⓓ	80 ⓐ ⓑ ⓒ ⓓ
6 ⓐ ⓑ ⓒ ⓓ	31 ⓐ ⓑ ⓒ ⓓ	56 ⓐ ⓑ ⓒ ⓓ	81 ⓐ ⓑ ⓒ ⓓ
7 ⓐ ⓑ ⓒ ⓓ	32 ⓐ ⓑ ⓒ ⓓ	57 ⓐ ⓑ ⓒ ⓓ	82 ⓐ ⓑ ⓒ ⓓ
8 ⓐ ⓑ ⓒ ⓓ	33 ⓐ ⓑ ⓒ ⓓ	58 ⓐ ⓑ ⓒ ⓓ	83 ⓐ ⓑ ⓒ ⓓ
9 ⓐ ⓑ ⓒ ⓓ	34 ⓐ ⓑ ⓒ ⓓ	59 ⓐ ⓑ ⓒ ⓓ	84 ⓐ ⓑ ⓒ ⓓ
10 ⓐ ⓑ ⓒ ⓓ	35 ⓐ ⓑ ⓒ ⓓ	60 ⓐ ⓑ ⓒ ⓓ	85 ⓐ ⓑ ⓒ ⓓ
11 ⓐ ⓑ ⓒ ⓓ	36 ⓐ ⓑ ⓒ ⓓ	61 ⓐ ⓑ ⓒ ⓓ	86 ⓐ ⓑ ⓒ ⓓ
12 ⓐ ⓑ ⓒ ⓓ	37 ⓐ ⓑ ⓒ ⓓ	62 ⓐ ⓑ ⓒ ⓓ	87 ⓐ ⓑ ⓒ ⓓ
13 ⓐ ⓑ ⓒ ⓓ	38 ⓐ ⓑ ⓒ ⓓ	63 ⓐ ⓑ ⓒ ⓓ	88 ⓐ ⓑ ⓒ ⓓ
14 ⓐ ⓑ ⓒ ⓓ	39 ⓐ ⓑ ⓒ ⓓ	64 ⓐ ⓑ ⓒ ⓓ	89 ⓐ ⓑ ⓒ ⓓ
15 ⓐ ⓑ ⓒ ⓓ	40 ⓐ ⓑ ⓒ ⓓ	65 ⓐ ⓑ ⓒ ⓓ	90 ⓐ ⓑ ⓒ ⓓ
16 ⓐ ⓑ ⓒ ⓓ	41 ⓐ ⓑ ⓒ ⓓ	66 ⓐ ⓑ ⓒ ⓓ	91 ⓐ ⓑ ⓒ ⓓ
17 ⓐ ⓑ ⓒ ⓓ	42 ⓐ ⓑ ⓒ ⓓ	67 ⓐ ⓑ ⓒ ⓓ	92 ⓐ ⓑ ⓒ ⓓ
18 ⓐ ⓑ ⓒ ⓓ	43 ⓐ ⓑ ⓒ ⓓ	68 ⓐ ⓑ ⓒ ⓓ	93 ⓐ ⓑ ⓒ ⓓ
19 ⓐ ⓑ ⓒ ⓓ	44 ⓐ ⓑ ⓒ ⓓ	69 ⓐ ⓑ ⓒ ⓓ	94 ⓐ ⓑ ⓒ ⓓ
20 ⓐ ⓑ ⓒ ⓓ	45 ⓐ ⓑ ⓒ ⓓ	70 ⓐ ⓑ ⓒ ⓓ	95 ⓐ ⓑ ⓒ ⓓ
21 ⓐ ⓑ ⓒ ⓓ	46 ⓐ ⓑ ⓒ ⓓ	71 ⓐ ⓑ ⓒ ⓓ	96 ⓐ ⓑ ⓒ ⓓ
22 ⓐ ⓑ ⓒ ⓓ	47 ⓐ ⓑ ⓒ ⓓ	72 ⓐ ⓑ ⓒ ⓓ	97 ⓐ ⓑ ⓒ ⓓ
23 ⓐ ⓑ ⓒ ⓓ	48 ⓐ ⓑ ⓒ ⓓ	73 ⓐ ⓑ ⓒ ⓓ	98 ⓐ ⓑ ⓒ ⓓ
24 ⓐ ⓑ ⓒ ⓓ	49 ⓐ ⓑ ⓒ ⓓ	74 ⓐ ⓑ ⓒ ⓓ	99 ⓐ ⓑ ⓒ ⓓ
25 ⓐ ⓑ ⓒ ⓓ	50 ⓐ ⓑ ⓒ ⓓ	75 ⓐ ⓑ ⓒ ⓓ	100 ⓐ ⓑ ⓒ ⓓ

TEAR HERE

Chapter 9

Sample Test 5

100 Questions • 50 Minutes

> **Directions:** Each of these test questions consists of three capitalized words and four lettered words enclosed in parentheses. Two of the capitalized words are related in some way. Find the two related words, and establish the nature of the relationship. Then study the four words lettered A, B, C, and D. Select the one lettered word that is related to the remaining capitalized word in the same way that the first two capitalized words are related. Mark the answer sheet for the letter preceding the word you select.

ROAD MAP

- *Answer Key*
- *Explanatory Answers*

1. FEAST : MEAL :: VELLUM : (A. paper, B. fur, C. cotton, D. forest)

2. (A. leave, B. audition, C. divide, D. correct) : APPLY :: PART : POSITION

3. OXEN : STRENGTH :: (A. furnace, B. animal, C. cattle, D. ants) : INDUSTRY

4. ASSIDUOUS : EGREGIOUS :: (A. leafy, B. desultory, C. diligent, D. bitter) : FLAGRANT

5. SHIP : (A. crow's nest, B. deck, C. prow, D. mast) :: COLUMN : CAPITAL

6. DAVID COPPERFIELD : TINY TIM :: (A. Joseph Andrews, B. Ahab, C. Becky Sharp, D. Little Nell) : OLIVER TWIST

7. CLEOPATRA : (A. Caesar, B. snake, C. Anthony, D. beauty) :: GOLIATH : STONE

8. (A. circle, B. heart, C. dissemination, D. artery) : CIRCULATE :: DITCH : IRRIGATE

9. BRIGHT : GAUDY :: (A. urged, B. implied, C. prevented, D. acquiesced) : COMPELLED

10. (A. dissidence, B. deficiency, C. irreverence, D. deference) : DISRESPECT :: IMBUE : EXTRACT

11. EGO : ID :: SELF : (A. desire, B. society, C. conscience, D. morality)

12. HIGH GEAR : (A. automobile, B. driver, C. speed, D. brake.) :: PROGRESS : RECESSION

13. (A. gem, B. spore, C. illegitimacy, D. superficiality) : SPURIOUS :: MONEY : COUNTERFEIT

14. AMIN : (A. Elizabeth II, B. Waldheim, C. Qaddafi, D. Adenauer) :: KING : BUNCHE

15. 225 : AREA :: (A. 2,744, B. 3,375, C. 38,416, D. 50,625) : VOLUME

16. QUEUE : (A. borough, B. tail, C. line, D. broom) :: CUE : BROUGHAM

17. COLONEL : REGIMENT :: (A. major, B. captain, C. private, D. general) : BATTALION

18. DILETTANTE : (A. thorough, B. painstaking, C. diplomatic, D. superficial) :: BOISTEROUS : LOUD

19. HANDLEBARS : SPOKE :: KEYBOARD : (A. sound, B. chip, C. music, D. retort)

20. (A. rectify, B. make, C. find, D. realize) : MISTAKE :: REGAIN : LOSS

21. INDEX : FRONTISPIECE :: MATURITY : (A. adolescence, B. infancy, C. puberty, D. adulthood)

22. TAUTOLOGICAL : REDUNDANT :: (A. mature, B. incipient, C. obnoxious, D. late) : INCHOATE

23. SQUARE : (A. triangle, B. triplet, C. poem, D. duet) :: QUADRUPLET : COUPLET

24. MAY : (A. horn, B. charity, C. tempest, D. despair) :: FEAR : COD

25. (A. m, B. p, C. l, D. t) : H :: W : S

26. CHOLERIC : AMIABLE :: (A. timid, B. blind, C. mute, D. temerarious) : CIRCUMSPECT

27. IRON : (A. hard, B. strong, C. steel, D. pig) :: OIL : CRUDE

28. (A. astronomy, B. play, C. symphony, D. clouds) : STAR :: CONCERT : SOLOIST

29. SALUTE : (A. motto, B. reveille, C. mess, D. orders) :: TROOP : EAGLE

30. PROVISIONS : QUARTERMASTER :: (A. cup, B. knife, C. saddle, D. manuscript) : SCRIVENER

31. ATLANTIS : (A. Pompeii, B. Xanadu, C. Byzantium, D. Zanzibar) :: SHANGRI-LA : EL DORADO

32. WIND : DEFICIT :: EROSION : (A. spending, B. appreciation, C. borrowing, D. employment)

33. (A. slot, B. note, C. band, D. harmony) : VALVE :: HARMONICA : TRUMPET

34. FLAUNT : (A. destructively, B. stupidly, C. willingly, D. boastfully) :: BETRAY : DECEPTIVELY

35. HOUYHNHNM : YAHOO :: REASON : (A. learning, B. intelligence, C. ignorance, D. genius)

36. DEFIED : ASTRIDE :: EARTH : (A. geography, B. zoology, C. birth, D. life)

37. ST. PETERSBURG : LENINGRAD :: (A. Stalingrad, B. Leningrad, C. Moscow, D. Odessa) : ST. PETERSBURG

38. (A. 1999, B. 1900, C. 1901, D. 1902) : 1910 :: 1950 : 1959

39. ADVOCATE : (A. impute, B. allude, C. imply, D. impugn) :: AMELIORATE : IMPAIR

40. HENRY MOORE : (A. Rodin, B. Pavlov, C. Van Gogh, D. Gertrude Stein) :: DONATELLO : BERNINI

41. HO CHI MINH : GANDHI :: FRANCE : (A. Indochina, B. Great Britain, C. Vietnam, D. India)

42. HEDGER : SHRUBBERY :: (A. snuffer, B. gardener, C. whittler, D. stickler) : STICK

43. MAN : (A. bird, B. centipede, C. elephant, D. Adam) :: WHEELBARROW : BICYCLE

44. (A. velocity, B. viscosity, C. temperature, D. density) : FLUID :: FRICTION : SOLID

45. CANTON : COUNTY :: (A. Ohio, B. Japan, C. Switzerland, D. China) : IRELAND

46. PECK : PINT :: 1 : (A. 4, B. 16, C. 8, D. 2)

47. TWEEZERS : BLEACH :: (A. steel, B. light, C. adding machine, D. eraser) : PICKPOCKET

48. HARANGUING : (A. persuade, B. filet, C. cleaning, D. arbitrate) :: FILIBUSTERING : OBSTRUCT

49. SHERRY : BEER :: PORT : (A. champagne, B. sauterne, C. claret, D. muscatel)

50. HONOR : GOVERNOR :: (A. Excellency, B. Majesty, C. Highness, D. Grace) : DUKE

51. ANDIRON : PEDESTAL :: (A. log, B. bucket, C. anvil, D. skillet) : STATUE

52. GENERAL : STARS :: COLONEL : (A. oak, B. silver, C. gold, D. eagle)

53. (A. insist, B. reply, C. demur, D. demand) : REFUSE :: LAZY : INERT

54. HEART : HEAD :: VENERY : (A. ribaldry, B. flesh, C. mortality, D. restraint)

55. CALORIE : (A. energy, B. weight, C. metabolism, D. food) :: CENTURY : TIME

56. FLORIDA : SAUDI ARABIA :: (A. Louisiana, B. Georgia, C. Arkansas, D. Iraq) : IRAN

57. *KING LEAR* : *DIE FLEDERMAUS* :: *MACBETH* : (A. *Tosca*, B. *Othello*, C. *Ruddigore*, D. *Les Misèrables*)

58. BOARDWALK : (A. Park Place, B. Atlantic City, C. display, D. escalator) :: STRAND : STORE

59. (A. Parliament, B. Congress, C. Great Britain, D. Senate) : LORDS :: HOUSE : COMMONS

60. 1789 : (A. Germany, B. France, C. England, D. Russia) :: 1776 : UNITED STATES

61. MALLARD : CANVASBACK :: (A. snow, B. north, C. drake, D. gander) : CANADA

62. WELL-FED : (A. penurious, B. healthy, C. wealthy, D. miserly) :: HUNGRY : IMPECUNIOUS

GO ON TO THE NEXT PAGE

63. LAERTES : (A. Odysseus, B. Polonius, C. Claudius, D. Ophelia) :: ICARUS : DAEDALUS

64. SYRACUSE : (A. Oneonta, B. Geneva, C. Raleigh, D. Sparta) :: CARTHAGE : ALEXANDRIA

65. DISPIRITED : DEPRESSED :: (A. obligato, B. innuendo, C. declaration, D. crescendo) : INSINUATION

66. ORGANISM : (A. plant, B. animal, C. bacteria, D. cell) :: LIGHT : WAVE

67. KOLN : WIEN :: COLOGNE : (A. Vienna, B. Prague, C. Warsaw, D. Hamburg)

68. DCX : MDCCCXXX :: (A. CLX, B. XLI, C. LCD, D. LXVII) : CXXIII

69. WISDOM : (A. lion, B. owl, C. fox, D. deer) :: SPRING : ROBIN

70. BUTTERFLY : (A. insect, B. silkworm, C. wings, D. summer) :: CHRYSALIS : COCOON

71. ICELAND : NORWAY :: (A. winter, B. queen, C. president, D. sovereign) : KING

72. ROME : (A. NATO, B. SEATO, C. SALT II, D. EEC) :: VERSAILLES : LEAGUE OF NATIONS

73. CYLINDER : LOCK :: MOTOR : (A. shaft, B. canal, C. tackle, D. escape)

74. BANANA : (A. sapphire, B. saltcellar, C. stone, D. tree) :: BUTTER : SKY

75. GNASH : TEETH :: (A. fold, B. clasp, C. gnarl, D. wring) : HANDS

76. (A. opossum, B. fox, C. beaver, D. lady) : KANGAROO :: CHICKEN : COCKROACH

77. APHRODITE : VENUS :: ARES : (A. Mercury, B. Mars, C. Apollo, D. Hermes)

78. METAPHYSICS : (A. humanities, B. medicine, C. logic, D. art) :: EPISTEMOLOGY : ETHICS

79. CLARINET : PIANO :: WIND : (A. reed, B. wood, C, percussion, D. pianist)

80. ELEVATOR : SKYSCRAPER :: (A. gangplank, B. companionway, C. bulkhead, D. bridge) : SHIP

81. PROPENSITY : (A. riches, B. weight, C. bias, D. thought) :: CLUB : MACE

82. SALZBURG : STRATFORD :: (A. Goethe, B. Avon, C. Mozart, D. Brahms) : SHAKESPEARE

83. FLAMMABLE : INFLAMMABLE :: PERTINENT : (A. impertinent, B. inopportune, C. incoherent, D. relevant)

84. (A. revolution, B. dance, C. torque, D. axis) : ROTATE :: FRICTION : RESIST

85. PRISM : (A. spectrum, B. reflection, C. light, D. binoculars) :: FAMINE : WANT

86. LOOP : HUB :: BEEF : (A. corn, B. beans, C. tobacco, D. cotton)

87. JANUARY : (A. Cleveland, B. June, C. Washington, D. Hermes) :: SUNDAY : MERCURY

88. LIFT : ELEVATOR :: (A. oil, B. grease, C. gas, D. petrol) : GASOLINE

89. (A. $\frac{1}{6}$, B. $\frac{4}{5}$, C. $\frac{2}{5}$, D. $\frac{2}{10}$) : $\frac{1}{10}$ :: $\frac{3}{4}$: $\frac{3}{16}$

90. TORT : LITIGATION :: CONTRACT : (A. signature, B. obligation, C. clause, D. equity)

91. BULL : (A. wolf, B. turtle, C. fish, D. snail) :: CRAB : LION

92. EQUINOX : SOLSTICE :: SEPTEMBER : (A. November, B. January, C. June, D. March)

93. (A. hand, B. brow, C. rose, D. soon) : KNIT :: DICTATION : TAKE

94. GARROTING : DEATH :: CANVASSING : (A. painting, B. shelter, C. votes, D. fight)

95. PUSILLANIMOUS : INVIDIOUS :: (A. paronomasia, B. slather, C. melodramatically, D. perfunctory) : SANCTIMONIOUS

96. SUN : JAPAN :: (A. scythe, B. crescent, C. Caspian, D. hammer) : TURKEY

97. CICERO : DEMOSTHENES :: ROOSEVELT : (A. MacArthur, B. Hemingway, C. Shaw, D. Churchill)

98. TYRO : (A. tyrant, B. master, C. amateur, D. dabbler) :: TURPITUDE : PROBITY

99. COKE : COAL :: (A. oil, B. planks, C. saw, D. lumberjack) : TIMBER

100. SHOE : (A. fly, B. cobbler, C. pair, D. bell) :: SAW : GEAR

ANSWER KEY

1. A	21. B	41. B	61. A	81. C
2. B	22. B	42. C	62. C	82. C
3. D	23. D	43. C	63. B	83. D
4. C	24. A	44. B	64. D	84. C
5. A	25. C	45. C	65. B	85. A
6. D	26. D	46. B	66. D	86. B
7. B	27. D	47. D	67. A	87. C
8. D	28. B	48. A	68. B	88. D
9. A	29. A	49. A	69. B	89. C
10. D	30. D	50. D	70. B	90. B
11. A	31. B	51. A	71. C	91. C
12. D	32. C	52. D	72. D	92. C
13. A	33. A	53. C	73. B	93. B
14. C	34. D	54. D	74. A	94. C
15. B	35. C	55. A	75. D	95. D
16. D	36. C	56. A	76. A	96. B
17. A	37. B	57. C	77. B	97. D
18. D	38. C	58. D	78. C	98. B
19. B	39. D	59. D	79. C	99. B
20. A	40. A	60. B	80. B	100. D

EXPLANATORY ANSWERS

1. FEAST : MEAL :: VELLUM : (A. paper, B. fur, C. cotton, D. forest)

(**A**) In this analogy of degree, a feast is a rich and expensive meal; vellum is a rich and expensive kind of paper.

2. (A. leave, B. audition, C. divide, D, correct) : APPLY :: PART : POSITION

(**B**) The correspondence is one of action to object. You apply for a position of employment; you audition for a part in a play.

3. OXEN : STRENGTH :: (A. furnace, B. animal, C. cattle, D. ants) : INDUSTRY

(**D**) In this association analogy, oxen are associated with strength; ants are associated with industry.

4. ASSIDUOUS : EGREGIOUS :: (A. leafy, B. desultory, C. diligent, D. bitter) : FLAGRANT

(**C**) In this synonym analogy, another word for *egregious* is *flagrant*. A synonym for *assiduous* is *diligent*.

5. SHIP : (A. crow's nest, B. deck, C. prow, D. mast) :: COLUMN : CAPITAL

(**A**) A crow's nest is a small observation platform near the top of the mast of a ship; a capital is the uppermost part of a column.

6. DAVID COPPERFIELD : TINY TIM :: (A. Joseph Andrews, B. Ahab, C. Becky Sharp, D. Little Nell) : OLIVER TWIST

(**D**) The relationship among David Copperfield, Tiny Tim, and Oliver Twist is that they are all fictional characters created by Charles Dickens. To complete the analogy, another Dickens character must be selected, and Little Nell is the correct choice.

7 CLEOPATRA : (A. Caesar, B. snake, C. Anthony, D. beauty) :: GOLIATH : STONE

(**B**) Goliath was killed by a stone; Cleopatra was killed by an asp by which she was bitten.

8. (A. circle, B. heart, C. dissemination, D. artery) : CIRCULATE :: DITCH : IRRIGATE

(**D**) In this object-to-action analogy, a ditch is the channel through which water flows to irrigate; an artery is the vessel or channel through which blood may circulate.

9. BRIGHT : GAUDY :: (A. urged, B. implied, C. prevented, D. acquiesced) : COMPELLED

(**A**) The relationship is one of degree because something that is gaudy is excessively bright; *compelled* is excessively *urged*.

10. (A. dissidence, B. deficiency, C. irreverence, D. deference) : DISRESPECT :: IMBUE : EXTRACT

(**D**) *Imbue,* meaning *to permeate,* is the opposite of *extract,* meaning *to draw out.* The opposite of *disrespect* is *deference.*

11. EGO : ID :: SELF : (A. desire, B. society, C. conscience, D. morality)

(**A**) *Ego* is a psychological term for *self; id* is a psychological term for *desire.* The psychological term for *conscience* is *superego.*

12. HIGH GEAR : (A. automobile, B. driver, C. speed, D. brake) :: PROGRESS : RECESSION

(D) A high gear and a brake have opposite functions; similarly, *progress* and *recession* are opposite in meaning.

13. (A. gem, B. spore, C. illegitimacy, D. superficiality) : SPURIOUS :: MONEY : COUNTERFEIT

(A) A gem is worthless when it is spurious—that is, false; money is worthless when it is counterfeit.

14. AMIN : (A. Elizabeth II, B. Waldheim, C. Qaddafi, D. Adenauer) :: KING : BUNCHE

(C) Martin Luther King and Ralph Bunche were both very reliable men working for peace. Idi Amin and Muammar el-Qaddafi are known for tyranny, ruthlessness, and erratic behavior. While Kurt Waldheim's behavior has also been questioned, his reputation does not fall into the same league as those of Amin and Qaddafi.

15. 225 : AREA :: (A. 2,744, B. 3,375, C. 38,416, D. 50,625) : VOLUME

(B) The area of a figure is 225 square units. With no additional given information, one must assume that the figure is a square. One side of the figure is 15 units long because the square root of 225 is 15. The analogy asks for the volume of the cube based upon the figure related to its area. $15 \times 15 \times 15 = 3{,}375$ cubic units.

16. QUEUE : (A. borough, B. tail, C. line, D. broom) :: CUE : BROUGHAM

(D) *Queue* and *cue* are homophones, different in meaning but pronounced the same; *broom* and *brougham* are also pronounced the same.

17. COLONEL : REGIMENT :: (A. major, B. captain, C. private, D. general) : BATTALION

(A) A colonel leads a regiment; a major leads a battalion.

18. DILETTANTE : (A. thorough, B. painstaking, C. diplomatic, D. superficial) :: BOISTEROUS : LOUD

(D) A boisterous person tends to be loud; a dilettante, a dabbler, tends to be superficial.

19. HANDLEBARS : SPOKE :: KEYBOARD : (A. sound, B. chip, C. music, D. retort)

(B) This is a part-to-part analogy. Handlebars and a spoke are both parts of a bicycle; a keyboard and a chip are parts of a computer.

20. (A. rectify, B. make, C. find, D. realize) : MISTAKE :: REGAIN : LOSS

(A) The relationship is one of action to object. To improve a poor or unfortunate condition, one may rectify a mistake, and one may regain a loss.

21. INDEX : FRONTISPIECE :: MATURITY : (A. adolescence, B. infancy, C. puberty, D. adulthood)

(B) In this sequence analogy, the index comes at the end of a book, and the frontispiece comes at the beginning; maturity comes in the latter part of life, and infancy comes in the beginning.

22. TAUTOLOGICAL : REDUNDANT :: (A. mature, B. incipient, C. obnoxious, D. late) : INCHOATE

(B) *Tautological* is a synonym for *redundant; inchoate,* which means *at an early state of development,* is a synonym for *incipient.*

23. SQUARE : (A. triangle, B. triplet, C. poem, D. duet) :: QUADRUPLET : COUPLET

(D) *Quadruplet* refers to a group of four; a couplet consists of two successive rhyming lines of verse. Because a square has four sides, a term involving a pair must be chosen to complete the analogy. A duet, a composition for two performers, is the only possible choice.

24. MAY : (A. horn, B. charity, C. tempest, D. despair) :: FEAR : COD

(A) In this place analogy, May, Fear, and Cod are all names of capes. To complete the analogy, another cape must be selected, and Cape Horn is the correct choice.

25. (A. m, B. p, C. l, D. t) : H :: W : S

(C) In the alphabet, W is the fourth letter after S; L is the fourth letter after H.

26. CHOLERIC : AMIABLE :: (A. timid, B. blind, C. mute, D. temerarious) : CIRCUMSPECT

(D) *Choleric,* which means *bad-tempered,* and *amiable,* meaning *agreeable,* are opposites; *temerarious,* which means *rash* and *reckless,* and *circumspect,* meaning *careful,* are opposites.

27. IRON : (A. hard, B. strong, C. steel, D. pig) :: OIL : CRUDE

(D) In this product-to-source analogy, oil in its rough state is called crude oil; iron in its rough state is called pig iron.

28. (A. astronomy, B. play, C. symphony, D. clouds) : STAR :: CONCERT : SOLOIST

(B) A star takes the leading role in a play; a soloist takes the leading role in a concert.

29. SALUTE : (A. motto, B. reveille, C. mess, D. orders) :: TROOP : EAGLE

(A) Salute, troop, and eagle are all things associated with the Boy Scouts. To complete the analogy, another element of scouting should be selected, and motto is the correct choice. Reveille and mess are associated with Boy Scout camping, but it is not necessary to extend to camping to complete this analogy.

30. PROVISIONS : QUARTERMASTER :: (A. cup, B. knife, C. saddle, D. manuscript) : SCRIVENER

(D) In this worker-to-job analogy, a quartermaster's job is to secure provisions for an army; a scrivener's job is to copy a manuscript.

31. ATLANTIS : (A. Pompeii, B. Xanadu, C. Byzantium, D. Zanzibar) :: SHANGRI-LA : EL DORADO

(B) Atlantis, Shangri-La, and El Dorado are related because each is an undocumented place. Xanadu, the only undocumented place among the answer choices, correctly completes this analogy.

32. WIND : DEFICIT :: EROSION : (A. spending, B. appreciation, C. borrowing, D. employment)

(C) In this cause-and-effect analogy, one effect of excessive wind is soil erosion; an effect of an excessive deficit is borrowing to make up for expenditures. Excessive spending is a cause of a deficit, not an effect.

33. (A. slot, B. note, C. band, D. harmony) : VALVE :: HARMONICA : TRUMPET

(A) The correspondence is one of part to whole. A valve is part of a trumpet; a slot is part of a harmonica.

34. FLAUNT : (A. destructively, B. stupidly, C. willingly, D. boastfully) :: BETRAY : DECEPTIVELY

(**D**) To flaunt is to act boastfully; to betray is to act deceptively.

35. HOUYHNHNM : YAHOO :: REASON : (A. learning, B. intelligence, C. ignorance, D. genius)

(**C**) In *Gulliver's Travels,* by Jonathan Swift, a houyhnhnm symbolizes intelligence and reason, whereas a yahoo symbolizes the opposite, stupidity or ignorance.

36. DEFIED : ASTRIDE :: EARTH : (A. geography, B. zoology, C. birth, D. life)

(**C**) In this nonsemantic rhyming analogy, *defied* rhymes with *astride; earth* rhymes with *birth.*

37. ST. PETERSBURG : LENINGRAD :: (A. Stalingrad, B. Leningrad, C. Moscow, D. Odessa) : ST. PETERSBURG

(**B**) The analogy is based on identity. The soviet name for the city was Leningrad. Before the Revolution and after the dissolution of the Soviet Union, the name for the city was and now is St. Petersburg.

38. (A. 1999, B. 1900, C. 1901, D. 1902) : 1910 :: 1950 : 1959

(**C**) In this sequence analogy, the difference between 1901 and 1910 is nine years; the difference between 1950 and 1959 is nine years. The mathematics of this problem is simple, but the use of dates is deceptive. When dates appear to be meaningless, you must look for a relationship along another dimension, just as when words appear unrelated you must seek a grammatical or nonsemantic relationship.

39. ADVOCATE : (A. impute, B. allude, C. imply, D. impugn) :: AMELIORATE : IMPAIR

(**D**) *Ameliorate,* meaning *to improve* or *to make better,* is the opposite of *impair,* meaning *to make worse.* The opposite of *advocate,* meaning *to support* or *to plead in favor of,* is *impugn,* meaning *to deny* or *to attack as false.*

40. HENRY MOORE : (A. Rodin, B. Pavlov, C. Van Gogh, D. Gertrude Stein) :: DONATELLO : BERNINI

(**A**) The connection among Henry Moore, Donatello, and Bernini is that they are all sculptors. To complete the analogy, another sculptor must be chosen, and Rodin is the correct choice.

41. HO CHI MINH : GANDHI :: FRANCE : (A. Indochina, B. Great Britain, C. Vietnam, D. India)

(**B**) Ho Chi Minh and Gandhi were both leaders of independence movements in countries colonized by European nations. Ho Chi Minh, a leftist revolutionary, fought to expel France from Indochina. Gandhi, an advocate of nonviolence and passive resistance, led the movement to expel Great Britain from India.

42. HEDGER : SHRUBBERY :: (A. snuffer, B. gardener, C. whittler, D. stickler) : STICK

(**C**) A hedger trims shrubbery; a whittler trims a stick.

43. MAN : (A. bird, B. centipede, C. elephant, D. Adam) :: WHEELBARROW : BICYCLE

(**C**) The relationship is a numerical ratio of one to two. A wheelbarrow has one wheel; a bicycle has two. Similarly, a man has two legs, and an elephant has four. Approach this analogy by looking first at the two adjacent capitalized words. You will instantly recognize that a wheelbarrow has one wheel and a bicycle has two. Man uses both a wheelbarrow and a bicycle, and none of the choices logically uses either, so you should begin to suspect a numerical analogy. A centipede with its 100 legs is a distracter that also serves as a clue. Because the wheel ratio is one to two, you must be careful not to choose the bird, which has the same number of legs as the man.

44. (A. velocity, B. viscosity, C. temperature, D. density) : FLUID :: FRICTION : SOLID

(**B**) Viscosity is the resistance of a fluid to flow, just as friction is the resistance to relative motion between two solids.

45. CANTON : COUNTY :: (A. Ohio, B. Japan, C. Switzerland, D. China) : IRELAND

(**C**) A canton is a territorial division in Switzerland; a county is a territorial division in Ireland.

46. PECK : PINT :: 1 : (A. 4, B. 16, C. 8, D. 2)

(**B**) In this measurement analogy, a peck is equal to 8 quarts. A pint is half of a quart; therefore, 1 peck is equal to 16 pints.

47. TWEEZERS : BLEACH :: (A. steel, B. light, C. adding machine, D. eraser) : PICKPOCKET

(**D**) The relationship among tweezers, bleach, and a pickpocket is that they all remove something. Among the choices, an eraser also removes something, a written mistake.

48. HARANGUING : (A. persuade, B. filet, C. cleaning, D. arbitrate) :: FILIBUSTERING : OBSTRUCT

(**A**) In this purpose analogy, a purpose of filibustering is to obstruct passage of legislation. The purpose of jawboning is to persuade or coax another party to accept your position.

49. SHERRY : BEER :: PORT : (A. champagne, B. sauterne, C. claret, D. muscatel)

(**A**) Sherry has no carbonation; beer has carbonation. Port has no carbonation; champagne has carbonation.

50. HONOR : GOVERNOR :: (A. Excellency, B. Majesty, C. Highness, D. Grace) : DUKE

(**D**) The proper way to refer to people in certain positions or ranks is to say his honor, the governor, and his grace, the duke.

51. ANDIRON : PEDESTAL :: (A. log, B. bucket, C. anvil, D. skillet) : STATUE

(**A**) An andiron holds a log; a pedestal holds a statue.

52. GENERAL : STARS :: COLONEL : (A. oak, B. silver, C. gold, D. eagle)

(**D**) In this association analogy, stars symbolize the rank of general; an eagle symbolizes the rank of colonel.

53. (A. insist, B. reply, C. demur, D. demand) : REFUSE :: LAZY : INERT

(**C**) The relationship is one of degree. *Lazy,* meaning *sluggish,* is a lesser degree of immobility than *inert.* To *demur,* meaning to *hesitate, delay,* or *object,* is a lesser degree of protestation than to *refuse.*

54. HEART : HEAD :: VENERY : (A. ribaldry, B. flesh, C. mortality, D. restraint)

(D) It is often said that the ways of the heart are the opposite to the ways of the head; the opposite of venery, the gratification of desires, is restraint.

55. CALORIE : (A. energy, B. weight, C. metabolism, D. food) :: CENTURY : TIME

(A) A calorie is a measure of the heat-producing or energy-producing value of food. A century is a measure of time.

56. FLORIDA : SAUDI ARABIA :: (A. Louisiana, B. Georgia, C. Arkansas, D. Iraq) : IRAN

(A) In this place analogy, Saudi Arabia and Iran are both countries bordering on the Persian Gulf; Florida and Louisiana are states that border on the Gulf of Mexico. And, just as Saudi Arabia and Iran do not border on each other, so also Florida and Louisiana do not have a common border.

57. *KING LEAR* : *DIE FLEDERMAUS* :: *MACBETH* : (A. *Tosca*, B. *Othello*, C. *Ruddigore*, D. *Les Misèrables*)

(C) *King Lear* and *Macbeth* are both Shakespearean tragedies. *Die Fledermaus* and *Ruddigore* are both comic operas. The writer of the two comedies is irrelevant because no other choice is a comedy.

58. BOARDWALK : (A. Park Place, B. Atlantic City, C. display, D. escalator) :: STRAND : STORE

(D) A boardwalk is a kind of walkway along a strand or beach; an escalator is a kind of walkway in a department store.

59. (A. Parliament, B. Congress, C. Great Britain, D. Senate) : LORDS :: HOUSE : COMMONS

(D) The Senate and the House of Lords are the upper houses of the U.S. Congress and the British Parliament, respectively; the House of Representatives and House of Commons are the lower houses.

60. 1789 : (A. Germany, B. France, C. England, D. Russia) :: 1776 : UNITED STATES

(B) The dates mark the beginnings of two highly significant revolutions. 1776 was the beginning of the revolution in what was to become the United States; 1789 was the beginning year of the revolution in France.

61. MALLARD : CANVASBACK :: (A. snow, B. north, C. drake, D. gander) : CANADA

(A) This is a part-to-part relationship. Mallard and canvasback both belong to the group "ducks." Canada and snow both belong to the group "geese."

62. WELL-FED : (A. penurious, B. healthy, C. wealthy, D. miserly) :: HUNGRY : IMPECUNIOUS

(C) The relationship is that of opposites. A well-fed person is not hungry; A wealthy person is not impecunious, or lacking money.

63. LAERTES : (A. Odysseus, B. Polonius, C. Claudius, D. Ophelia) :: ICARUS : DAEDALUS

(B) In Greek mythology, Icarus is the son of Daedalus; in Shakespeare's play *Hamlet,* Laertes is the son of Polonius.

64. SYRACUSE : (A. Oneonta, B. Geneva, C. Raleigh, D. Sparta) :: CARTHAGE : ALEXANDRIA

(D) Syracuse, Sparta, Carthage, and Alexandria are all names of ancient historical communities.

65. DISPIRITED : DEPRESSED :: (A. obligato, B. innuendo, C. declaration, D. crescendo) : INSINUATION

(**B**) *Dispirited* and *depressed* are synonyms; *innuendo* and *insinuation* are also synonyms.

66. ORGANISM : (A. plant, B. animal, C. bacteria, D. cell) :: LIGHT : WAVE

(**D**) In this whole-to-part analogy, an organism is made up of cells; light consists physically of waves.

67. KOLN : WIEN :: COLOGNE : (A. Vienna, B. Prague, C. Warsaw, D. Hamburg)

(**A**) The German name for Cologne is Koln; the German name for Vienna is Wien.

68. DCX : MDCCCXXX :: (A. CLX, B. XLI, C. LCD, D. LXVII) : CXXIII

(**B**) If you are required to perform mathematical calculations with large Roman numerals, you may be pretty certain that the calculations will be very simple ones. Begin by translating into Arabic numerals. DCX = 610. MDCCCXXX = 1,830. By inspection you can see that $610 \times 3 = 1,830$. Now translate the third Roman numeral. CXXIII = 123. The fourth term must be one-third of 123 or 41, which is XLI.

69. WISDOM : (A. lion, B. owl, C. fox, D. deer) :: SPRING : ROBIN

(**B**) The relationship is one of association. A robin is associated with the coming of spring; an owl is associated with great wisdom.

70. BUTTERFLY : (A. insect, B. silkworm, C. wings, D. summer) :: CHRYSALIS : COCOON

(**B**) An early stage in the development of the butterfly is the chrysalis; an early stage in the development of the silkworm is the cocoon. *Chrysalis* and *cocoon* are synonyms. *Butterfly* and *silkworm* are not synonyms, but they do bear the same sequential relationship to the enveloped stage of development.

71. ICELAND : NORWAY :: (A. winter, B. queen, C. president, D. sovereign) : KING

(**C**) Norway is a monarchy headed by a king; Iceland is a republic headed by a president.

72. ROME : (A. NATO, B. SEATO, C. SALT II, D. EEC) :: VERSAILLES : LEAGUE OF NATIONS

(**D**) The groundwork for the League of Nations was laid out in the Treaty of Versailles in 1919. The initial planning for the EEC (European Economic Community) was drafted in the Treaty of Rome in 1957. The NATO (North Atlantic Treaty Organization) alliance was forged in Washington, D.C., in 1949: SEATO (Southeast Asia Treaty Organization) in Manila in 1954; and SALT II (Strategic Arms Limitation Treaty II) in Vienna in 1979.

73. CYLINDER : LOCK :: MOTOR : (A. shaft, B. canal, C. tackle, D. escape)

(**B**) A cylinder is part of a motor; a lock is part of a canal. This is a difficult analogy because a cylinder is also part of a lock. However, if you begin and stick with this relationship, you can then choose only that a shaft is part of a motor, which is a reverse relationship and creates an incorrect analogy.

74. BANANA : (A. sapphire, B. saltcellar, C. stone, D. tree) :: BUTTER : SKY

(**A**) Butter is yellow, and sky is blue; because a banana is yellow, the task is to find the choice that is blue: a sapphire.

158   Master the Miller Analogies Test

75. GNASH : TEETH :: (A. fold, B. clasp, C. gnarl, D. wring) : HANDS

(**D**) In this action-to-object analogy, you may gnash your teeth or wring your hands in anger or dismay. All of the other choices are also activities that can be done with your hands, but they are not characteristically a sign of anger or dismay.

76. (A. opossum, B. fox, C. beaver, D. lady) : KANGAROO :: CHICKEN : COCKROACH

(**A**) A chicken and a cockroach are both related as oviparous or egg-bearing. An opossum and a kangaroo are both classified as marsupials, pouched mammals.

77. APHRODITE : VENUS :: ARES : (A. Mercury, B. Mars, C. Apollo, D. Hermes)

(**B**) Aphrodite is the Greek goddess of love and beauty; Venus is her Roman counterpart. Ares is the Greek god of war; Mars is his Roman counterpart.

78. METAPHYSICS : (A. humanities, B. medicine, C. logic, D. art) :: EPISTEMOLOGY : ETHICS

(**C**) The four terms of this analogy are all related in that epistemology, ethics, metaphysics, and logic constitute four of the five branches of philosophy. The fifth is aesthetics.

79. CLARINET : PIANO :: WIND : (A. reed, B. wood, C. percussion, D. pianist)

(**C**) A clarinet is a wind instrument; a piano is a percussion instrument.

80. ELEVATOR : SKYSCRAPER :: (A. gangplank, B. companionway, C. bulkhead, D. bridge) : SHIP

(**B**) An elevator is used to ascend and descend once inside a skyscraper; a companionway, a ship's staircase, is used for the same purpose in a ship.

81. PROPENSITY : (A. riches, B. weight, C. bias, D. thought) :: CLUB : MACE

(**C**) In this degree analogy, a propensity is a lesser degree of opinion than is a bias; a club is a less ominous weapon than a mace, which is a spiked club.

82. SALZBURG : STRATFORD :: (A. Goethe, B. Avon, C. Mozart, D. Brahms) : SHAKESPEARE

(**C**) Stratford is the birthplace of Shakespeare; Salzburg is the birthplace of Mozart.

83. FLAMMABLE : INFLAMMABLE :: PERTINENT : (A. impertinent, B. inopportune, C. incoherent, D. relevant)

(**D**) *Flammable* and *inflammable* are synonyms; *pertinent* and *relevant* are also synonyms.

84. (A. revolution, B. dance, C. torque, D. axis) : ROTATE :: FRICTION : RESIST

(**C**) In this cause-and-effect analogy, friction causes something to resist moving; torque causes something to rotate. The effects are opposite, but the cause-to-effect relationship is the same.

85. PRISM : (A. spectrum, B. reflection, C. light, D. binoculars) :: FAMINE : WANT

(**A**) In this product-source analogy, a spectrum is created by a prism; want is produced by a famine, which is a scarcity.

86. LOOP : HUB :: BEEF : (A. corn, B. beans, C. tobacco, D. cotton)

(**B**) The loop and the hub are nicknames for the downtown business districts of Chicago and Boston, respectively; Chicago is known for its beef, and Boston is known for its beans.

87. JANUARY : (A. Cleveland, B. June, C. Washington, D. Hermes) :: SUNDAY : MERCURY

(**C**) We have a number of firsts here: January is the first month; Sunday is the first day of the week; Mercury is the first planet in distance from the sun; and Washington was the first U.S. president.

88. LIFT : ELEVATOR :: (A. oil, B. grease, C. gas, D. petrol) : GASOLINE

(**D**) *Lift* is the British word for an elevator; *petrol* is the British word for gasoline.

89. (A. $\frac{1}{6}$, B. $\frac{4}{5}$, C. $\frac{2}{5}$, D. $\frac{2}{10}$) : $\frac{1}{10}$ :: $\frac{3}{4}$ :: $\frac{3}{16}$

(**C**) In this numerical analogy, $\frac{1}{4}$ of $\frac{3}{4}$ is $\frac{3}{16}$; $\frac{1}{4}$ of $\frac{2}{5}$ is $\frac{1}{10}$.

90. TORT : LITIGATION :: CONTRACT : (A. signature, B. obligation, C. clause, D. equity)

(**B**) A tort is a wrong that entails litigation; a contract is an agreement that entails obligation.

91. BULL : (A. wolf, B. turtle, C. fish, D. snail) :: CRAB : LION

(**C**) The bull (Taurus), fish (Pisces), crab (Cancer), and lion (Leo) are all signs of the zodiac.

92. EQUINOX : SOLSTICE :: SEPTEMBER : (A. November, B. January, C. June, D. March)

(**C**) *Equinox* refers to either of the two times each year when the sun crosses the equator and day and night are everywhere of equal length, occurring about March 21 and September 23. *Solstice* refers to one of the two points at which the sun's apparent position on the celestial sphere reaches its greatest distance above or below the celestial equator, occurring about June 22 and December 22.

93. (A. hand, B. brow, C. rose, D. soon) : KNIT :: DICTATION : TAKE

(**B**) In this action-to-object analogy, one may knit a brow, and one may take dictation.

94. GARROTING : DEATH :: CANVASSING : (A. painting, B. shelter, C. votes, D. fight)

(**C**) The correspondence is one of cause and effect. Garroting (strangling) commonly causes death; canvassing (soliciting for support) commonly results in votes.

95. PUSILLANIMOUS : INVIDIOUS :: (A. paronomasia, B. slather, C. melodramatically, D. perfunctory) : SANCTIMONIOUS

(**D**) The Miller Analogies Test tends to get into some esoteric vocabulary, but not much. If the words seem excessively long or obscure, look for another relationship before trying to define and determine meaningful relationships. In this analogy based upon grammar, *pusillanimous, invidious,* and *sanctimonious* are all adjectives. The only choice that is an adjective is *perfunctory*. With *paronomasia,* you should know by its ending that it is a noun; *slather* is a verb or a noun; and *melodramatically* is an adverb.

96. SUN : JAPAN :: (A. scythe, B. crescent, C. Caspian, D. hammer) : TURKEY

(**B**) The crescent is a symbol associated with Turkey just as the rising sun is a symbol associated with Japan.

97. CICERO : DEMOSTHENES :: ROOSEVELT : (A. MacArthur, B. Hemingway, C. Shaw, D. Churchill)

(D) Cicero and Demosthenes are related as orators; Roosevelt and Churchill are related as statesmen.

98. TYRO : (A. tyrant, B. master, C. amateur, D. dabbler) :: TURPITUDE : PROBITY

(B) The opposite of *turpitude,* which means *baseness,* is *probity,* meaning *uprightness.* An antonym for *tyro,* a beginner, is *master.* If you are unfamiliar with the meaning of a particular word, such as *tyro,* but understand the relationship between the remaining pair of words, closely examine the relationship between the four answer choices. In most analogy problems, if two answer choices are synonymous, neither is likely to be correct. In this case, *amateur* and *dabbler* are synonyms, and both can be eliminated from consideration.

99. COKE : COAL :: (A. oil, B. planks, C. saw, D. lumberjack) : TIMBER

(B) In this product-source analogy, coke is obtained by heating coal; planks are formed by cutting timber.

100. SHOE : (A. fly, B. cobbler, C. pair, D. bell) :: SAW : GEAR

(D) A saw and a gear both have teeth; a shoe and a bell both have a tongue.

SAMPLE TEST 6
Answer Sheet

1. ⓐ ⓑ ⓒ ⓓ
2. ⓐ ⓑ ⓒ ⓓ
3. ⓐ ⓑ ⓒ ⓓ
4. ⓐ ⓑ ⓒ ⓓ
5. ⓐ ⓑ ⓒ ⓓ
6. ⓐ ⓑ ⓒ ⓓ
7. ⓐ ⓑ ⓒ ⓓ
8. ⓐ ⓑ ⓒ ⓓ
9. ⓐ ⓑ ⓒ ⓓ
10. ⓐ ⓑ ⓒ ⓓ
11. ⓐ ⓑ ⓒ ⓓ
12. ⓐ ⓑ ⓒ ⓓ
13. ⓐ ⓑ ⓒ ⓓ
14. ⓐ ⓑ ⓒ ⓓ
15. ⓐ ⓑ ⓒ ⓓ
16. ⓐ ⓑ ⓒ ⓓ
17. ⓐ ⓑ ⓒ ⓓ
18. ⓐ ⓑ ⓒ ⓓ
19. ⓐ ⓑ ⓒ ⓓ
20. ⓐ ⓑ ⓒ ⓓ
21. ⓐ ⓑ ⓒ ⓓ
22. ⓐ ⓑ ⓒ ⓓ
23. ⓐ ⓑ ⓒ ⓓ
24. ⓐ ⓑ ⓒ ⓓ
25. ⓐ ⓑ ⓒ ⓓ

26. ⓐ ⓑ ⓒ ⓓ
27. ⓐ ⓑ ⓒ ⓓ
28. ⓐ ⓑ ⓒ ⓓ
29. ⓐ ⓑ ⓒ ⓓ
30. ⓐ ⓑ ⓒ ⓓ
31. ⓐ ⓑ ⓒ ⓓ
32. ⓐ ⓑ ⓒ ⓓ
33. ⓐ ⓑ ⓒ ⓓ
34. ⓐ ⓑ ⓒ ⓓ
35. ⓐ ⓑ ⓒ ⓓ
36. ⓐ ⓑ ⓒ ⓓ
37. ⓐ ⓑ ⓒ ⓓ
38. ⓐ ⓑ ⓒ ⓓ
39. ⓐ ⓑ ⓒ ⓓ
40. ⓐ ⓑ ⓒ ⓓ
41. ⓐ ⓑ ⓒ ⓓ
42. ⓐ ⓑ ⓒ ⓓ
43. ⓐ ⓑ ⓒ ⓓ
44. ⓐ ⓑ ⓒ ⓓ
45. ⓐ ⓑ ⓒ ⓓ
46. ⓐ ⓑ ⓒ ⓓ
47. ⓐ ⓑ ⓒ ⓓ
48. ⓐ ⓑ ⓒ ⓓ
49. ⓐ ⓑ ⓒ ⓓ
50. ⓐ ⓑ ⓒ ⓓ

51. ⓐ ⓑ ⓒ ⓓ
52. ⓐ ⓑ ⓒ ⓓ
53. ⓐ ⓑ ⓒ ⓓ
54. ⓐ ⓑ ⓒ ⓓ
55. ⓐ ⓑ ⓒ ⓓ
56. ⓐ ⓑ ⓒ ⓓ
57. ⓐ ⓑ ⓒ ⓓ
58. ⓐ ⓑ ⓒ ⓓ
59. ⓐ ⓑ ⓒ ⓓ
60. ⓐ ⓑ ⓒ ⓓ
61. ⓐ ⓑ ⓒ ⓓ
62. ⓐ ⓑ ⓒ ⓓ
63. ⓐ ⓑ ⓒ ⓓ
64. ⓐ ⓑ ⓒ ⓓ
65. ⓐ ⓑ ⓒ ⓓ
66. ⓐ ⓑ ⓒ ⓓ
67. ⓐ ⓑ ⓒ ⓓ
68. ⓐ ⓑ ⓒ ⓓ
69. ⓐ ⓑ ⓒ ⓓ
70. ⓐ ⓑ ⓒ ⓓ
71. ⓐ ⓑ ⓒ ⓓ
72. ⓐ ⓑ ⓒ ⓓ
73. ⓐ ⓑ ⓒ ⓓ
74. ⓐ ⓑ ⓒ ⓓ
75. ⓐ ⓑ ⓒ ⓓ

76. ⓐ ⓑ ⓒ ⓓ
77. ⓐ ⓑ ⓒ ⓓ
78. ⓐ ⓑ ⓒ ⓓ
79. ⓐ ⓑ ⓒ ⓓ
80. ⓐ ⓑ ⓒ ⓓ
81. ⓐ ⓑ ⓒ ⓓ
82. ⓐ ⓑ ⓒ ⓓ
83. ⓐ ⓑ ⓒ ⓓ
84. ⓐ ⓑ ⓒ ⓓ
85. ⓐ ⓑ ⓒ ⓓ
86. ⓐ ⓑ ⓒ ⓓ
87. ⓐ ⓑ ⓒ ⓓ
88. ⓐ ⓑ ⓒ ⓓ
89. ⓐ ⓑ ⓒ ⓓ
90. ⓐ ⓑ ⓒ ⓓ
91. ⓐ ⓑ ⓒ ⓓ
92. ⓐ ⓑ ⓒ ⓓ
93. ⓐ ⓑ ⓒ ⓓ
94. ⓐ ⓑ ⓒ ⓓ
95. ⓐ ⓑ ⓒ ⓓ
96. ⓐ ⓑ ⓒ ⓓ
97. ⓐ ⓑ ⓒ ⓓ
98. ⓐ ⓑ ⓒ ⓓ
99. ⓐ ⓑ ⓒ ⓓ
100. ⓐ ⓑ ⓒ ⓓ

TEAR HERE

Chapter 10

Sample Test 6

100 Questions • 50 Minutes

Directions: Each of these test questions consists of three capitalized words and four lettered words enclosed in parentheses. Two of the capitalized words are related in some way. Find the two related words, and establish the nature of the relationship. Then study the four words lettered A, B, C, and D. Select the one lettered word that is related to the remaining capitalized word in the same way that the first two capitalized words are related. Mark the answer sheet for the letter preceding the word you select.

ROAD MAP

- *Answer Key*
- *Explanatory Answers*

1. SHINGLE : (A. siding, B. hair, C. thatch, D. roof) :: TILE : SLATE

2. SCRUB : SHINE :: (A. turn, B. top, C, spiral, D. dance) : SPIN

3. (A. larva, B. embryo, C. caduceus, D. tadpole) : FROG :: CATERPILLAR : BUTTERFLY

4. LEAP : STRIDE :: JUMP : (A. fall, B. step, C. skip, D. bound)

5. CAT : MOUSE :: (A. polar bear, B. lion, C. orca, D. rat) : ANTELOPE

6. MERCURY : MICA :: QUICKSILVER : (A. formica, B. saltpeter, C. isinglass, D. hydroxide)

7. ROMEO : JULIET :: (A. Pyramus, B. Hercules, C. Endymion, D. Philemon) : THISBE

8. QUEENSLAND : (A. Kingscote, B. Brisbane, C. Victoria, D. Melbourne) :: ALBERTA : ONTARIO

9. BOUILLABAISSE : L'ORANGE :: (A. paella, B. a la mode, C. custard, D. chowder) : PEKING

10. (A. Annapolis, B. William, C. Baltimore, D. McHenry) : MARYLAND :: PENN : PENNSYLVANIA

11. $\frac{1}{2}$: .5 :: $\frac{5}{20}$: (A. $\frac{1}{5}$, B. .02, C. $\frac{1}{4}$, D. .25)

12. HYDE PARK : ROOSEVELT :: OYSTER BAY : (A. Kennedy, B. Tyler, C. Coolidge, D. Roosevelt)

13. PEPSIN : PTYALIN :: PROTEIN : (A. meat, B. starch, C. saliva, D. vitamins)

14. RAPHAEL : MICHELANGELO :: (A. Monet, B. Hockney, C. Braque, D. Veronese) : PICASSO

15. GOBI : (A. Mojave, B. Swahili, C. Masai, D. Azalea) :: TIGRIS : EUPHRATES

16. CAPON : (A. rooster, B. turkey, C. chicken, D. steer) :: MULE : TANGELO

17. 12:3 :: 44 : (A. 33, B. 3, C. 11, D. 22)

18. GO : WENT :: READ : (A. write, B. learned, C. listen, D. read)

19. (A. "Lycidas," B. "Thanatopsis," C. "Adonais," D. "Astrophel") : "ELEGY" :: BRYANT : GRAY

20. *MAINE* : (A. Spanish-American War, B. Pearl Harbor, C. War of 1812, D. Civil War) :: ALAMO : TEXAS WAR OF INDEPENDENCE

21. PLUTO : URANUS :: (A. Ursa, B. Mercury, C. Haley, D. Sirius) :: POLARIS

22. TRUMAN : (A. reconstruction, B. policy, C. containment, D. rearmament) :: CHAMBERLAIN : APPEASEMENT

23. JOHN : IRVING :: (A. Toni, B. Carol, C. Betty, D. Mary) : MORRISON

24. SAMISEN : (A. junk, B. sampan, C. teapot, D. banjo) :: AMOEBA : PARAMECIUM

25. BIENNIAL : BIANNUAL :: TWO : (A. one, B. one half, C. two, D. eight)

26. *PYGMALION* : *MY FAIR LADY* :: (A. *A Doll's House*, B. *The Pawnbroker*, C. *The Matchmaker*, D. *A House Is Not a Home*) : *HELLO, DOLLY!*

27. JACKSON : VAN BUREN :: WILSON : (A. Buchanan, B. Tyler, C. Taft, D. Ford)

28. (A. Algeria, B. Zimbabwe, C. Zambia, D. Liberia) : SIERRA LEONE :: ANGOLA : MOZAMBIQUE

29. FISSION : ENERGY :: (A. fusion, B. inertia, C. mass, D. entropy) : ENERGY

30. CHRISTIE : (A. Queen, B. Holmes, C. Seaman, D. Gardner) :: POIROT : MASON

31. BACH : HANDEL :: MONET : (A. Brontë, B. Kant, C. Cassatt, D. Sibelius)

32. 9 : 27 :: 4 : (A. 9, B. 8, C. 18, D. 3)

33. (A. C.S.A., B. O.S.S., C. A.C.W., D. O.P.A.) : C.I.A. :: I.W.W. : C.I.O.

34. SUNNITE : SHIITE :: (A. Presbyterian, B. Hindu, C. Catholic, D. Protestant) : EPISCOPALIAN

35. *ANIMAL FARM* : (A. Eric Blair, B. William Blair, C. William Porter, D. Thomas Wolfe) :: *PUDD'NHEAD WILSON* : SAMUEL LANGHORNE CLEMENS

36. STRIKE : LOCKOUT :: CONTRADICT : (A. appeal, B. repeat, C. agree, D. annul)

37. COLLIER : MINER :: (A. phobia, B. remission, C. bracelet, D. talisman) : AMULET

38. LOBSTER : SPIDER :: (A. arthropod, B. crayfish, C. clam, D. crustacean) : ARACHNID

39. HOMER : (A. Pindar, B. Ovid, C. Heraclitus, D. Aeneas) :: HERODOTUS : THUCYDIDES

40. HAIL : HALE :: (A. pale, B. pair, C. pear, D. whale) : PARE

41. MANET : *PROUST* :: GAINSBOROUGH : (A. Goya, B. *La Maja*, C. *Blue Boy*, D. Addison)

42. INFLAMMABLE : COMBUSTIBLE :: INVALUABLE : (A. priceless, B. worthless, C. untrue, D. deteriorating)

43. 3,280.8 ft. : (A. mile, B. kilometer, C. fathom, D. league) :: 946 ml. : QUART

44. OIL : (A. sun, B. gasoline, C. fuel, D. olive) :: COAL : WIND

45. (A. Brahms, B. Beethoven, C. Debussy, D. Haydn) : TCHAIKOVSKY :: *PASTORALE* : *PATHETIQUE*

46. ESTONIA : RUSSIA :: (A. Georgia, B. China, C. Cuba, D. Monaco) : CZECHOSLOVAKIA

47. FLAMINGO : (A. horned owl, B. flicker, C. catbird, D. demoiselle) :: CHICKEN : TURKEY

48. 1^2 :1 :: 5^2 : (A. 3, B. 25, C. 1, D. 10)

49. SCOTLAND : UNITED KINGDOM :: HOLLAND : (A. The Netherlands, B. Flanders, C. Europe, D. Belgium)

50. (A. griffin, B. giraffe, C. zebra, D. dinosaur) : DODO :: UNICORN : MASTODON

51. ANOPHELES : MALARIA :: AEDES : (A. cholera, B. dengue, C. bubonic plague, D. typhus)

52. OVOLO : CAVETTO :: (A. fertile, B. sheepish, C. convex, D. poetic) : CONCAVE

53. CANTERBURY : (A. Chaucer, B. Hemingway, C. Updike, D. Forster) :: CASTERBRIDGE : HARDY

54. (A. laugh, B. weep, C. cringe, D. geese) : QUAIL :: GAGGLE : COVEY

55. MANY : RAINDROPS :: MUCH : (A. flood, B. snowflakes, C. puddle, D. water)

56. HEART : STOMACH :: (A. veins, B. arteries, C. intestines, D. capillaries) : DUODENUM

57. BRISTLES : (A. razor, B. toothbrush, C. monkey, D. flower) :: FEATHERS : DUSTER

58. CHEETAH : LEOPARD :: WOLF : (A. feline, B. canine, C. dog, D. lupus)

59. TILES : (A. checkers, B. faucet, C. badminton, D. mah-jongg) :: DICE : BACKGAMMON

60. (A. statehouse, B. battlement, C. church, D. fortress) : CHURCH :: CITADEL : CATHEDRAL

61. 5 : $\sqrt{36}$ :: 8 : (A. 9, B. $\sqrt{81}$, C. $\sqrt{9}$, D. $\sqrt{64}$)

62. (A. crime, B. punishment, C. jury, D. verdict) : SENTENCE :: ANTEPENULT : PENULT

63. PANDA : (A. condor, B. bear, C. goldfish, D. ostrich) :: RACCOON : CROW

64. *LUSITANIA* : BRITAIN :: 007 : (A. Japan, B. Korea, C. USSR, D. James Bond)

65. YARD : FATHOM :: (A. eclipse, B. new, C. half, D. moon) : FULL

66. LANGSTON HUGHES : DOUGHTRY LONG :: (A. Marianne Moore, B. Gwendolyn Brooks, C. Gertrude Stein, D. Emily Dickinson) : MAYA ANGELOU

67. SAT® : (A. PEP, B. ACT®, C. TAT, D. NTE®) :: GRE® : MAT

68. TULIP : ASTER :: SPRING : (A. chicken, B. jump, C. fall, D. well)

69. BOLL WEEVIL : GYPSY MOTH :: (A. bee, B. termite, C. cockroach, D. louse) : PRAYING MANTIS

70. GHENT : (A. American Revolution, B. World War I, C. War of 1812, D. Hundred Years' War) :: P'ANMUNJOM : KOREAN WAR

71. (A. Nymph, B. Syrinx, C. Naiad, D. Chaos) : PAN :: ECHO : NARCISSUS

72. (A. terrapin, B. terrestrial, C. teuton, D. termagant) : SYCOPHANT :: VIRAGO : TOADY

73. KNESSET : ISRAEL :: DIET : (A. Kashrut, B. Luther, C. Japan, D. Congress)

74. *LES MISÈRABLES* : VICTOR HUGO :: (A. *Le Rouge et le Noir*, B. *Notre Dame de Paris*, C. *Les Trois Mousquetaires*, D. *Madame Bovary*) : ALEXANDRE DUMAS

75. ITS : IT'S :: (A. their, B. their's, C. there, D. there's) : THEY'RE

76. NICTATE : WINK :: (A. oscillate, B. osculate, C. ossify, D. oscultate) : KISS

77. INFLUENZA : VIRUS :: HODGKIN'S DISEASE : (A. schizophrenia, B. kidney disease, C. leprosy, D. cancer)

78. 28 : 82 :: 56 : (A. 54, B. 30, C. 65, D. 136)

79. *MAMA LUCIA* : (A. *Lucia de Lamermoor*, B. *Cavalleria Rusticana*, C. *Marriage of Figaro*, D. *Tosca*) :: *FIGARO* : *BARBER OF SEVILLE*

80. MINNEAPOLIS : NEW ORLEANS :: ALBANY : (A. Boston, B. Cleveland, C. New York, D. Louisiana)

81. STAG : BILLY :: DOE : (A. William, B. Hinny, C. Kid, D. Nanny)

82. ROGET : (A. bridge, B. synonyms, C. thesaurus, D. quiz shows) :: MILLER : ANALOGIES

83. OCULIST : OPHTHALMOLOGIST :: CHIROPODIST : (A. chiropractor, B. pediatrician, C. osteopath, D. podiatrist)

84. GNU : GNAT :: (A. koala, B. knight, C. kestrell, D. kangaroo) : KNAVE

85. ALLAH : (A. Islam, B. Mohammed, C. Christianity, D. God) :: HORUS : NEPTUNE

86. 15 : 5 :: 23 : (A. 1, B. 2, C. 5, D. 6)

87. CYRILLIC : RUSSIAN :: ROMAN : (A. Gypsy, B. English, C. numerals, D. Arabic)

88. PASTERN : (A. flank, B. rural, C. horse, D. duck) :: PISTIL : STAMEN

89. @ : & :: 2 : (A. #, B. 5, C. 7, D. $\frac{1}{2}$)

90. SADAT : JERUSALEM :: (A. Mao Tse-tung, B. Nixon, C. Ho Chi Minh, D. Sun Yat Sen) : CHINA

91. (A. Alice, B. Medusa, C. King Arthur, D. Minerva) : ADONIS :: QUASIMODO : SNOW WHITE

92. ANTHROPOLOGY : MARGARET MEAD :: (A. archeology, B. history, C. philosophy, D. psychology) : HOWARD CARTER

93. AMBITION : MACBETH :: JEALOUSY : (A. Caesar, B. Brutus, C. Othello, D. Shylock)

94. *FAUST* : (A. Mephistopheles, B. Goethe, C. folklore, D. underworld) :: *WASTELAND* : ELIOT

95. (A. ibid., B. etc., C. asst., D. dz.) : ET AL. :: OP. CIT. : CF

96. YALTA : ROOSEVELT :: (A. Munich, B. Potsdam, C. Bastogne, D. Corregidor) : TRUMAN

97. *THE MAGIC FLUTE* : (A. *Iolanthe*, B. *Turandot*, C. *Il Trovatore*, D. *Don Giovanni*) :: *AIDA* : *DON CARLOS*

98. OXYGEN : (A. air, B. water, C. carbon dioxide, D. carbon monoxide) :: FAUNA : FLORA

99. (A. Sleeping Beauty, B. Cinderella, C. Rapunzel, D. Goldilocks) : PRINCE CHARMING :: FROG : PRINCESS

100. 9 : 104 :: BEETHOVEN : (A. Mozart, B. Sibelius, C. Haydn, D. Casals)

ANSWER KEY

1. C	21. D	41. C	61. B	81. D
2. A	22. C	42. A	62. D	82. B
3. D	23. A	43. B	63. A	83. D
4. B	24. D	44. A	64. B	84. B
5. B	25. B	45. B	65. C	85. D
6. C	26. C	46. A	66. B	86. D
7. A	27. B	47. D	67. B	87. B
8. C	28. B	48. B	68. C	88. A
9. D	29. A	49. A	69. A	89. C
10. C	30. D	50. A	70. C	90. B
11. D	31. C	51. B	71. B	91. B
12. D	32. B	52. C	72. D	92. A
13. B	33. B	53. A	73. C	93. C
14. C	34. A	54. D	74. C	94. B
15. A	35. A	55. D	75. A	95. A
16. D	36. C	56. B	76. B	96. B
17. C	37. D	57. B	77. D	97. D
18. D	38. D	58. C	78. C	98. C
19. B	39. A	59. D	79. B	99. A
20. A	40. B	60. D	80. C	100. C

Sample Test 6

EXPLANATORY ANSWERS

1. SHINGLE : (A. siding, B. hair, C. thatch, D. roof) :: TILE : SLATE

(**C**) The analogy is one of part to part. Tile and slate are both roofing materials; shingle and thatch are roofing materials as well.

2. SCRUB : SHINE :: (A. turn, B. top, C. spiral, D. dance) : SPIN

(**A**) In this cause-and-effect analogy, to scrub something causes it to shine, and to turn something causes it to spin.

3. (A. larva, B. embryo, C. caduceus, D. tadpole) : FROG :: CATERPILLAR : BUTTERFLY

(**D**) This is a sequential analogy; the tadpole stage precedes the frog, and a caterpillar precedes a butterfly.

4. LEAP : STRIDE :: JUMP : (A. fall, B. step, C. skip, D. bound)

(**B**) The relationship is one of degree. A leap is a very large jump; a stride is a very large step.

5. CAT : MOUSE :: (A. polar bear, B. lion, C. orca, D. rat) : ANTELOPE

(**B**) The relationship of cat to mouse is that of predator to prey. An antelope is preyed upon by lions.

6. MERCURY : MICA :: QUICKSILVER : (A. formica, B. saltpeter, C. isinglass, D. hydroxide)

(**C**) The relationship is that of synonyms. Mercury is often known as quicksilver; mica is often called isinglass.

7. ROMEO : JULIET :: (A. Pyramus, B. Hercules, C. Endymion, D. Philemon) : THISBE

(**A**) Romeo and Juliet were tragic lovers whose parents forbade their marriage. This story closely parallels that of the mythological Pyramus and Thisbe, whose love was also thwarted by their parents.

8. QUEENSLAND : (A. Kingscote, B. Brisbane, C. Victoria, D. Melbourne) :: ALBERTA : ONTARIO

(**C**) The relationship is that of part to part. Alberta and Ontario are both Canadian provinces; Queensland and Victoria are both Australian provinces.

9. BOUILLABAISSE : L'ORANGE :: (A. paella, B. a la mode, C. custard, D. chowder) : PEKING

(**D**) L'orange and Peking are ways of preparing duck; bouillabaisse and chowder are different kinds of fish stews.

10. (A. Annapolis, B. William, C. Baltimore, D. McHenry) : MARYLAND :: PENN : PENNSYLVANIA

(**C**) William Penn established the colony that later became the state of Pennsylvania; Lord Baltimore established the colony that became the state of Maryland.

11. $\frac{1}{2}$: .5 :: $\frac{5}{20}$: (A. $\frac{1}{5}$, B. .02, C. $\frac{1}{4}$, D. .25)

(**D**) The relationship is that of a fraction to its decimal equivalent. $\frac{1}{2} = .5$; $\frac{5}{20} = .25$.

12. HYDE PARK : ROOSEVELT :: OYSTER BAY : (A. Kennedy, B. Tyler, C. Coolidge, D. Roosevelt)

(D) Hyde Park was the family home of Franklin D. Roosevelt; Oyster Bay was the family home of Theodore Roosevelt.

13. PEPSIN : PTYALIN :: PROTEIN : (A. meat, B. starch, C. saliva, D. vitamins)

(B) Pepsin is an enzyme that breaks down protein into amino acids; ptyalin is the enzyme that decomposes starch. The analogy is one of function.

14. RAPHAEL : MICHELANGELO :: (A. Monet, B. Hockney, C. Braque, D. Veronese) : PICASSO

(C) Raphael and Michelangelo are both artists from the Renaissance Era. Braque and Picasso are both Cubist artists from the early twentieth century.

15. GOBI : (A. Mojave, B. Swahili, C. Masai, D. Azalea) :: TIGRIS : EUPHRATES

(A) Gobi and Mojave are both deserts; Tigris and Euphrates are both rivers.

16. CAPON : (A. rooster, B. turkey, C. chicken, D. steer) :: MULE : TANGELO

(D) The analogy is one of shared characteristic. Mule and tangelo share the characteristic that both are man-made hybrids. Capon and steer also share a characteristic: Both are castrated males of their species that are raised specially for their meat.

17. 12 : 3 :: 44 : (A. 33, B. 3, C. 11, D. 22)

(C) The analogy stems from the divisibility of the first number by the second and the answer yielded by the division. 12 ÷ 3 = 4; 44 ÷ 11 = 4. The sign "::" does not necessarily mean "equals."

18. GO : WENT :: READ : (A. write, B. learned, C. listen, D. read)

(D) This is a grammatical analogy. *Went* is the past tense of *go; read* is the past tense of *read*.

19. (A. "Lycidas," B. "Thanatopsis," C. "Adonais," D. "Astrophel") : "ELEGY" :: BRYANT : GRAY

(B) Thomas Gray wrote "Elegy Written in a Country Churchyard," commonly known as Gray's "Elegy"; William Cullen Bryant wrote "Thanatopsis."

20. MAINE : (A. Spanish-American War, B. Pearl Harbor, C. War of 1812, D. Civil War) :: ALAMO : TEXAS WAR OF INDEPENDENCE

(A) The battle of the Alamo, a mission in Texas at which all defenders were killed, was the turning point of the Texas War of Independence. The rallying cry of the Texans was "Remember the Alamo." The sinking of the battleship *Maine* in Havana Harbor brought the United States into the Spanish-American War. The American call to battle was "Remember the *Maine*."

21. PLUTO : URANUS :: (A. Ursa, B. Mercury, C. Haley, D. Sirius) : POLARIS

(D) Pluto and Uranus are both planets; Sirius (the dog star) and Polaris (the north star) are both stars.

22. TRUMAN : (A. reconstruction, B. policy, C. containment, D. rearmament) :: CHAMBERLAIN : APPEASEMENT

(C) In this analogy of association, just as British Prime Minister Neville Chamberlain is associated with the policy of appeasement, so President Harry Truman is associated with the policy of Soviet containment.

23. JOHN : IRVING :: (A. Toni, B. Carol, C. Betty, D. Mary) : MORRISON

(A) The relationship is between the first and last name of a well-known contemporary author. John Irving is the author of *The World According to Garp* and *The Cider House Rules*. Toni Morrison is the author of *Beloved* and *Tar Baby*.

24. SAMISEN : (A. junk, B. sampan, C. teapot, D. banjo) :: AMOEBA : PARAMECIUM

(D) An amoeba and a paramecium are both simple water organisms; a samisen and a banjo are both simple stringed instruments.

25. BIENNIAL : BIANNUAL :: TWO : (A. one, B. one half, C. two, D. eight)

(B) A biennial event happens once every two years; a biannual event occurs twice a year or every one-half year.

26. *PYGMALION* : *MY FAIR LADY* :: (A. *A Doll's House*, B. *The Pawnbroker*, C. *The Matchmaker*, D. *A House Is Not a Home*) : *HELLO, DOLLY!*

(C) *Pygmalion* is the George Bernard Shaw play upon which the musical *My Fair Lady* was based; *The Matchmaker* is the Thornton Wilder play upon which the musical *Hello, Dolly!* was based.

27. JACKSON : VAN BUREN :: WILSON : (A. Buchanan, B. Tyler, C. Taft, D. Ford)

(B) Jackson and Van Buren both entered the White House as widowers and remained single throughout their tenure; both Wilson and Tyler married second wives while in the White House.

28. (A. Algeria, B. Zimbabwe, C. Zambia, D. Liberia) : SIERRA LEONE :: ANGOLA : MOZAMBIQUE

(B) Angola and Mozambique were colonies of Portugal before they achieved their independence; Sierra Leone and Zimbabwe were British colonies. Algeria was French; Zambia was Belgian; Liberia was always independent.

29. FISSION : ENERGY :: (A. fusion, B. inertia, C. mass, D. entropy) : ENERGY

(A) This is a cause-and-effect analogy. Both nuclear fission and nuclear fusion create energy. None of the other choices creates energy.

30. CHRISTIE : (A. Queen, B. Holmes, C. Seaman, D. Gardner) :: POIROT : MASON

(D) In this analogy, there is a relationship between the mystery writer and the character created by the author. Agatha Christie is the creator of Hercule Poirot; Erle Stanley Gardner is the creator of Perry Mason.

31. BACH : HANDEL :: MONET : (A. Brontë, B. Kant, C. Cassatt, D. Sibelius)

(C) Bach and Handel are both well-known Baroque composers. Monet and Cassatt are both well-known Impressionist artists.

32. 9 : 27 :: 4 : (A. 9, B. 8, C. 18, D. 3)

(**B**) The relationship is based upon a mathematical relationship: 9 is equal to 3^2, whereas 27 is equal to 3^3. 4 is equal to 2^2 whereas 8 is equal to 2^3.

33. (A. C.S.A., B. O.S.S., C. A.C.W., D. O.P.A.) : C.I.A. :: I.W.W. : C.I.O.

(**B**) This is a sequence analogy. The O.S.S. (Office of Strategic Services) was an intelligence-gathering unit during World War II and was a forerunner of the C.I.A. (Central Intelligence Agency). The I.W.W. (Industrial Workers of the World) was an early labor union and was a forerunner of the C.I.O. (Congress of Industrial Organizations).

34. SUNNITE : SHIITE :: (A. Presbyterian, B. Hindu, C. Catholic, D. Protestant) : EPISCOPALIAN

(**A**) The Sunnites and the Shi'ites are all Moslems. The two sects broke apart over a disagreement on succession after the death of Mohammed. Presbyterians and Episcopalians are both Protestant groups.

35. *ANIMAL FARM* : (A. Eric Blair, B. William Blair, C. William Porter, D. Thomas Wolfe) :: *PUDD'NHEAD WILSON* : SAMUEL LANGHORNE CLEMENS

(**A**) *Pudd'nhead Wilson* is a book written by Samuel Langhorne Clemens, whose pen name was Mark Twain; *Animal Farm* is a book written by Eric Blair, whose pen name was George Orwell.

36. STRIKE : LOCKOUT :: CONTRADICT : (A. appeal, B. repeat, C. agree, D. annul)

(**C**) This analogy is based upon antonyms. In a strike, management welcomes the workers, but the workers refuse to work. In a lockout, the workers are willing, but management does not allow them to work. *Contradict* is the antonym of *agree*.

37. COLLIER : MINER :: (A. phobia, B. remission, C. bracelet, D. talisman) : AMULET

(**D**) This analogy is based upon synonyms. A collier is a coal miner; a talisman is a good luck charm, as is an amulet.

38. LOBSTER : SPIDER :: (A. arthropod, B. crayfish, C. clam, D. crustacean) : ARACHNID

(**D**) A spider is an arachnid, a member of the class Arachnida of the phylum Arthropoda. A lobster is a crustacean, a member of the class Crustacea of the phylum Arthropoda.

39. HOMER : (A. Pindar, B. Ovid, C. Heraclitus, D. Aeneas) :: HERODOTUS : THUCYDIDES

(**A**) Herodotus and Thucydides were both Greek historians; Homer and Pindar were both Greek poets. Ovid was a Roman poet.

40. HAIL : HALE :: (A. pale, B. pair, C. pear, D. whale) : PARE

(**B**) This is a nonsemantic relationship. The words of the first pair *hail* and *hale* are homonyms. Both answers B and C create a pair of homonyms with *pare;* however, answer B is the best choice because its spelling is analogous to that of the first member of the initial word pair.

41. MANET : *PROUST* :: GAINSBOROUGH : (A. Goya, B. *La Maja,* C. *Blue Boy,* D. Addison)

(**C**) The artist Manet painted a portrait of the novelist Marcel Proust; the artist Gainsborough painted a famous portrait of a young man in blue called *Blue Boy.*

42. INFLAMMABLE : COMBUSTIBLE :: INVALUABLE : (A. priceless, B. worthless, C. untrue, D. deteriorating)

(**A**) *Inflammable* and *combustible* are synonyms; *invaluable* and *priceless* are synonyms. Often, the prefix "in" means *not,* but in both these instances, the initial "in" does not mean that the word is negative.

43. 3,280.8 ft. : (A. mile, B. kilometer, C. fathom, D. league) :: 946 ml. : QUART

(**B**) 946 ml. is equal to one quart; 3,280.8 ft. is equal to one kilometer.

44. OIL : (A. sun, B. gasoline, C. fuel, D. olive) :: COAL : WIND

(**A**) Coal is a fossil fuel; wind is a nonfossil power source. Oil is a fossil fuel, while the sun is a nonfossil power source.

45. (A. Brahms, B. Beethoven, C. Debussy, D. Haydn) : TCHAIKOVSKY :: *PASTORALE* : *PATHETIQUE*

(**B**) Tchaikovsky's sixth symphony is named the *Pathetique;* Beethoven's sixth symphony is named the *Pastorale*.

46. ESTONIA : RUSSIA :: (A. Georgia, B. China, C. Cuba, D. Monaco) : CZECHOSLOVAKIA

(**A**) Estonia and Russia were both constituent republics of the now defunct USSR (Union of Soviet Socialist Republics). Georgia and Czechoslovakia were also member states of the USSR.

47. FLAMINGO : (A. horned owl, B. flicker, C. catbird, D. crane) :: CHICKEN : TURKEY

(**D**) The chicken and turkey are both barnyard fowl. The flamingo and crane are both wading birds.

48. 1^2 : 1 :: 5^2 : (A. 3, B. 25, C. 1, D. 10)

(**B**) This analogy is simply that of the square of a number to the number.

49. SCOTLAND : UNITED KINGDOM :: HOLLAND : (A. The Netherlands, B. Flanders, C. Europe, D. Belgium)

(**A**) Scotland is a constituent country of the United Kingdom. Holland is one province of the Netherlands.

50. (A. griffin, B. giraffe, C. zebra, D. dinosaur) : DODO :: UNICORN : MASTODON

(**A**) A unicorn is a mythological animal; a mastodon is an extinct animal. A griffin is a mythological animal; a dodo is an extinct animal.

51. ANOPHELES : MALARIA :: AEDES : (A. cholera, B. dengue, C. bubonic plague, D. typhus)

(**B**) The anopheles mosquito transmits malaria; the aedes mosquito transmits dengue and yellow fever.

52. OVOLO : CAVETTO :: (A. fertile, B. sheepish, C. convex, D. poetic) : CONCAVE

(**C**) Ovolo and cavetto are moldings. Ovolo is a convex molding; cavetto is a concave molding.

53. CANTERBURY : (A. Chaucer, B. Hemingway, C. Updike, D. Forster) :: CASTERBRIDGE : HARDY

(**A**) Canterbury is the destination in Chaucer's work *The Canterbury Tales;* Casterbridge is the city in the Thomas Hardy novel *The Mayor of Casterbridge*.

54. (A. laugh, B. weep, C. cringe, D. geese) : QUAIL :: GAGGLE : COVEY

(D) A covey is a flock of quail; a gaggle is a flock of geese.

55. MANY : RAINDROPS :: MUCH : (A. flood, B. snowflakes, C. puddle, D. water)

(D) This is a grammatical analogy. The adjective *many* is used to describe a quantity of an object that can be counted; the adjective *much* is used to describe a volume that cannot be counted.

56. HEART : STOMACH :: (A. veins, B. arteries, C. intestines, D. capillaries) : DUODENUM

(B) The contents of the stomach empty directly into the duodenum (the top part of the small intestine); blood from the heart goes directly into arteries for distribution.

57. BRISTLES : (A. razor, B. toothbrush, C. monkey, D. flower) :: FEATHERS : DUSTER

(B) Feathers are part of a feather duster; bristles are part of a toothbrush. This is a part-to-whole analogy.

58. CHEETAH : LEOPARD :: WOLF : (A. feline, B. canine, C. dog, D. lupus)

(C) This is a part-to-part analogy. The cheetah and leopard are both members of the feline family; the wolf and dog are both members of the canine family.

59. TILES : (A. checkers, B. faucet, C. badminton, D. mah-jongg) :: DICE : BACKGAMMON

(D) This is an analogy of part-to-whole. Tiles are used in the game of mah-jongg; dice are used in the game of backgammon. Although checkers uses round game pieces, they are not traditionally known as tiles.

60. (A. statehouse, B. battlement, C. church, D. fortress) : CHURCH :: CITADEL : CATHEDRAL

(D) A cathedral is a church; a citadel is a fortress.

61. $5 : \sqrt{36} :: 8 :$ (A. 9, B. $\sqrt{81}$, C. $\sqrt{9}$, D. $\sqrt{64}$)

(B) The relationship is between a number and the expression of a square root. 5 is one less than the square root of 36; 8 is one less than the square root of 81. Therefore, the analogy should read, $5 : \sqrt{36} :: 8 : \sqrt{81}$. Choice A makes a correct statement but is not a perfect analogy. If choice B were not offered, then A would suffice. However, you must always choose the answer that creates the most perfect analogy.

62. (A. crime, B. punishment, C. jury, D. verdict) : SENTENCE :: ANTEPENULT : PENULT

(D) This is a sequential analogy. The antepenult is the third syllable from the end of a word; the penult is the next-to-the-last syllable of a word. In the sequence of events from crime to punishment, verdict comes immediately before sentence.

63. PANDA : (A. condor, B. bear, C. goldfish, D. ostrich) :: RACCOON : CROW

(A) The raccoon and crow are both plentiful, common creatures; the panda and condor are both members of endangered species.

64. *LUSITANIA* : BRITAIN :: 007 : (A. Japan, B. Korea, C. USSR, D. James Bond)

(B) The *Lusitania* was a British ship that was sunk by the Germans; flight 007 was a Korean airplane that was shot down and sunk by the Soviets in the Sea of Japan. The salient relationship is that between the vessel and the country to which it belonged.

65. YARD : FATHOM :: (A. eclipse, B. new, C. half, D. moon) : FULL

(C) In the parlance of measurement, a yard (3 feet) is half of a fathom (6 feet). In speaking of the moon, a half moon is half of a full moon.

66. LANGSTON HUGHES : DOUGHTRY LONG :: (A. Marianne Moore, B. Gwendolyn Brooks, C. Gertrude Stein, D. Emily Dickinson) : MAYA ANGELOU

(B) Langston Hughes and Doughtry Long are both black male poets; Gwendolyn Brooks and Maya Angelou are both black female poets.

67. SAT® : (A. PEP, B. ACT®, C. TAT, D. NTE®) :: GRE® : MAT

(B) The GRE (Graduate Record Exam) and MAT (Miller Analogies Test) are both qualifying examinations for graduate school; the SAT (Scholastic Assessment Test) and ACT (American College Testing Program) are both qualifying examinations for college admission.

68. TULIP : ASTER :: SPRING : (A. chicken, B. jump, C. fall, D. well)

(C) The nature of the relationship is association. A tulip is a flower associated with spring; an aster is a flower associated with fall.

69. BOLL WEEVIL : GYPSY MOTH :: (A. bee, B. termite, C. cockroach, D. louse) : PRAYING MANTIS

(A) A boll weevil and a gypsy moth are both harmful insects. A bee and a praying mantis are both beneficial insects that prey upon harmful insects.

70. GHENT : (A. American Revolution, B. World War I, C. War of 1812, D. Hundred Years' War) :: P'ANMUNJOM : KOREAN WAR

(C) Panmunjom was the site of the signing of the Peace Treaty ending the Korean War; Ghent (in Belgium) was the site of the signing of the Peace Treaty ending the War of 1812.

71. (A. Nymph, B. Syrinx, C. Naiad, D. Chaos) : PAN :: ECHO : NARCISSUS

(B) Echo was a nymph loved by Narcissus; Syrinx was a nymph loved by Pan.

72. (A. terrapin, B. terrestrial, C. teuton, D. termagant) : SYCOPHANT :: VIRAGO : TOADY

(D) On each side of the proportion, the words are synonyms. A virago is a quarrelsome woman, a shrew, or a termagant; a toady is a fawning person, a flatterer, or a sycophant.

73. KNESSET : ISRAEL :: DIET : (A. Kashrut, B. Luther, C. Japan, D. Congress)

(C) The Knesset is the lawmaking body of the government of Israel; the Diet serves as the congressional arm of the government of Japan.

74. *LES MISÈRABLES* : VICTOR HUGO :: (A. *Le Rouge et le Noir*, B. *Notre Dame de Paris*, C. *Les Trois Mousquetaires*, D. *Madame Bovary*) : ALEXANDRE DUMAS

(C) *Les Misèrables* is a novel written by Victor Hugo; *Les Trois Mousquetaires* is a novel written by Alexandre Dumas.

75. ITS : IT'S :: (A. their, B. their's, C. there, D. there's) : THEY'RE

(A) This is a grammatical analogy. Simply stated, the relationship on both sides of the proportion is possessive: contraction. *Its* is the possessive of *it,* while *it's* is the contraction for *it is; their* is the possessive of *they,* while *they're* is the contraction for *they are.*

76. NICTATE : WINK :: (A. oscillate, B. osculate, C. ossify, D. oscultate) : KISS

(B) The analogy is based upon synonyms. To nictate is to wink; to osculate is to kiss.

77. INFLUENZA : VIRUS :: HODGKIN'S DISEASE : (A. schizophrenia, B. kidney disease, C. leprosy, D. cancer)

(D) Influenza is one type of virus; Hodgkin's Disease is a form of cancer.

78. 28 : 82 :: 56 : (A. 54, B. 30, C. 65, D. 136)

(C) The relationship of the numbers is a nonmathematical one. The second number is merely a mirror image of the first.

79. MAMA LUCIA : (A. *Lucia de Lamermoor,* B. *Cavalleria Rusticana,* C. *Marriage of Figaro,* D. *Tosca*) :: FIGARO : BARBER OF SEVILLE

(B) Figaro is a character in the opera *Barber of Seville;* Mama Lucia is a character in the opera *Cavalleria Rusticana.*

80. MINNEAPOLIS : NEW ORLEANS :: ALBANY : (A. Boston, B. Cleveland, C. New York, D. Louisiana)

(C) The source of the Mississippi River is in Minnesota very close to the city of Minneapolis, while the mouth of the Mississippi River is at New Orleans; the source of the Hudson River is very close to the city of Albany, while the mouth of the Hudson River is at New York City.

81. STAG : BILLY :: DOE : (A. William, B. Hinny, C. Kid, D. Nanny)

(D) This analogy is based upon gender, that is, the relationship of male to female. A stag is a male deer; a doe is a female deer. *Billy* is the commonly used term referring to a male goat; *nanny* is the counterpart for a female goat.

82. ROGET : (A. bridge, B. synonyms, C. thesaurus, D. quiz shows) :: MILLER : ANALOGIES

(B) The subject of the examination devised by W.S. Miller is analogies; the subject of the book compiled by Roget is synonyms.

83. OCULIST : OPHTHALMOLOGIST :: CHIROPODIST : (A. chiropractor, B. pediatrician, C. osteopath, D. podiatrist)

(D) The analogy is based upon similarity of function. Both an oculist and an ophthalmologist are eye doctors; both a chiropodist and a podiatrist are foot doctors.

84. GNU : GNAT :: (A. koala, B. knight, C. kestrell, D. kangaroo) : KNAVE

(B) This is a nonsemantic analogy. Both a gnu and a gnat are creatures whose names begin with a silent letter "g"; both a knight and a knave are persons whose names begin with a silent letter "k."

85. ALLAH : (A. Islam, B. Mohammed, C. Christianity, D. God) :: HORUS : NEPTUNE

(**D**) Horus and Neptune are both gods in polytheistic religions; both Allah and God are the deities of monotheistic religions.

86. 15 : 5 :: 23 : (A. 1, B. 2, C. 5, D. 6)

(**D**) This is a different style of relationship, found by multiplying the two numbers in each double-digit number (15 and 23). $1 \times 5 = 5$; $2 \times 3 = 6$.

87. CYRILLIC : RUSSIAN :: ROMAN : (A. Gypsy, B. English, C. numerals, D. Arabic)

(**B**) The Russian language is written in the Cyrillic alphabet; the English language is written in the Roman alphabet.

88. PASTERN : (A. flank, B. rural, C. horse, D. duck) :: PISTIL : STAMEN

(**A**) The pistil and stamen are both parts of a flower; the pastern and flank are both parts of a horse. The relationship is that of part to part.

89. @ : & :: 2 : (A. #, B. 5, C. 7, D. $\frac{1}{2}$)

(**C**) This analogy is based upon the location of certain symbols on the keyboard. The "@" symbol is on the same key as the 2; the "&" symbol shares a key with the 7.

90. SADAT : JERUSALEM :: (A. Mao Tse-tung, B. Nixon, C. Ho Chi Minh, D. Sun Yat Sen) : CHINA

(**B**) You might call the area of commonality "improbable visits." Anwar Sadat, an Egyptian hard-liner, visited Jerusalem. Richard Nixon, a conservative president, went to China. Mao Tse-tung and Sun Yat Sen were Chinese leaders.

91. (A. Alice, B. Medusa, C. King Arthur, D. Minerva) : ADONIS :: QUASIMODO : SNOW WHITE

(**B**) The analogy is between hideous ugliness and great beauty. Quasimodo was the hunchback in Victor Hugo's *Hunchback of Notre Dame,* while Snow White was a beautiful fairy tale heroine. Medusa, in Greek mythology, was a Gorgon and very ugly, while Adonis, also from Greek mythology, was the epitome of male beauty.

92. ANTHROPOLOGY : MARGARET MEAD :: (A. archaeology, B. history, C. philosophy, D. psychology) : HOWARD CARTER

(**A**) Margaret Mead was a famous anthropologist; Howard Carter was an English archaeologist.

93. AMBITION : MACBETH :: JEALOUSY : (A. Caesar, B. Brutus, C. Othello, D. Shylock)

(**C**) Ambition was the force that drove Macbeth; jealousy was the force that drove Othello.

94. *FAUST* : (A. Mephistopheles, B. Goethe, C. folklore, D. underworld) :: *WASTELAND* : ELIOT

(**B**) The analogy is one of product to its creator. The dramatic poem *Faust* was written by Goethe; the classic poem *The Wasteland* was written by T.S. Eliot.

95. (A. ibid., B. etc., C. asst., D. dz.) : ET AL. :: OP. CIT. : CF

(**A**) The analogy is based upon the location in which the abbreviation is likely to be found. Op. cit. (in the work cited) and cf (compare) are both abbreviations from the Latin commonly used in footnotes. Ibid. (in the same place) and et al. (and others) are also footnote abbreviations.

96. YALTA : ROOSEVELT :: (A. Munich, B. Potsdam, C. Bastogne. D. Corregidor) : TRUMAN

(**B**) Yalta was the site of a conference of the three major allies of World War II at which President Roosevelt represented the United States; Potsdam was the site of a later conference at which President Truman represented the United States.

97. *THE MAGIC FLUTE* : (A. *Iolanthe*, B. *Turandot*, C. *Il Trovatore*, D. *Don Giovanni*) :: *AIDA* : *DON CARLOS*

(**D**) *Aida* and *Don Carlos* are both operas written by Verdi; *The Magic Flute* and *Don Giovanni* are operas written by Mozart.

98. OXYGEN : (A. air, B. water, C. carbon dioxide, D. carbon monoxide) :: FAUNA : FLORA

(**C**) The relationship of fauna (animal life) to oxygen is that animals breathe oxygen. The relationship of flora (plant life) to carbon dioxide is that plants breathe carbon dioxide.

99. (A. Sleeping Beauty, B. Cinderella, C. Rapunzel, D. Goldilocks) : PRINCE CHARMING :: FROG : PRINCESS

(**A**) The frog was under a wicked spell that was broken by the kiss of the princess; Sleeping Beauty was under a wicked spell that was broken by the kiss of Prince Charming.

100. 9 : 104 :: BEETHOVEN : (A. Mozart, B. Sibelius, C. Haydn, D. Casals)

(**C**) Beethoven wrote 9 symphonies; Haydn was very prolific and wrote 104.

SAMPLE TEST 7

Answer Sheet

1. ⓐ ⓑ ⓒ ⓓ
2. ⓐ ⓑ ⓒ ⓓ
3. ⓐ ⓑ ⓒ ⓓ
4. ⓐ ⓑ ⓒ ⓓ
5. ⓐ ⓑ ⓒ ⓓ
6. ⓐ ⓑ ⓒ ⓓ
7. ⓐ ⓑ ⓒ ⓓ
8. ⓐ ⓑ ⓒ ⓓ
9. ⓐ ⓑ ⓒ ⓓ
10. ⓐ ⓑ ⓒ ⓓ
11. ⓐ ⓑ ⓒ ⓓ
12. ⓐ ⓑ ⓒ ⓓ
13. ⓐ ⓑ ⓒ ⓓ
14. ⓐ ⓑ ⓒ ⓓ
15. ⓐ ⓑ ⓒ ⓓ
16. ⓐ ⓑ ⓒ ⓓ
17. ⓐ ⓑ ⓒ ⓓ
18. ⓐ ⓑ ⓒ ⓓ
19. ⓐ ⓑ ⓒ ⓓ
20. ⓐ ⓑ ⓒ ⓓ
21. ⓐ ⓑ ⓒ ⓓ
22. ⓐ ⓑ ⓒ ⓓ
23. ⓐ ⓑ ⓒ ⓓ
24. ⓐ ⓑ ⓒ ⓓ
25. ⓐ ⓑ ⓒ ⓓ
26. ⓐ ⓑ ⓒ ⓓ
27. ⓐ ⓑ ⓒ ⓓ
28. ⓐ ⓑ ⓒ ⓓ
29. ⓐ ⓑ ⓒ ⓓ
30. ⓐ ⓑ ⓒ ⓓ
31. ⓐ ⓑ ⓒ ⓓ
32. ⓐ ⓑ ⓒ ⓓ
33. ⓐ ⓑ ⓒ ⓓ
34. ⓐ ⓑ ⓒ ⓓ
35. ⓐ ⓑ ⓒ ⓓ
36. ⓐ ⓑ ⓒ ⓓ
37. ⓐ ⓑ ⓒ ⓓ
38. ⓐ ⓑ ⓒ ⓓ
39. ⓐ ⓑ ⓒ ⓓ
40. ⓐ ⓑ ⓒ ⓓ
41. ⓐ ⓑ ⓒ ⓓ
42. ⓐ ⓑ ⓒ ⓓ
43. ⓐ ⓑ ⓒ ⓓ
44. ⓐ ⓑ ⓒ ⓓ
45. ⓐ ⓑ ⓒ ⓓ
46. ⓐ ⓑ ⓒ ⓓ
47. ⓐ ⓑ ⓒ ⓓ
48. ⓐ ⓑ ⓒ ⓓ
49. ⓐ ⓑ ⓒ ⓓ
50. ⓐ ⓑ ⓒ ⓓ
51. ⓐ ⓑ ⓒ ⓓ
52. ⓐ ⓑ ⓒ ⓓ
53. ⓐ ⓑ ⓒ ⓓ
54. ⓐ ⓑ ⓒ ⓓ
55. ⓐ ⓑ ⓒ ⓓ
56. ⓐ ⓑ ⓒ ⓓ
57. ⓐ ⓑ ⓒ ⓓ
58. ⓐ ⓑ ⓒ ⓓ
59. ⓐ ⓑ ⓒ ⓓ
60. ⓐ ⓑ ⓒ ⓓ
61. ⓐ ⓑ ⓒ ⓓ
62. ⓐ ⓑ ⓒ ⓓ
63. ⓐ ⓑ ⓒ ⓓ
64. ⓐ ⓑ ⓒ ⓓ
65. ⓐ ⓑ ⓒ ⓓ
66. ⓐ ⓑ ⓒ ⓓ
67. ⓐ ⓑ ⓒ ⓓ
68. ⓐ ⓑ ⓒ ⓓ
69. ⓐ ⓑ ⓒ ⓓ
70. ⓐ ⓑ ⓒ ⓓ
71. ⓐ ⓑ ⓒ ⓓ
72. ⓐ ⓑ ⓒ ⓓ
73. ⓐ ⓑ ⓒ ⓓ
74. ⓐ ⓑ ⓒ ⓓ
75. ⓐ ⓑ ⓒ ⓓ
76. ⓐ ⓑ ⓒ ⓓ
77. ⓐ ⓑ ⓒ ⓓ
78. ⓐ ⓑ ⓒ ⓓ
79. ⓐ ⓑ ⓒ ⓓ
80. ⓐ ⓑ ⓒ ⓓ
81. ⓐ ⓑ ⓒ ⓓ
82. ⓐ ⓑ ⓒ ⓓ
83. ⓐ ⓑ ⓒ ⓓ
84. ⓐ ⓑ ⓒ ⓓ
85. ⓐ ⓑ ⓒ ⓓ
86. ⓐ ⓑ ⓒ ⓓ
87. ⓐ ⓑ ⓒ ⓓ
88. ⓐ ⓑ ⓒ ⓓ
89. ⓐ ⓑ ⓒ ⓓ
90. ⓐ ⓑ ⓒ ⓓ
91. ⓐ ⓑ ⓒ ⓓ
92. ⓐ ⓑ ⓒ ⓓ
93. ⓐ ⓑ ⓒ ⓓ
94. ⓐ ⓑ ⓒ ⓓ
95. ⓐ ⓑ ⓒ ⓓ
96. ⓐ ⓑ ⓒ ⓓ
97. ⓐ ⓑ ⓒ ⓓ
98. ⓐ ⓑ ⓒ ⓓ
99. ⓐ ⓑ ⓒ ⓓ
100. ⓐ ⓑ ⓒ ⓓ

TEAR HERE

Chapter 11

Sample Test 7

100 Questions • 50 Minutes

> **Directions:** Each of these test questions consists of three capitalized words and four lettered words enclosed in parentheses. Two of the capitalized words are related in some way. Find the two related words, and establish the nature of the relationship. Then study the four words lettered A, B, C, and D. Select the one lettered word that is related to the remaining capitalized word in the same way that the first two capitalized words are related. Mark the answer sheet for the letter preceding the word you select.

ROAD MAP

- *Answer Key*
- *Explanatory Answers*

1. TINY : (A. dwarf, B. small, C. infinitesimal, D. huge) :: BIG : ENORMOUS

2. LAMP : LIGHT :: CHAIR : (A. stool, B. table, C. back, D. seat)

3. (A. bud, B. spring, C. flower, D. blossom) : BLOOM :: FADE : FALL

4. BLUE : (A. gold, B. gray, C. red, D. green) :: NORTH : SOUTH

5. DOCKET : COURT :: (A. agenda, B. itinerary, C. calendar, D. route) : TRIP

6. NEITHER : WEIRD :: (A. friend, B. yield, C. receipt, D. height) : LEISURE

7. BERING STRAIT : SEWARD PENINSULA :: STRAIT OF MAGELLAN : (A. Trazos-Montes, B. Tierra del Fuego, C. Matan, D. Malay Peninsula)

8. *LORD OF THE FLIES* : *LORD OF THE RINGS* :: GOLDING : (A. Swift, B. King Arthur, C. Tolkien, D. Beckett)

9. ATROPHY : (A. eyes, B. muscles, C. teeth, D. veins) :: INFLAMED : JOINTS

10. ERNEST : RUDYARD :: HEMINGWAY : (A. Proust, B. Lotus, C. Kipling, D. Brecht)

11. $\frac{4}{8} : \frac{8}{4} :: \frac{5}{15} :$ (A. $\frac{1}{3}$, B. $\frac{2}{3}$, C. $\frac{15}{5}$, D. $\frac{3}{1}$)

12. MAY DAY : (A. Labor Day, B. Christmas, C. Bastille Day, D. Tet) :: RAMADAN : LENT

13. INGENUOUS : (A. frank, B. aloof, C. clever, D. pretty) :: INIQUITOUS : WICKED

14. PROTRACTOR : ANGLES :: COMPASS : (A. tones, B. area, C. topography, D. direction)

15. TENNESSEE WILLIAMS : *THE GLASS MENAGERIE* :: (A. Thornton Wilder, B. Luigi Pirandello, C. Maxwell Anderson, D. Noel Coward) : *SIX CHARACTERS IN SEARCH OF AN AUTHOR*

16. INJURY : PARAPLEGIA :: STROKE : (A. aphasia, B. quadriplegia, C. fantasia, D. hemiplegia)

17. LIKES : EVERYONE :: (A. indifferent, B. wish, C. loves, D. care) : NOBODY

18. SEPTEMBER : (A. October, B. January, C. Thursday, D. planting) :: HARVEST MOON : HUNTER'S MOON

19. ERATO : THALIA :: (A. movies, B. sleep, C. poetry, D. death) : COMEDY

20. (A. anglophile, B. bibliophile, C. oenophile, D. vines) : WINE :: FRANCOPHILE : FRANCE

21. 6 : –6 :: 31 : (A. –2, B. 3, C. –13, D. 19)

22. RIVE GAUCHE : PARIS :: (A. New Jersey, B. Albany, C. Riker's Island, D. Brooklyn) : NEW YORK

23. SURINAME : (A. Guyana, B. British Honduras, C. Belize, D. Dutch Guiana.) :: ZIMBABWE : RHODESIA

24. BAROQUE : VIVALDI :: (A. Classical, B. Romantic, C. Rococo, D. Impressionist) : SCHUMANN

25. OBSEQUIOUS : OBSTINATE :: DIFFIDENT : (A. indifferent, B. shy, C. distinct, D. defiant)

26. SHIITE : (A. Arab, B. Muslim, C. Sunni, D. Iran) :: ROMAN CATHOLIC : PROTESTANT

27. HONOR : CITATION :: SPEEDING : (A. citation, B. hurry, C. race, D. stop)

28. *HEDDA GABLER* : (A. *The Cherry Orchard*, B. *Riders to the Sea*, C. *An Enemy of the People*, D. *Blood Wedding*) :: *ANNA CHRISTIE* : *MOON FOR THE MISBEGOTTEN*

29. YELLOW : (A. jonquil, B. cornflower, C. rose, D. jacket) :: RED : SALVIA

30. ANODE : CATHODE :: OXIDATION : (A. erosion, B. reduction, C. carbonization, D. hydrogenation)

31. CELLO : VIOLIN :: (A. clarinet, B. French horn, C. accordion, D. rebec) : SAXOPHONE

32. JOAN OF ARC : (A. Pope, B. stake, C. king, D. saint) :: GALILEO : SUN

33. (A. Yeats, B. Shakespeare, C. Chaucer, D. Tennyson) : SONNETS :: NASH : LIMERICKS

34. RACQUETBALL : PLATFORM TENNIS :: HOCKEY : (A. badminton, B. rugby, C. volleyball, D. curling)

35. ST. PETERSBURG : HERMITAGE :: (A. Spain, B. Majorca, C. Madrid, D. Seville) : PRADO

36. ABSCISSA : (A. ordinate, B. mantissa, C. coordinate, D. precision) :: X : Y

37. SKINNER : BEHAVIORISM :: (A. Adler, B. Terman, C. Kant, D. Wertheimer) : GESTALT

38. HESTER : INFIDELITY :: (A. Cordelia, B. Goneril, C. Ophelia, D. Cassandra) : DEVOTION

39. CAPILLARIES : CIRCULATION :: VILLI : (A. respiration, B. digestion, C. recreation, D. procreation)

40. SAN MARINO : ITALY :: (A. Ethiopia, B. Capetown, C. Lesotho, D. Swaziland) : SOUTH AFRICA

41. (A. Florida, B. New Mexico, C. Puerto Rico, D. Texas) : ALASKA :: SPAIN : RUSSIA

42. KEYNES : ECONOMICS :: DEWEY : (A. zoology, B. electronics, C. medicine, D. education)

43. NEIL ARMSTRONG : YURI GAGARIN :: CHARLES LINDBERGH : (A. George Washington, B. Albert Einstein, C. Orville Wright, D. Guglielmo Marconi)

44. *PILGRIM'S PROGRESS* : (A. *Inferno*, B. *Paradise Lost*, C. *De Monarchia*, D. *Divine Comedy*) :: BUNYAN : DANTE

45. GENGHIS KHAN : MONGOLS :: ATTILA : (A. Roman Empire, B. Germany, C. Huns, D. Tatars)

46. HARE : (A. rabbit, B. tortoise, C. terrapin, D. hart) :: FOX : GRAPES

47. 4 : 6 :: (A. 10, B. 6, C. 9, D. 16) : 36

48. THOMAS MANN : *BUDDENBROOKS* :: THOMAS WOLFE : (A. *Death in Venice*, B. *Look Homeward, Angel*, C. *The Magic Mountain*, D. *Joseph and His Brothers*)

49. (A. Earth, B. moon, C. Russia, D. Stalin) : SPUTNIK :: JUPITER : IO

50. FREYA : ASGARD :: (A. Hera, B. Venus, C. Minerva, D. Aphrodite) : OLYMPUS

51. (A. isosceles, B. scalene, C. right, D. obtuse) : EQUILATERAL :: DUPLE : TRIPLE

52. ELWAY : JORDAN :: (A. football, B. baseball, C. hockey, D. horseracing) : BASKETBALL

53. OBVERSE : (A. coin, B. sweater, C. reverse, D. crochet) :: KNIT : PURL

54. PASTEL : MUTED :: LIGHT : (A. sound, B. voice, C. trumpet, D. wheel)

55. (A. one, B. two, C. three, D. nine) : BETWEEN :: SIX : AMONG

56. XENOPHOBIA : PREJUDICE :: PECCATOPHOBIA : (A. tantrums, B. bad habits, C. clumsiness, D. virtue)

57. HARPSICHORD : VIRGINAL :: (A. piccolo, B. saxophone, C. sousaphone, D. oboe) : CLARINET

58. LEAGUE : YARD :: MILES : (A. inches, B. feet, C. yards, D. furlongs)

59. ATOM : MOLECULE :: GENE : (A. heredity, B. genetics, C. DNA, D. chromosome)

60. FIRE : SMOKE :: (A. pipe, B. hose, C. leak, D. break) : STAIN

GO ON TO THE NEXT PAGE

61. BUTTER : MARGARINE :: SUGAR : (A. salt, B. strychnine, C. aspartame, D. vinegar)

62. TOM SAWYER : (A. Mark Twain, B. Samuel Langhorne Clemens, C. Becky Thatcher, D. David Copperfield) :: PORTHOS : ATHOS

63. (A. white, B. bluing, C. blanch, D. yellow) : BLEACH :: HENNA : ANIL

64. CHECKERS : RICHARD NIXON :: TRAVELER : (A. Robert E. Lee, B. Franklin Roosevelt, C. Dwight Eisenhower, D. Aristotle Onassis)

65. BRUTE : SQUIRE :: TUBER : (A. leaves, B. yams, C. quires, D. sterns)

66. $\frac{1}{8}$: 12.5% :: (A. $\frac{1}{6}$, B. $\frac{3}{11}$, C. $\frac{2}{7}$, D. $\frac{3}{8}$) : 37.5%

67. CRETACEOUS : DINOSAURS :: TERTIARY : (A. vampires, B. fish, C. reptiles, D. mammals)

68. MAPLE : (A. syrup, B. oak, C. cyanide, D. leaf) :: PRIVET : HEMLOCK

69. (A. Washington, B. Jefferson, C. Franklin, D. Lincoln) : MADISON :: DECLARATION OF INDEPENDENCE : CONSTITUTION

70. ALZHEIMER'S DISEASE : HANSEN'S DISEASE :: (A. cerebral palsy, B. copper deficiency, C. dementia, D. lymphatic cancer) : LEPROSY

71. SALVADOR DALI : RENE MAGRITTE :: (A. e.e. cummings, B. William Wordsworth, C. Jack London, D. Leo Tolstoy) : DON MARQUIS

72. INDEPENDENCE : COOPERATION :: PHOTOSYNTHESIS : (A. parasitism, B. parthenogenesis, C. symbiosis, D. carbohydrates)

73. (A. stars, B. restaurants, C. tires, D. highways) : MICHELIN :: GASOLINE : MOBIL

74. SWIFT : (A. Barrie, B. Kipling, C. Dorothy, D. Baum) :: LILLIPUT : OZ

75. FOUR : BASEBALL :: (A. ten, B. eleven, C. fifty, D. one hundred twenty) : FOOTBALL

76. (A. remuneration, B. stipend, C. pay, D. overtime) : SALARY :: COMMISSION : ROYALTY

77. LAWYER : BARRISTER :: ATTORNEY : (A. judge, B. juror, C. advocate, D. appellant)

78. KOALA : (A. eucalyptus, B. wallaby, C. bamboo, D. mulberry) :: WHALE : PLANKTON

79. DEER : (A. deer, B. moose, C. dear, D. swan) :: GOOSE : GEESE

80. 27 : (A. 3, B. 9, C. 5.19, D. 729) :: 125 : 5

81. EGG : CHICKEN :: CHICKEN : (A. rooster, B. capon, C. egg, D. hen)

82. PARIS : FRANCE :: (A. Tripoli, B. Rabat, C. Marseilles, D. Dakar) : SENEGAL

83. CCC : TVA :: FDIC : (A. OPA, B. WMC, C. OSS, D. FHA)

84. ELABORATE : (A. streamlined, B. boring, C. oblique, D. obligatory) :: SERIF : SANS SERIF

85. BULL RUN : MANASSAS :: STREAM : (A. battle, B. town, C. war, D. tribe)

86. GREENWICH VILLAGE : (A. London, B. Kensington, C. New York, D. Piccadilly Circus) :: MONTMARTRE : PARIS

87. UNITED STATES : DOW JONES :: JAPAN : (A. Hang Seng, B. Nikkei, C. Tokyo, D. Kyoto)

88. ZOLA : *NANA* :: (A. Humbert Humbert, B. Don Juan, C. Don Quixote, D. Nabokov) : *LOLITA*

89. KANT : CATEGORICAL IMPERATIVE :: (A. Descartes, B. Nietzsche, C. Sartre, D. Mill) : UTILITY

90. NOON : EVENING :: (A. snack, B. lunch, C. brunch, D. afternoon) : DINNER

91. MENTICIDE : BRAINWASHING :: OPPROBRIUM : (A. commendation, B. reproach, C. indoctrination, D. repression)

92. CALPURNIA : (A. Oedipus, B. Caesar, C. King Lear, D. Cicero) :: CRESSIDA : TROILUS

93. BLIND : DEAF :: (A. Milton, B. Scott, C. Mozart, D. Justice) : BEETHOVEN

94. REMUS : (A. Brer Rabbit, B. Aquarius, C. Quisling, D. Romulus) :: CASTOR : POLLUX

95. DOG : FLEA :: HORSE : (A. rider, B. fly, C. mane, D. shoe)

96. 10 : (A. decimal, B. common, C. unnatural, D. metric) :: e : NATURAL

97. BROUGHAM : CARRIAGE :: HOME : (A. horse, B. town, C. domicile, D. family)

98. DRACHMA · (A. Brazil, B. Nigeria, C. Greece, D. India) :: LIRA : ITALY

99. (A. Shangri-La, B. Lilliput, C. Atlantis, D. Ilium) : BRIGADOON :: FOUNTAIN OF YOUTH : NEVER-NEVER LAND

100. PARTHENON : PANTHEON :: (A. Taj Mahal, B. St. Paul's, C. Angkor Wat, D. Erechtheum) : SISTINE CHAPEL

ANSWER KEY

1. C	21. D	41. A	61. C	81. C
2. D	22. D	42. D	62. C	82. D
3. A	23. D	43. C	63. B	83. D
4. B	24. B	44. D	64. A	84. A
5. B	25. D	45. C	65. C	85. B
6. D	26. C	46. B	66. D	86. C
7. B	27. A	47. D	67. D	87. B
8. C	28. C	48. B	68. B	88. D
9. B	29. A	49. A	69. B	89. D
10. C	30. B	50. D	70. C	90. B
11. C	31. A	51. A	71. A	91. B
12. A	32. C	52. A	72. C	92. B
13. A	33. B	53. C	73. C	93. A
14. D	34. D	54. A	74. D	94. D
15. B	35. C	55. B	75. A	95. B
16. D	36. A	56. D	76. B	96. B
17. C	37. D	57. D	77. C	97. C
18. A	38. A	58. B	78. A	98. C
19. C	39. B	59. D	79. A	99. A
20. C	40. C	60. C	80. A	100. D

EXPLANATORY ANSWERS

1. TINY : (A. dwarf, B. small, C. infinitesimal, D. huge) :: BIG : ENORMOUS

(**C**) This is an analogy of degree. Enormous is an intense degree of big; infinitesimal is an intense degree of tiny.

2. LAMP : LIGHT :: CHAIR : (A. stool, B. table, C. back, D. seat)

(**D**) This is an analogy not of true synonyms but of synonyms as used in common parlance. Thus, "turn on a light" is used interchangeably with "turn on a lamp," and "have a seat" is used interchangeably with "have a chair."

3. (A. bud, B. spring, C. flower, D. blossom) : BLOOM :: FADE : FALL

(**A**) This analogy is based upon sequence. A flower must fade before it falls. The same flower must bud before it can bloom. The sequence is bud, bloom, fade, fall.

4. BLUE : (A. gold, B. gray, C. red, D. green) :: NORTH : SOUTH

(**B**) During the Civil War, the uniforms of the North were blue, and the uniforms of the South were gray. This is an analogy of association.

5. DOCKET : COURT :: (A. agenda, B. itinerary, C. calendar, D. route) : TRIP

(**B**) The court docket is the official register of cases to be tried; the trip itinerary is the step-by-step schedule for a trip including the route to be traveled, sights to be seen, and stops to be made.

6. NEITHER : WEIRD :: (A. friend, B. yield, C. receipt, D. height) : LEISURE

(**D**) This is a grammatical analogy. It is based upon the fact that the related words are all exceptions to the "*i* before *e* except after *c*" spelling rule. *Neither* and *weird* are both exceptions to this rule; so are *height* and *leisure*.

7. BERING STRAIT : SEWARD PENINSULA :: STRAIT OF MAGELLAN : (A. Trazos-Montes, B. Tierra del Fuego, C. Matan, D. Malay Peninsula)

(**B**) The Bering Strait separates the Seward Peninsula from Russia; the Strait of Magellan separates Tierra del Fuego from mainland South America.

8. *LORD OF THE FLIES* : *LORD OF THE RINGS* :: GOLDING : (A. Swift, B. King Arthur, C. Tolkien, D. Beckett)

(**C**) Golding is the author of *Lord of the Flies;* Tolkien is the author of *Lord of the Rings*.

9. ATROPHY : (A. eyes, B. muscles, C. teeth, D. veins) :: INFLAMED : JOINTS

(**B**) The analogy is based upon the association of body part to malady. Joints can become inflamed; muscles can atrophy or waste away.

10. ERNEST : RUDYARD :: HEMINGWAY : (A. Proust, B. Lotus, C. Kipling, D. Brecht)

(**C**) In this literary analogy, the relationship is based upon association of first and last names. Ernest Hemingway was an author, as was Rudyard Kipling.

11. $\frac{4}{8} : \frac{8}{4} :: \frac{5}{15} :$ (A. $\frac{1}{3}$, B. $\frac{2}{3}$, C. $\frac{15}{5}$, D. $\frac{3}{1}$)

(C) This is a simple relationship. The second term is the reciprocal of the first. $\frac{8}{4}$ is the reciprocal of $\frac{4}{8}$; $\frac{15}{5}$ is the reciprocal of $\frac{5}{15}$.

12. MAY DAY : (A. Labor Day, B. Christmas, C. Bastille Day, D. Tet) :: RAMADAN : LENT

(A) Ramadan and Lent are both prolonged periods of fasting and prayer—Ramadan for the Moslems, and Lent for Christians. May Day and Labor Day are both secular holidays in celebration of labor.

13. INGENUOUS : (A. frank, B. aloof, C. clever, D. pretty) :: INIQUITOUS : WICKED

(A) This is an analogy of synonyms. *Iniquitous* means *wicked*; *ingenuous* means *frank* or *open*.

14. PROTRACTOR : ANGLES :: COMPASS : (A. tones, B. area, C. topography, D. direction)

(D) This analogy is based upon function. The function of a protractor is to measure angles; the function of a compass is to measure direction.

15. TENNESSEE WILLIAMS : *THE GLASS MENAGERIE* :: (A. Thornton Wilder, B. Luigi Pirandello, C. Maxwell Anderson, D. Noel Coward) : *SIX CHARACTERS IN SEARCH OF AN AUTHOR*

(B) Tennessee Williams is the author of *The Glass Menagerie;* Luigi Pirandello is the author of *Six Characters in Search of an Author*.

16. INJURY : PARAPLEGIA :: STROKE : (A. aphasia, B. quadriplegia, C. fantasia, D. hemiplegia)

(D) An injury to the spinal column may cause paralysis of the lower half of the body—paraplegia; a stroke may cause paralysis of either the right or left half of the body—hemiplegia.

17. LIKES : EVERYONE :: (A. indifferent, B. wish, C. loves, D. care) : NOBODY

(C) This analogy is a grammatical one. *Everyone* is a singular pronoun that takes the singular form of the verb *likes; nobody* is a singular pronoun that takes the singular form of the verb *loves*.

18. SEPTEMBER : (A. October, B. January, C. Thursday, D. planting) :: HARVEST MOON : HUNTER'S MOON

(A) The Harvest Moon, the full moon following the autumnal equinox, generally falls in September; the Hunter's Moon, the next full moon following the Harvest Moon, generally falls in October.

19. ERATO : THALIA :: (A. movies, B. sleep, C. poetry, D. death) : COMEDY

(C) Erato and Thalia are both muses. Erato is the muse of poetry; Thalia is the muse of comedy.

20. (A. anglophile, B. bibliophile, C. oenophile, D. vines) : WINE :: FRANCOPHILE : FRANCE

(C) A francophile loves France. An oenophile loves wine.

21. 6 : –6 :: 31 : (A. –2, B. 3, C. –13, D. 19)

(D) The only feasible mathematical relationship is that of subtraction. 6 – 12 = –6; 31 – 12 = 19. The analogy is correct because on both sides of the proportion, 12 was subtracted from the first number to yield the second number.

22. RIVE GAUCHE : PARIS :: (A. New Jersey, B. Albany, C. Riker's Island, D. Brooklyn) : NEW YORK

(D) The Rive Gauche is a part of Paris located across the river from the main business part of the city; Brooklyn is a part of New York City located across the river from the main business section.

23. SURINAME : (A. Guyana, B. British Honduras, C. Belize, D. Dutch Guiana) :: ZIMBABWE : RHODESIA

(D) Zimbabwe is the current name for that African country that used to be called Rhodesia; Suriname is the name taken when that South American country gained its independence and ceased being Dutch Guiana. Belize was formerly known as British Honduras.

24. BAROQUE : VIVALDI :: (A. Classical, B. Romantic, C. Rococo, D. Impressionist) : SCHUMANN

(B) The music composed by Vivaldi was of the Baroque style; Schumann was strictly a Romantic composer.

25. OBSEQUIOUS : OBSTINATE :: DIFFIDENT : (A. indifferent, B. shy, C. distinct, D. defiant)

(D) This is an analogy of antonyms. The obsequious person is spineless and overly agreeable, whereas the obstinate person is stubborn and stands his or her ground. The diffident person is shy and lacking in self-confidence, while the defiant person is confident and bold.

26. SHIITE : (A. Arab, B. Muslim, C. Sunni, D. Iran) :: ROMAN CATHOLIC : PROTESTANT

(C) Roman Catholic and Protestant are two leading branches of Christianity. Shiite and Sunni are two leading branches of Islam.

27. HONOR : CITATION :: SPEEDING : (A. citation, B. hurry, C. race, D. stop)

(A) The relationship in the analogy is one of cause and effect. When you are to be honored, you receive a citation, which is a formal document describing your achievements. When you are stopped for speeding, you receive a citation, which is an official summons to appear in court. *Citation* is a word with two very different meanings.

28. *HEDDA GABLER* : (A. *The Cherry Orchard*, B. *Riders to the Sea*, C. *An Enemy of the People*, D. *Blood Wedding*) :: *ANNA CHRISTIE* : *MOON FOR THE MISBEGOTTEN*

(C) *Anna Christie* and *Moon for the Misbegotten* are both plays written by Eugene O'Neill; *Hedda Gabler* and *An Enemy of the People* are both plays written by Henrik Ibsen.

29. YELLOW : (A. jonquil, B. cornflower, C. rose, D. jacket) :: RED : SALVIA

(A) This analogy is one of characteristic. The characteristic color of salvia is flaming red; the characteristic color of a jonquil is yellow. A cornflower is blue.

30. ANODE : CATHODE :: OXIDATION : (A. erosion, B. reduction, C. carbonization, D. hydrogenation)

(B) The anode is the site of oxidation in an electrical cell; the cathode is the site of reduction in that same electrical cell.

31. CELLO : VIOLIN :: (A. clarinet, B. French horn, C. accordion, D. rebec) : SAXOPHONE

(A) The cello and violin are both stringed instruments; the clarinet and saxophone are both woodwinds with sounds produced by reeds. A rebec is an ancient stringed instrument.

32. JOAN OF ARC : (A. Pope, B. stake, C. king, D. saint) :: GALILEO : SUN

(C) Galileo fell out of favor with the church because of his insistence that the sun was the center of the universe; Joan of Arc fell out of favor with the church because of her defense of the king as the ruler on earth.

33. (A. Yeats, B. Shakespeare, C. Chaucer, D. Tennyson) : SONNETS :: NASH : LIMERICKS

(B) Ogden Nash is well known as a writer of limericks; Shakespeare is well known for his sonnets as well as for his plays.

34. RACQUETBALL : PLATFORM TENNIS :: HOCKEY : (A. badminton, B. rugby, C. volleyball, D. curling)

(D) Racquetball and platform tennis are both racquet sports played within an enclosed court; hockey and curling both take place on the ice.

35. ST. PETERSBURG : HERMITAGE :: (A. Spain, B. Majorca, C. Madrid, D. Seville) : PRADO

(C) The Hermitage is a famous art gallery in the city of St. Petersburg; the Prado is a famous art gallery in the city of Madrid.

36. ABSCISSA : (A. ordinate, B. mantissa, C. coordinate, D. precision) :: X : Y

(A) In coordinate geometry, an abscissa is the horizontal coordinate of a point in a plane obtained by measuring parallel to the X-axis; an ordinate is obtained by measuring parallel to the Y-axis.

37. SKINNER : BEHAVIORISM :: (A. Adler, B. Terman, C. Kant, D. Wertheimer) : GESTALT

(D) B.F. Skinner is a psychologist closely associated with the school of psychology called behaviorism; Max Wertheimer was the founder of the Gestalt school of psychology.

38. HESTER : INFIDELITY :: (A. Cordelia, B. Goneril, C. Ophelia, D. Cassandra) : DEVOTION

(A) This analogy is based upon characteristics. Hester Prynne in Hawthorne's *Scarlet Letter* was an adulteress; therefore infidelity was one of her characteristics. Cordelia in Shakespeare's *King Lear* was known for her devotion.

39. CAPILLARIES : CIRCULATION :: VILLI : (A. respiration, B. digestion, C. recreation, D. procreation)

(B) Capillaries, the smallest blood vessels, are part of the circulatory system; villi, fingerlike projections in the small intestine that help absorb nutrients, are part of the digestive system.

40. SAN MARINO : ITALY :: (A. Ethiopia, B. Capetown, C. Lesotho, D. Swaziland) : SOUTH AFRICA

(C) San Marino is a tiny independent country that exists entirely within the boundaries of Italy; Lesotho is a small independent country entirely bordered by South Africa.

41. (A. Florida, B. New Mexico, C. Puerto Rico, D. Texas) : ALASKA :: SPAIN : RUSSIA

(A) Alaska was purchased from Russia; Florida was purchased from Spain.

42. KEYNES : ECONOMICS :: DEWEY : (A. zoology, B. electronics, C. medicine, D. education)

(D) John Maynard Keynes formulated and published controversial and influential theories in economics; John Dewey was equally influential for his novel theories in education.

43. NEIL ARMSTRONG : YURI GAGARIN :: CHARLES LINDBERGH : (A. George Washington, B. Albert Einstein, C. Orville Wright, D. Guglielmo Marconi)

(C) The four analogous people were all pioneers in flight. Neil Armstrong was the first person to fly to the moon and then walk upon it; Yuri Gagarin, a Soviet, was the first person to go into outer space; Charles Lindbergh was the first aviator to cross the Atlantic alone; and Orville Wright was the first person to fly in an airplane.

44. *PILGRIM'S PROGRESS* : (A. *Inferno*, B. *Paradise Lost*, C. *De Monarchia*, D. *Divine Comedy*) :: BUNYAN : DANTE

(D) *Pilgrim's Progress* is a religious allegory written by John Bunyan; *Divine Comedy* is an allegorical autobiography heavily religious in content, written by Dante.

45. GENGHIS KHAN : MONGOLS :: ATTILA : (A. Roman Empire, B. Germany, C. Huns, D. Tatars)

(C) Genghis Khan was leader of the Mongols, conquerors of the thirteenth century; Attila was leader of the Huns, who conquered most of the Roman Empire in the middle of the fifth century.

46. HARE : (A. rabbit, B. tortoise, C. terrapin, D. hart) :: FOX : GRAPES

(B) The analogy is based upon the association of significant elements in two of *Aesop's Fables*. The fox attempts to reach the grapes; the hare attempts to win a race with the tortoise.

47. 4 : 6 :: (A. 10, B. 6, C. 9, D. 16) : 36

(D) This is an A : C :: B : D correspondence. 6 squared is 36; 4 squared is 16. On one side of the proportion are the square roots; on the other side, in the same order, are the squares.

48. THOMAS MANN : *BUDDENBROOKS* :: THOMAS WOLFE : (A. *Death in Venice*, B. *Look Homeward, Angel*, C. *The Magic Mountain*, D. *Joseph and His Brothers*)

(B) Thomas Mann is the author of *Buddenbrooks*; Thomas Wolfe is the author of *Look Homeward, Angel*.

49. (A. Earth, B. moon, C. Russia, D. Stalin) : SPUTNIK :: JUPITER : IO

(A) Io is the first moon of the planet Jupiter. A moon is a satellite. Sputnik was the first man-made satellite of the planet Earth.

50. FREYA : ASGARD :: (A. Hera, B. Venus, C. Minerva, D. Aphrodite) : OLYMPUS

(D) The Norse gods live at Asgard; the Norse goddess of love and beauty is Freya. The Greek gods live at Olympus; the Greek goddess of love and beauty is Aprhodite.

51. (A. isosceles, B. scalene, C. right, D. obtuse) : EQUILATERAL :: DUPLE : TRIPLE

(A) In music, duple time is time that is divisible by 2; triple time is time that is divisible by 3 (into equal segments). An isosceles triangle is one in which two sides are equal; all three sides of an equilateral triangle are of equal length.

52. ELWAY : JORDAN :: (A. football, B. baseball, C, hockey, D. horseracing) : BASKETBALL

(A) This analogy is based upon the association between the athlete and the sport in which he excels. John Elway played football and Michael Jordan played basketball. Both led their teams to victory in multiple championship games.

53. OBVERSE : (A. coin, B. sweater, C. reverse, D. crochet) :: KNIT : PURL

(C) Knit and purl are basically opposite stitches, although the entire activity is called knitting. Obverse and reverse are the opposite sides of a coin.

54. PASTEL : MUTED :: LIGHT : (A. sound, B. voice, C. trumpet, D. wheel)

(A) Color is created by light waves. A pastel color is one that has been softened. Thus, pastel color is softened light waves. When a sound has been softened, we say that it has been muted.

55. (A. one, B. two, C. three, D. nine) : BETWEEN :: SIX : AMONG

(B) This is a grammatical analogy. The preposition *among* is used for comparison of more than two persons or things; the preposition *between* is used for comparisons between only two persons or things.

56. XENOPHOBIA : PREJUDICE :: PECCATOPHOBIA : (A. tantrums, B. bad habits, C. clumsiness, D. virtue)

(D) This is a cause-and-effect relationship. Xenophobia (fear of strangers) leads to prejudice; peccatophobia (fear of sinning) leads to virtue.

57. HARPSICHORD : VIRGINAL :: (A. piccolo, B. saxophone, C. sousaphone, D. oboe) : CLARINET

(D) A harpsichord is a manual double-keyboard instrument, while a virginal is a single-keyboard instrument closely related to the harpsichord; the oboe is a double-reed wind instrument, while the clarinet is a single-reed woodwind.

58. LEAGUE : YARD :: MILES : (A. inches, B. feet, C. yards, D. furlongs)

(B) The analogy is based on a proportional part-to-whole relationship. A league is composed of 3 miles, and a yard is composed of 3 feet.

59. ATOM : MOLECULE :: GENE : (A. heredity, B. genetics, C. DNA, D. chromosome)

(D) This analogy is based upon a part-to-whole relationship. An atom is a constituent part of a molecule; a gene is a constituent part of a chromosome.

60. FIRE : SMOKE :: (A. pipe, B. hose, C. leak, D. break) : STAIN

(C) Smoke is presumptive evidence of fire; a stain is presumptive evidence of a leak.

61. BUTTER : MARGARINE :: SUGAR : (A. salt, B. strychnine, C. aspartame, D. vinegar)

(C) Margarine is a synthetic shortening used in place of butter that closely resembles butter in taste and color; aspartame is a synthetic sweetener used in place of sugar. Strychnine is a poison.

62. TOM SAWYER : (A. Mark Twain, B. Samuel Langhorne Clemens, C. Becky Thatcher, D. David Copperfield) :: PORTHOS : ATHOS

(C) The analogy is based upon the friendship of two characters in the same novel. Athos and Porthos are two major characters in Alexandre Dumas' novel *The Three Musketeers;* Tom Sawyer and Becky Thatcher are two major characters in Mark Twain's novel *The Adventures of Tom Sawyer.*

63. (A. white, B. bluing, C. blanch, D. yellow) : BLEACH :: HENNA : ANIL

(B) Henna and anil are both plants that yield dyeing agents. Bluing and bleach are both agents that serve to whiten or remove dye.

64. CHECKERS : RICHARD NIXON :: TRAVELER : (A. Robert E. Lee, B. Franklin Roosevelt, C. Dwight Eisenhower, D. Aristotle Onassis)

(A) This analogy is based upon animals and the famous persons with whom their names are closely associated. Checkers was Richard Nixon's dog. Traveler was Robert E. Lee's horse.

65. BRUTE : SQUIRE :: TUBER : (A. leaves, B. yams, C. quires, D. stems)

(C) This nonsemantic analogy is based upon anagrams. *Tuber* is an anagram of *brute; quires* is an anagram of *squire*. The fact that there is absolutely no meaningful relationship between any two of the capitalized words should immediately alert you to a nonsemantic analogy. All the words are nouns, although *brute* could be an adjective and *squire* a verb, so no grammatical analogy is feasible. The *qu* in *squire* leads you directly to the correct answer.

66. $\frac{1}{8}$: 12.5% :: (A. $\frac{1}{6}$, B. $\frac{3}{11}$, C. $\frac{2}{7}$, D. $\frac{3}{8}$) : 37.5%

(D) The relationship here is between the fraction and its percent equivalent. $\frac{1}{8}$ is equivalent to 12.5%; $\frac{3}{8}$ is equivalent to 37.5%.

67. CRETACEOUS : DINOSAURS :: TERTIARY : (A. vampires, B. fish, C. reptiles, D. mammals)

(D) This analogy refers to geologic periods. During the Cretaceous period, dinosaurs were the predominant animal form; during the Tertiary period, mammals were predominant.

68. MAPLE : (A. syrup, B. oak, C. cyanide, D. leaf) :: PRIVET : HEMLOCK

(B) The analogy is based upon function. Privet and hemlock serve as hedges on or between properties; maple and oak serve as shade trees.

69. (A. Washington, B. Jefferson, C. Franklin, D. Lincoln) : MADISON :: DECLARATION OF INDEPENDENCE : CONSTITUTION

(B) The relationship in this analogy is between the author and the document. Although both documents were the products of many men's thinking, the acknowledged author of the Constitution is Madison, and the authorship of the Declaration of Independence is attributed to Jefferson.

70. ALZHEIMER'S DISEASE : HANSEN'S DISEASE :: (A. cerebral palsy, B. copper deficiency, C. dementia, D. lymphatic cancer) : LEPROSY

(C) This analogy is based upon alternative names for the same disease. Hansen's Disease is leprosy; Alzheimer's Disease is a form of dementia.

71. SALVADOR DALI : RENE MAGRITTE :: (A. e.e. cummings, B. William Wordsworth, C. Jack London, D. Leo Tolstoy) : DON MARQUIS

(A) Salvador Dali and Rene Magritte are both famous Surrealist painters; e.e. cummings and Don Marquis are both writers who are famous for writing only in lowercase.

72. INDEPENDENCE : COOPERATION :: PHOTOSYNTHESIS : (A. parasitism, B. parthenogenesis, C. symbiosis, D. carbohydrates)

(C) Photosynthesis is the independent creation of food (carbohydrates) by chlorophyll-bearing plants; symbiosis is the cooperative arrangement by which two plants, two animals, or an animal and a plant live together and mutually supply each other's needs.

73. (A. stars, B. restaurants, C. tires, D. highways) : MICHELIN :: GASOLINE : MOBIL

(C) Gasoline is the chief product of Mobil; tires are the chief product of Michelin.

74. SWIFT : (A. Barrie, B. Kipling, C. Dorothy, D. Baum) :: LILLIPUT : OZ

(D) In this analogy, fictional countries are paired with their creators. Jonathan Swift was the creator of Lilliput in his social novel *Gulliver's Travels;* Frank Baum created the land of Oz in *The Wizard of Oz.*

75. FOUR : BASEBALL :: (A. ten, B. eleven, C. fifty, D. one hundred twenty) : FOOTBALL

(A) Four balls in baseball entitle the batter to walk to first base; the game then continues without the team's changing positions. Ten yards in football constitutes a first down; the game continues with the same team in possession of the ball.

76. (A. remuneration, B. stipend, C. pay, D. overtime) : SALARY :: COMMISSION : ROYALTY

(B) Commission and royalty are both forms of payment that are based upon a percentage of the money brought in; salary and stipend are both fixed rates of payment.

77. LAWYER : BARRISTER :: ATTORNEY : (A. judge, B. juror, C. advocate, D. appellant)

(C) All four words are synonyms or near synonyms. *Lawyer* and *attorney* are terms most often used in the United States, while *barrister* and *advocate* are more often used in England.

78. KOALA : (A. eucalyptus, B. wallaby, C. bamboo, D. mulberry) :: WHALE : PLANKTON

(A) The chief food of the whale is plankton; the sole food of the koala is leaves of the eucalyptus tree.

79. DEER : (A. deer, B. moose, C. dear, D. swan) :: GOOSE : GEESE

(A) This is a grammatical analogy. On both sides of the proportion are words that form their plurals in an irregular manner. The plural of goose is geese; the plural of deer is deer.

80. 27 : (A. 3, B. 9, C. 5.19, D. 729) :: 125 : 5

(A) 125 is the cube of 5; 27 is the cube of 3. Conversely, 5 is the cube root of 125; 3 is the cube root of 27.

81. EGG : CHICKEN :: CHICKEN : (A. rooster, B. capon, C. egg, D. hen)

(C) The relationship in this analogy is not only sequential, but it also is circular. There is a conundrum, "Which came first, the chicken or the egg?" The answer is that the chicken comes from an egg, and an egg comes from a chicken. The sequence is analogous on both sides of the proportion.

82. PARIS : FRANCE :: (A. Tripoli, B. Rabat, C. Marseilles, D. Dakar) : SENEGAL

(**D**) The relationship is that of the capital city to the country of which it is the capital. Paris is the capital of France; Dakar is the capital of Senegal.

83. CCC : TVA :: FDIC : (A. OPA, B. WMC, C. OSS, D. FHA)

(**D**) All four related terms are agencies that were set up early in the Franklin D. Roosevelt administration to help the nation to recover from the Depression. CCC is the Civilian Conservation Corps; TVA is the Tennessee Valley Authority; FDIC is the Federal Deposit Insurance Corporation; and FHA is the Federal Housing Administration. OPA (Office of Price Administration) and OSS (Office of Security Services) were World War II agencies. WMC is the Women's Marine Corps.

84. ELABORATE : (A. streamlined, B. boring, C. oblique, D. obligatory) :: SERIF : SANS SERIF

(**A**) *Serif* and *sans serif* refer to typefaces. Serif type has elaborate little cross strokes at the tops and bottoms of capital letters. Sans serif type has no such embellishments, hence it is streamlined.

85. BULL RUN : MANASSAS :: STREAM : (A. battle, B. town, C. war, D. tribe)

(**B**) In Civil War histories, the labels First Battle of Bull Run and Battle of Manassas are used interchangeably to refer to the same battle. Northerners named battles for streams; Southerners called the battles by the names of the towns they were in or near.

86. GREENWICH VILLAGE : (A. London, B. Kensington, C. New York, D. Piccadilly Circus) :: MONTMARTRE : PARIS

(**C**) Montmartre is traditionally known as the artists' district of Paris; Greenwich Village is traditionally known as the artists' district of New York City.

87. UNITED STATES : DOW JONES :: JAPAN : (A. Hang Seng, B. Nikkei, C. Tokyo, D. Kyoto)

(**B**) The analogy is one of country to major stock market index. The Dow Jones average is the major index of the United States stock market and is widely quoted as an indicator of market performance; the Nikkei average is the major index of Japan's market performance. The Hang Seng is the index of Hong Kong.

88. ZOLA : NANA :: (A. Humbert Humbert, B. Don Juan, C. Don Quixote, D. Nabokov) : LOLITA

(**D**) Emile Zola is the author of the novel *Nana;* Vladimir Nabokov is the author of the novel *Lolita.*

89. KANT : CATEGORICAL IMPERATIVE :: (A. Descartes, B. Nietzsche, C. Sartre, D. Mill) : UTILITY

(**D**) Kant's test of the morality of an action was the categorical imperative, the test of whether the action would be pleasing to another person in a particular situation; Mill's test of the morality of an action was its utility—that is, whether it would be pleasing to the greatest number of people.

90. NOON : EVENING :: (A. snack, B. lunch, C. brunch, D. afternoon) : DINNER

(**B**) This is a sequential relationship. Noon comes before evening; lunch comes before dinner. Or, you may see the relationship as being one of characteristic. At noon, one will have lunch; in the evening, one will have dinner. A snack can be eaten at any time. Brunch is a combination of breakfast and lunch.

91. MENTICIDE : BRAINWASHING :: OPPROBRIUM : (A. commendation, B. reproach, C. indoctrination, D. repression)

(B) This is an analogy based on synonyms. Menticide is brainwashing; opprobrium is reproach.

92. CALPURNIA : (A. Oedipus, B. Caesar, C. King Lear, D. Cicero) :: CRESSIDA : TROILUS

(B) On both sides of this analogy, we find women who warned their men of impending danger. In Shakespeare's *Troilus and Cressida,* Cressida warns her brother Troilus of the perils of fighting the Greeks. In Shakespeare's *Julius Caesar,* Calpurnia warns her husband Caesar of the dangers of going to the Senate.

93. BLIND : DEAF :: (A. Milton, B. Scott, C. Mozart, D. Justice) : BEETHOVEN

(A) This is an analogy of characteristic. The composer Beethoven was deaf; the poet Milton was blind.

94. REMUS : (A. Brer Rabbit, B. Aquarius, C. Quisling, D. Romulus) :: CASTOR : POLLUX

(D) Castor and Pollux are mythological twins and are the astronomical constellations that make up the zodiac sign Gemini; Remus and Romulus were mythological twins who founded the city of Rome. The analogy is based upon the fact that both pairs are twins.

95. DOG : FLEA :: HORSE : (A. rider, B. fly, C. mane, D. shoe)

(B) This analogy is based upon the relationship of object to actor, with a very special relationship between the two. The actor acts as irritant to the object. Thus, a flea irritates a dog; a fly irritates a horse. The rider may at times irritate the horse, though not as consistently as the fly.

96. 10 : (A. decimal, B. common, C. unnatural, D. metric) :: e : NATURAL

(B) A logarithm to the base is a natural logarithm; a logarithm to the base 10 is a common logarithm.

97. BROUGHAM : CARRIAGE :: HOME : (A. horse, B. town, C. domicile, D. family)

(C) The terms in this analogy are synonyms. A brougham is a carriage; a home is a domicile.

98. DRACHMA : (A. Brazil, B. Nigeria, C. Greece, D. India) :: LIRA : ITALY

(C) This analogy is based upon country to currency. The national currency of Italy is the lira; the national currency of Greece is the drachma. Brazil uses the real, Nigeria uses the naira, and India uses the rupee.

99. (A. Shangri-La, B. Lilliput, C. Atlantis, D. Ilium) : BRIGADOON :: FOUNTAIN OF YOUTH : NEVER-NEVER LAND

(A) The four related terms are all places in which time stands still and people never age.

100. PARTHENON : PANTHEON :: (A. Taj Mahal, B. St. Paul's, C. Angkor Wat, D. Erechtheum) : SISTINE CHAPEL

(D) In this analogy, the association is one of place and function. The Pantheon and the Sistine Chapel are both famous places of worship in Rome; the Parthenon and the Erechtheum are both famous temples in Athens.

PART 4

GRE Verbal Analogies

PREVIEW

CHAPTER 12 *Practice for the GRE*

Chapter 12

Practice for the GRE

The analogy question is acknowledged to be one of the most sensitive measures of general intelligence and of reasoning ability. As such, it is used on many standardized examinations for graduate-level study and for higher-level employment.

The examinations that large corporations and foundations have designed for their own use for making employment and grant-recipient decisions often combine a measure of specific knowledge with the measure of reasoning ability. Among standardized exams, the most well-known of such exams is the Minnesota Engineering Analogies Test (MEAT). The subject matter of the MEAT is strictly confined to science and mathematics. The examination presupposes more than a superficial background in these areas, and the questions become increasingly technical. The format of the MEAT is similar to that of the MAT: three given terms and a choice of one of four to complete the analogy. In the MEAT, the fourth term is always the missing term, and the choices are numbered rather than lettered. Thus, a MEAT item reads: A : B :: C : 1, 2, 3, or 4.

Of the nationally distributed graduate-level exams that utilize the analogy question, the best-known and most widely used is the Graduate Record Examination (GRE). Questions on the GRE are intended to measure only reasoning ability and vocabulary. The GRE does not test knowledge in specific fields such as literature, philosophy, or chemistry. In measuring breadth of vocabulary, however, the GRE analogy questions do reach into the vocabulary of the various fields.

The GRE and some other exams present the analogy question in a format somewhat different from that of the MAT. Instead of supplying only one missing term, as on the MAT, you must select a pair of words whose relationship to each other most closely parallels the relationship expressed by the first word pair.

Sample analogy pair:

> **Q** SNAPSHOT : SCRAPBOOK ::
> (A) memo : file
> (B) photograph : book jacket
> (C) camera : case
> (D) film : frame
> (E) career : portfolio
>
> (A) (B) (C) ● (E)

ROAD MAP

- *Test 1*
- *Test 2*
- *Test 3*
- *Test 4*
- *Test 5*
- *Test 6*
- *Test 7*
- *Answer Key*
- *Explanatory Answers*

> **NOTE**
> Analogy questions appear on so many exams because the analogy section is almost an intelligence exam in itself. Performance on analogy questions is a good indicator of general knowledge, extent of reading, mental flexibility, and reasoning ability.

Answer: **(A)** A snapshot is stored for future reference in a scrapbook in the same way that a memo is stored in a file.

Although the format of these analogy problems differs from the format of MAT problems, the same strategies apply. First, you must determine the nature of the relationship between the terms of the given word pair, and then you must select the one pair from the choices offered in which the terms are related in exactly the same way.

Let us "walk together" through a typical analogy problem of the missing pair format.

Q SPANIEL : DOG ::
(A) kitten : cat
(B) lion : tiger
(C) spider : fly
(D) robin : bird
(E) fish : trout

Ⓐ Ⓑ Ⓒ ● Ⓔ

The words are familiar ones, so you can slip right through the definition-of-terms phase. Now look at the initial pair. A spaniel is a specific kind of dog. Look at the answer choices. You are seeking a choice in which the first word is a specific kind of the second word. Begin by eliminating the answers that are obviously incorrect. Answers B and C may both be eliminated because a lion is not a specific type of tiger, and a spider is not a specific type of fly. Now return to choice A. A kitten is a young cat. If there were no better answer offered, you might consider marking answer A, but you must not be satisfied with a dubiously correct answer without carefully searching for a truly correct one; a kitten really is not a specific type of cat.

At first glance, both answers D and E might appear to be correct. A robin is a specific type of bird; a trout is a specific type of fish. However, answer E reverses the sequence of the original relationship. In answer E, fish is the larger group of which trout is a specific kind, whereas in the original pair, the specific kind is named before the larger group. Thus answer D, which maintains the relationship in the same sequence, is the correct completion of this analogy.

The A : C :: B : D relationship occurs much less frequently among analogies in which you choose pairs rather than single words. However, this relationship is not precluded by the pair format, and you must not rule out the possibility when you cannot find a relationship between A and B.

> **CAUTION**
> Don't get bogged down in meaning. Often, the words in one pair are totally unrelated to the words in the analogous pair. The words in the pairs may come from totally different disciplines. However, the relationship between the words on both sides of the analogy will be the same. In analogy questions, only the relationship matters.

You'll get plenty of practice with the paired analogy problems in the pages that follow. The practice questions are divided into short tests to allow you to complete a set even when you have only a few minutes to spare. At the end of the chapter, you will find both answers and explanations for all questions. Be sure to study *all* the explanations—each has something to teach in terms of vocabulary, relationships, or reasoning processes.

If you will be taking the GRE, these exercises are a *must* for you. If not, try them anyway and gain whatever benefits you can.

Answer Sheet

GRE Verbal Analogies Test 1

1 Ⓐ Ⓑ Ⓒ Ⓓ Ⓔ   5 Ⓐ Ⓑ Ⓒ Ⓓ Ⓔ   9 Ⓐ Ⓑ Ⓒ Ⓓ Ⓔ   13 Ⓐ Ⓑ Ⓒ Ⓓ Ⓔ   17 Ⓐ Ⓑ Ⓒ Ⓓ Ⓔ
2 Ⓐ Ⓑ Ⓒ Ⓓ Ⓔ   6 Ⓐ Ⓑ Ⓒ Ⓓ Ⓔ   10 Ⓐ Ⓑ Ⓒ Ⓓ Ⓔ   14 Ⓐ Ⓑ Ⓒ Ⓓ Ⓔ   18 Ⓐ Ⓑ Ⓒ Ⓓ Ⓔ
3 Ⓐ Ⓑ Ⓒ Ⓓ Ⓔ   7 Ⓐ Ⓑ Ⓒ Ⓓ Ⓔ   11 Ⓐ Ⓑ Ⓒ Ⓓ Ⓔ   15 Ⓐ Ⓑ Ⓒ Ⓓ Ⓔ   19 Ⓐ Ⓑ Ⓒ Ⓓ Ⓔ
4 Ⓐ Ⓑ Ⓒ Ⓓ Ⓔ   8 Ⓐ Ⓑ Ⓒ Ⓓ Ⓔ   12 Ⓐ Ⓑ Ⓒ Ⓓ Ⓔ   16 Ⓐ Ⓑ Ⓒ Ⓓ Ⓔ   20 Ⓐ Ⓑ Ⓒ Ⓓ Ⓔ

GRE Verbal Analogies Test 2

1 Ⓐ Ⓑ Ⓒ Ⓓ Ⓔ   5 Ⓐ Ⓑ Ⓒ Ⓓ Ⓔ   9 Ⓐ Ⓑ Ⓒ Ⓓ Ⓔ   13 Ⓐ Ⓑ Ⓒ Ⓓ Ⓔ   17 Ⓐ Ⓑ Ⓒ Ⓓ Ⓔ
2 Ⓐ Ⓑ Ⓒ Ⓓ Ⓔ   6 Ⓐ Ⓑ Ⓒ Ⓓ Ⓔ   10 Ⓐ Ⓑ Ⓒ Ⓓ Ⓔ   14 Ⓐ Ⓑ Ⓒ Ⓓ Ⓔ   18 Ⓐ Ⓑ Ⓒ Ⓓ Ⓔ
3 Ⓐ Ⓑ Ⓒ Ⓓ Ⓔ   7 Ⓐ Ⓑ Ⓒ Ⓓ Ⓔ   11 Ⓐ Ⓑ Ⓒ Ⓓ Ⓔ   15 Ⓐ Ⓑ Ⓒ Ⓓ Ⓔ   19 Ⓐ Ⓑ Ⓒ Ⓓ Ⓔ
4 Ⓐ Ⓑ Ⓒ Ⓓ Ⓔ   8 Ⓐ Ⓑ Ⓒ Ⓓ Ⓔ   12 Ⓐ Ⓑ Ⓒ Ⓓ Ⓔ   16 Ⓐ Ⓑ Ⓒ Ⓓ Ⓔ   20 Ⓐ Ⓑ Ⓒ Ⓓ Ⓔ

GRE Verbal Analogies Test 3

1 Ⓐ Ⓑ Ⓒ Ⓓ Ⓔ   5 Ⓐ Ⓑ Ⓒ Ⓓ Ⓔ   9 Ⓐ Ⓑ Ⓒ Ⓓ Ⓔ   13 Ⓐ Ⓑ Ⓒ Ⓓ Ⓔ   17 Ⓐ Ⓑ Ⓒ Ⓓ Ⓔ
2 Ⓐ Ⓑ Ⓒ Ⓓ Ⓔ   6 Ⓐ Ⓑ Ⓒ Ⓓ Ⓔ   10 Ⓐ Ⓑ Ⓒ Ⓓ Ⓔ   14 Ⓐ Ⓑ Ⓒ Ⓓ Ⓔ   18 Ⓐ Ⓑ Ⓒ Ⓓ Ⓔ
3 Ⓐ Ⓑ Ⓒ Ⓓ Ⓔ   7 Ⓐ Ⓑ Ⓒ Ⓓ Ⓔ   11 Ⓐ Ⓑ Ⓒ Ⓓ Ⓔ   15 Ⓐ Ⓑ Ⓒ Ⓓ Ⓔ   19 Ⓐ Ⓑ Ⓒ Ⓓ Ⓔ
4 Ⓐ Ⓑ Ⓒ Ⓓ Ⓔ   8 Ⓐ Ⓑ Ⓒ Ⓓ Ⓔ   12 Ⓐ Ⓑ Ⓒ Ⓓ Ⓔ   16 Ⓐ Ⓑ Ⓒ Ⓓ Ⓔ   20 Ⓐ Ⓑ Ⓒ Ⓓ Ⓔ

GRE Verbal Analogies Test 4

1 Ⓐ Ⓑ Ⓒ Ⓓ Ⓔ   5 Ⓐ Ⓑ Ⓒ Ⓓ Ⓔ   9 Ⓐ Ⓑ Ⓒ Ⓓ Ⓔ   13 Ⓐ Ⓑ Ⓒ Ⓓ Ⓔ   17 Ⓐ Ⓑ Ⓒ Ⓓ Ⓔ
2 Ⓐ Ⓑ Ⓒ Ⓓ Ⓔ   6 Ⓐ Ⓑ Ⓒ Ⓓ Ⓔ   10 Ⓐ Ⓑ Ⓒ Ⓓ Ⓔ   14 Ⓐ Ⓑ Ⓒ Ⓓ Ⓔ   18 Ⓐ Ⓑ Ⓒ Ⓓ Ⓔ
3 Ⓐ Ⓑ Ⓒ Ⓓ Ⓔ   7 Ⓐ Ⓑ Ⓒ Ⓓ Ⓔ   11 Ⓐ Ⓑ Ⓒ Ⓓ Ⓔ   15 Ⓐ Ⓑ Ⓒ Ⓓ Ⓔ   19 Ⓐ Ⓑ Ⓒ Ⓓ Ⓔ
4 Ⓐ Ⓑ Ⓒ Ⓓ Ⓔ   8 Ⓐ Ⓑ Ⓒ Ⓓ Ⓔ   12 Ⓐ Ⓑ Ⓒ Ⓓ Ⓔ   16 Ⓐ Ⓑ Ⓒ Ⓓ Ⓔ   20 Ⓐ Ⓑ Ⓒ Ⓓ Ⓔ

GRE Verbal Analogies Test 5

1 Ⓐ Ⓑ Ⓒ Ⓓ Ⓔ   5 Ⓐ Ⓑ Ⓒ Ⓓ Ⓔ   9 Ⓐ Ⓑ Ⓒ Ⓓ Ⓔ   13 Ⓐ Ⓑ Ⓒ Ⓓ Ⓔ   17 Ⓐ Ⓑ Ⓒ Ⓓ Ⓔ
2 Ⓐ Ⓑ Ⓒ Ⓓ Ⓔ   6 Ⓐ Ⓑ Ⓒ Ⓓ Ⓔ   10 Ⓐ Ⓑ Ⓒ Ⓓ Ⓔ   14 Ⓐ Ⓑ Ⓒ Ⓓ Ⓔ   18 Ⓐ Ⓑ Ⓒ Ⓓ Ⓔ
3 Ⓐ Ⓑ Ⓒ Ⓓ Ⓔ   7 Ⓐ Ⓑ Ⓒ Ⓓ Ⓔ   11 Ⓐ Ⓑ Ⓒ Ⓓ Ⓔ   15 Ⓐ Ⓑ Ⓒ Ⓓ Ⓔ   19 Ⓐ Ⓑ Ⓒ Ⓓ Ⓔ
4 Ⓐ Ⓑ Ⓒ Ⓓ Ⓔ   8 Ⓐ Ⓑ Ⓒ Ⓓ Ⓔ   12 Ⓐ Ⓑ Ⓒ Ⓓ Ⓔ   16 Ⓐ Ⓑ Ⓒ Ⓓ Ⓔ   20 Ⓐ Ⓑ Ⓒ Ⓓ Ⓔ

GRE Verbal Analogies Test 6

1 Ⓐ Ⓑ Ⓒ Ⓓ Ⓔ   5 Ⓐ Ⓑ Ⓒ Ⓓ Ⓔ   9 Ⓐ Ⓑ Ⓒ Ⓓ Ⓔ   13 Ⓐ Ⓑ Ⓒ Ⓓ Ⓔ   17 Ⓐ Ⓑ Ⓒ Ⓓ Ⓔ
2 Ⓐ Ⓑ Ⓒ Ⓓ Ⓔ   6 Ⓐ Ⓑ Ⓒ Ⓓ Ⓔ   10 Ⓐ Ⓑ Ⓒ Ⓓ Ⓔ   14 Ⓐ Ⓑ Ⓒ Ⓓ Ⓔ   18 Ⓐ Ⓑ Ⓒ Ⓓ Ⓔ
3 Ⓐ Ⓑ Ⓒ Ⓓ Ⓔ   7 Ⓐ Ⓑ Ⓒ Ⓓ Ⓔ   11 Ⓐ Ⓑ Ⓒ Ⓓ Ⓔ   15 Ⓐ Ⓑ Ⓒ Ⓓ Ⓔ   19 Ⓐ Ⓑ Ⓒ Ⓓ Ⓔ
4 Ⓐ Ⓑ Ⓒ Ⓓ Ⓔ   8 Ⓐ Ⓑ Ⓒ Ⓓ Ⓔ   12 Ⓐ Ⓑ Ⓒ Ⓓ Ⓔ   16 Ⓐ Ⓑ Ⓒ Ⓓ Ⓔ   20 Ⓐ Ⓑ Ⓒ Ⓓ Ⓔ

GRE Verbal Analogies Test 7

1. Ⓐ Ⓑ Ⓒ Ⓓ Ⓔ
2. Ⓐ Ⓑ Ⓒ Ⓓ Ⓔ
3. Ⓐ Ⓑ Ⓒ Ⓓ Ⓔ
4. Ⓐ Ⓑ Ⓒ Ⓓ Ⓔ
5. Ⓐ Ⓑ Ⓒ Ⓓ Ⓔ
6. Ⓐ Ⓑ Ⓒ Ⓓ Ⓔ
7. Ⓐ Ⓑ Ⓒ Ⓓ Ⓔ
8. Ⓐ Ⓑ Ⓒ Ⓓ Ⓔ
9. Ⓐ Ⓑ Ⓒ Ⓓ Ⓔ
10. Ⓐ Ⓑ Ⓒ Ⓓ Ⓔ
11. Ⓐ Ⓑ Ⓒ Ⓓ Ⓔ
12. Ⓐ Ⓑ Ⓒ Ⓓ Ⓔ
13. Ⓐ Ⓑ Ⓒ Ⓓ Ⓔ
14. Ⓐ Ⓑ Ⓒ Ⓓ Ⓔ
15. Ⓐ Ⓑ Ⓒ Ⓓ Ⓔ
16. Ⓐ Ⓑ Ⓒ Ⓓ Ⓔ
17. Ⓐ Ⓑ Ⓒ Ⓓ Ⓔ
18. Ⓐ Ⓑ Ⓒ Ⓓ Ⓔ
19. Ⓐ Ⓑ Ⓒ Ⓓ Ⓔ
20. Ⓐ Ⓑ Ⓒ Ⓓ Ⓔ

TEST 1

20 Questions • 10 Minutes

Directions: Each of these test questions begins with two capitalized words that are related to each other in some way. Find out how they are related. Then study the five pairs of words that follow. They are lettered (A), (B), (C), (D), (E). Select the two words that are related to each other in the same way that the two capitalized words are related.

1. TROT : GALLOP ::
    (A) jog : walk
    (B) swim : run
    (C) paddle : row
    (D) pace : step
    (E) lope : scurry

2. TRELLIS : PROP ::
    (A) ladder : climb
    (B) pillar : buttress
    (C) flowerpot : plant
    (D) seed : sow
    (E) buoy : moor

3. CROWN : ROYAL ::
    (A) gun : imperial
    (B) cola : sweet
    (C) crucifix : religious
    (D) wrap : ermine
    (E) staff : general

4. ISLAND : OCEAN ::
    (A) hill : stream
    (B) forest : valley
    (C) oasis : desert
    (D) tree : field
    (E) house : lawn

5. MATHEMATICS : NUMEROLOGY ::
    (A) biology : botany
    (B) psychology : physiology
    (C) anatomy : medicine
    (D) astronomy : astrology
    (E) magic : science

6. BUCOLIC : URBAN ::
    (A) dense : sparse
    (B) rural : ephemeral
    (C) elastic : plastic
    (D) rustic : toxic
    (E) mist : smog

7. DISLIKABLE : ABHORRENT ::
    (A) trustworthy : helpful
    (B) difficult : arduous
    (C) silly : young
    (D) tender : hard
    (E) ugly : beautiful

8. WOOD : CORD ::
    (A) tree : pasture
    (B) nature : industry
    (C) milk : quart
    (D) leaf : cow
    (E) fire : string

9. DROUGHT : THIRST ::
    (A) blizzard : snow blindness
    (B) food : hunger
    (C) music : sorrow
    (D) heat : light
    (E) aridity : dryness

10. MINARET : MOSQUE ::
    (A) religion : laity
    (B) steeple : church
    (C) dainty : grotesque
    (D) modem : classic
    (E) tent : house

GO ON TO THE NEXT PAGE

11. WHEAT : CHAFF ::
    (A) wine : dregs
    (B) bread : roll
    (C) laughter : raillery
    (D) oat : oatmeal
    (E) whiskey : vodka

12. DEVIOUS : SPY ::
    (A) productive : farmer
    (B) orthodox : heretic
    (C) balanced : reporter
    (D) normal : psychologist
    (E) practical : nurse

13. EBB : WAX ::
    (A) rise : fall
    (B) spring : fall
    (C) abate : recede
    (D) slacken : grow
    (E) tide : paraffin

14. DRAMA : DIRECTOR ::
    (A) class : principal
    (B) magazine : editor
    (C) actor : playwright
    (D) tragedy : producer
    (E) leader : group

15. COMMONPLACE : CLICHÉ ::
    (A) serious : play
    (B) annoying : pun
    (C) appreciated : gift
    (D) terse : maxim
    (E) ordinary : miracle

16. PLEASED : THRILLED ::
    (A) tipsy : drunk
    (B) sensible : lively
    (C) intelligent : dumb
    (D) liberal : tolerant
    (E) happy : despairing

17. GROVE : WILLOW ::
    (A) stack : novel
    (B) fence : shrub
    (C) pine : stand
    (D) thicket : blackberry
    (E) glen : birch

18. MORAL : SIN ::
    (A) civil : court
    (B) popular : law
    (C) legal : crime
    (D) silent : priest
    (E) social : philosopher

19. ELLIPSE : CURVE ::
    (A) stutter : speech
    (B) triangle : base
    (C) revolution : distance
    (D) square : polygon
    (E) sun : moon

20. SILK : RAYON ::
    (A) candy : cake
    (B) butter : margarine
    (C) cane : stalk
    (D) spice : pepper
    (E) vitamin : nutrient

TEST 2

20 Questions • 10 Minutes

Directions: Each of these test questions begins with two capitalized words that are related to each other in some way. Find out how they are related. Then study the five pairs of words that follow. They are lettered (A), (B), (C), (D), (E). Select the two words that are related to each other in the same way that the two capitalized words are related.

1. REQUEST : DEMAND ::
   (A) reply : respond
   (B) regard : reject
   (C) inquire : require
   (D) wish : crave
   (E) accept : question

2. PHOTOGRAPH : ALBUM ::
   (A) skillet : stove
   (B) presents : tree
   (C) money : wallet
   (D) chair : veranda
   (E) receptacle : recipient

3. WATER : FAUCET ::
   (A) fuel : throttle
   (B) H$_2$O : O
   (C) kitchen : sink
   (D) steam : solid
   (E) vapor : tub

4. HOLOCAUST : FIRE ::
   (A) drum : water
   (B) hanging : noose
   (C) murder : knife
   (D) sleep : pill
   (E) trial : jury

5. OSCILLATE : PENDULUM ::
   (A) obligate : promise
   (B) catch : fish
   (C) turn : car
   (D) spin : gyroscope
   (E) learn : student

6. HERB : DILL ::
   (A) plantain : berry
   (B) legume : tuber
   (C) conifer : fir
   (D) fruit : vegetable
   (E) tree : bark

7. INTESTINE : DIGESTIVE ::
   (A) trapezium : tent
   (B) cerebellum : skeletal
   (C) pores : excretory
   (D) lungs : circulatory
   (E) intestate : alimentary

8. FLASK : BOTTLE ::
   (A) whiskey : food
   (B) metal : glass
   (C) pamphlet : book
   (D) quart : pint
   (E) stopper : sink

9. MONEY : AVARICE ::
   (A) finance : greed
   (B) property : insolence
   (C) dollar sign : capitalism
   (D) food : voracity
   (E) wages : overtime

10. HAIR : BALDNESS ::
    (A) wig : head
    (B) egg : eggshell
    (C) rain : drought
    (D) skin : scar
    (E) mammal : bird

GO ON TO THE NEXT PAGE

11. BOAT : SHIP ::
    (A) book : tome
    (B) canoe : paddle
    (C) oar : water
    (D) aft : stem
    (E) river : ocean

12. SCYTHE : DEATH ::
    (A) fall : winter
    (B) knife : murder
    (C) heart : love
    (D) harvest : crops
    (E) flag : war

13. KENNEL : DOG ::
    (A) fennel : channel
    (B) stall : horse
    (C) hangar : vehicle
    (D) nest : stork
    (E) cubby : cub

14. CARNIVORE : ANIMALS ::
    (A) omnivore : omelets
    (B) vegetarian : vegetables
    (C) trace : minerals
    (D) herbivore : health
    (E) death : life

15. LIBEL : SLANDER ::
    (A) chair : office
    (B) telephone : computer
    (C) brick : paper
    (D) copier : plagiarist
    (E) oak : spruce

16. ENTRY : DICTIONARY ::
    (A) pedal : bike
    (B) wheel : car
    (C) note : score
    (D) car : sedan
    (E) fold : fan

17. MAUVE : COLOR ::
    (A) basil : spice
    (B) art : photography
    (C) form : function
    (D) tan : brown
    (E) gold : sunset

18. MUFFLE : SILENCE ::
    (A) cover : clang
    (B) sound : hear
    (C) cry : guffaw
    (D) stymie : defeat
    (E) snuggle : confront

19. WHALE : FISH ::
    (A) poodle : dog
    (B) fly : insect
    (C) bat : bird
    (D) clue : trace
    (E) mako : shark

20. VERB : ACTION ::
    (A) grammar : word
    (B) speech : discourse
    (C) adverb : adjective
    (D) pronoun : person
    (E) proverb : reaction

TEST 3

20 Questions • 10 Minutes

Directions: Each of these test questions begins with two capitalized words that are related to each other in some way. Find out how they are related. Then study the five pairs of words that follow. They are lettered (A), (B), (C), (D), (E). Select the two words that are related to each other in the same way that the two capitalized words are related.

1. PLUTOCRAT : WEALTH ::
   (A) autocrat : industry
   (B) theocrat : religion
   (C) oligarch : ruler
   (D) technocrat : popularity
   (E) republican : conservation

2. NEWS REPORT : DESCRIPTIVE ::
   (A) weather report : unpredictable
   (B) editorial : bias
   (C) story : newsworthy
   (D) security guard : protective
   (E) fact : fiction

3. PROPHYLACTIC : PREVENT ::
   (A) toothbrush : clean
   (B) aspirin : throb
   (C) therapeutic : cure
   (D) surgery : cut
   (E) alcohol : harm

4. RIGGING : ROPE ::
   (A) barrels : brass
   (B) figurehead : hewn
   (C) sails : canvas
   (D) ship : steam
   (E) portage : weight

5. MATRICULATE : GRADUATION ::
   (A) grow : harvest
   (B) enlist : discharge
   (C) boil : canning
   (D) endow : bestowal
   (E) register : election

6. WATER : HYDRAULIC ::
   (A) energy : atomic
   (B) power : electric
   (C) air : pneumatic
   (D) pressure : compressed
   (E) gas : politic

7. RABIES : HYDROPHOBIA ::
   (A) pneumonia : grippe
   (B) chill : bronchitis
   (C) rhinitis : influenza
   (D) measles : rubeola
   (E) scurvy : rickets

8. STABLE : HORSE ::
   (A) barn : silo
   (B) sty : hog
   (C) fold : ram
   (D) hen : coop
   (E) shed : tools

9. PETAL : BLOSSOM ::
   (A) cone : pine tree
   (B) vane : windmill
   (C) flower : shrub
   (D) sill : window
   (E) clock : digit

10. ROLE : ACTOR ::
    (A) aria : soprano
    (B) private : soldier
    (C) composition : singer
    (D) position : ballplayer
    (E) hierarchy : bureaucrat

GO ON TO THE NEXT PAGE

11. *ILIAD* : EPIC ::
    (A) *Hamlet* : tragedy
    (B) Dickens : novel
    (C) *Cinderella* : plot
    (D) *Macbeth* : prosody
    (E) sonnet : narration

12. SILO : FODDER ::
    (A) barn : corn
    (B) farm : crops
    (C) tractor : fuel
    (D) cask : wine
    (E) vine : grapes

13. KILT : SARI ::
    (A) gown : robe
    (B) senator : fakir
    (C) man : woman
    (D) tartan : plaid
    (E) skirt : blouse

14. PROW : SHIP ::
    (A) caboose : train
    (B) nose : airplane
    (C) bird : beak
    (D) wheel : car
    (E) tail : cat

15. TRESS : HAIR ::
    (A) pat : butter
    (B) slice : fox
    (C) flock : geese
    (D) land : cotton
    (E) skein : wool

16. EPOXY : AFFIX ::
    (A) crowbar : pry
    (B) glue : freshen
    (C) tongs : secure
    (D) proxy : fix
    (E) stone : lift

17. DISCIPLINE : ORDER ::
    (A) military : rank
    (B) authority : follower
    (C) parent : child
    (D) training : preparation
    (E) form : formlessness

18. SUFFICIENT : OVERABUNDANT ::
    (A) few : many
    (B) scarce : absent
    (C) insufficient : abundant
    (D) empty : full
    (E) left : sinister

19. WATERMARK : PAPER ::
    (A) buoy : stamp
    (B) birthmark : person
    (C) tide : character
    (D) line : signal
    (E) document : certificate

20. BRIGHT : BRILLIANT ::
    (A) color : red
    (B) yellow : sparkly
    (C) happy : overjoyed
    (D) light : fire
    (E) sun : star

TEST 4

20 Questions • 10 Minutes

Directions: Each of these test questions begins with two capitalized words that are related to each other in some way. Find out how they are related. Then study the five pairs of words that follow. They are lettered (A), (B), (C), (D), (E). Select the two words that are related to each other in the same way that the two capitalized words are related.

1. XYLOPHONE : PERCUSSION ::
    (A) wood : brass
    (B) cylinder : planar
    (C) bassoon : wind
    (D) bass : treble
    (E) string : cello

2. STALLION : GELDING ::
    (A) mare : filly
    (B) buck : deer
    (C) pig : boar
    (D) bull : steer
    (E) trotter : pacer

3. GRIPPING : PLIERS ::
    (A) chisel : gouging
    (B) breaking : hammer
    (C) elevating : jack
    (D) killing : knife
    (E) glue : attaching

4. RADIUS : CIRCLE ::
    (A) rubber : tire
    (B) spoke : wheel
    (C) equator : earth
    (D) cord : circumference
    (E) center : navel

5. ZODIAC : SIGN ::
    (A) auto : wheel
    (B) year : month
    (C) hand : finger
    (D) team : tackle
    (E) country : land

6. AXIOM : TRANSITIVITY ::
    (A) feeling : sensitivity
    (B) theorem : Pythagorean
    (C) longevity : exercise
    (D) commutativity : association
    (E) proof : acceptance

7. ALLAY : FEARS ::
    (A) alloy : metals
    (B) bandage : stomach
    (C) pacify : infant
    (D) terminate : clause
    (E) placate : relaxation

8. ALCOVE : ROOM ::
    (A) roof : house
    (B) county : nation
    (C) censure : excommunication
    (D) cave : mountain
    (E) recess : school

9. DINOSAUR : CROCODILE ::
    (A) zebra : horse
    (B) woolly mammoth : elephant
    (C) exotic : mundane
    (D) deer : elk
    (E) learning : hyena

10. MISDEMEANOR : FELONY ::
    (A) pilfer : steal
    (B) thief : burglar
    (C) murder : manslaughter
    (D) cracked : smashed
    (E) accident : oversight

GO ON TO THE NEXT PAGE

11. EROSION : FLOODING ::
    (A) timber : fire
    (B) population : explosion
    (C) knell : death
    (D) contamination : pollution
    (E) movement : agility

12. HYGROMETER : HUMIDITY ::
    (A) thermometer : temperature
    (B) valve : pressure
    (C) rate : speed
    (D) barometer : weather
    (E) tide : mist

13. MEAL : REPAST ::
    (A) drink : beverage
    (B) later : prior
    (C) ship : truck
    (D) rain : snow
    (E) food : drink

14. CULL : INFERIOR ::
    (A) reject : regular
    (B) select : choice
    (C) affect : voice
    (D) predict : abnormal
    (E) benefit : imperfect

15. BALLAD : SONG ::
    (A) major : minor
    (B) oil : olives
    (C) medal : wreath
    (D) broadloom : carpet
    (E) shoe : necklace

16. POD : WHALES ::
    (A) herd : animals
    (B) pride : pigeons
    (C) den : foxes
    (D) spell : witches
    (E) brace : ducks

17. HIGHWAY : ROAD MAP ::
    (A) sky : chart
    (B) wall : painting
    (C) hallway : blueprint
    (D) avenue : bus stop
    (E) planet : topographic map

18. MONARCH : REGAL ::
    (A) lord : masterful
    (B) serf : lowly
    (C) king : courtly
    (D) royalty : gentle
    (E) vassal : popular

19. BOLD : COWED ::
    (A) daring : intrepid
    (B) demanding : satisfied
    (C) loving : selfish
    (D) good : delicious
    (E) thriving : hearty

20. GALLON : MILK ::
    (A) metric ton : automobile
    (B) bushel : fuel
    (C) yard : fabric
    (D) milligram : flour
    (E) dram : cider

TEST 5

20 Questions • 10 Minutes

Directions: Each of these test questions begins with two capitalized words that are related to each other in some way. Find out how they are related. Then study the five pairs of words that follow. They are lettered (A), (B), (C), (D), (E). Select the two words that are related to each other in the same way that the two capitalized words are related.

1. EXPOSITORY : ARTICLE ::
   (A) epistolary : conjunction
   (B) shocking : news
   (C) narrative : story
   (D) lyrical : music
   (E) persuasive : poem

2. GOLD : PROSPECTOR ::
   (A) medicine : doctor
   (B) prayer : preacher
   (C) wood : carpenter
   (D) clues : detective
   (E) coal : fire

3. DEXTROSE : SUGAR ::
   (A) sucrose : sweetener
   (B) corn : maize
   (C) fat : lipid
   (D) enzyme : protein
   (E) heart attack : embolism

4. SWARM : APIARY ::
   (A) eagles : aerie
   (B) ants : anthill
   (C) herd : field
   (D) flock : aviary
   (E) family : home

5. LATCH : GATE ::
   (A) lock : key
   (B) hasp : jar
   (C) knob : door
   (D) lever : stone
   (E) buckle : belt

6. STYLUS : INCISE ::
   (A) stiletto : sharpen
   (B) penknife : whittle
   (C) block : pound
   (D) bread : knead
   (E) ax : hone

7. COCKPIT : INTERIOR ::
   (A) aileron : exterior
   (B) propeller : rolling
   (C) elevator : supportive
   (D) tail : yawing
   (E) rudder : pitching

8. VICAR : CLERGY ::
   (A) president : judicial
   (B) dragoon : military
   (C) Catholic : Protestant
   (D) rabbi : synagogue
   (E) rancher : farm

9. GARNER : WEALTH ::
   (A) assemble : glue
   (B) steal : money
   (C) collate : pages
   (D) achieve : intelligence
   (E) plant : sheaves

10. STREET : SIDEWALK ::
    (A) beach : boardwalk
    (B) highway : off ramp
    (C) downtown : crosstown
    (D) stoplight : pedestrian
    (E) track : finish line

GO ON TO THE NEXT PAGE

11. GLUTTON : UNDISCRIMINATING ::
    (A) wisdom : epicurean
    (B) spaghetti : edible
    (C) atrophy : empathetic
    (D) good : plenty
    (E) gourmet : selective

12. COUPLET : POEM ::
    (A) page : poster
    (B) sentence : paragraph
    (C) number : alphabet
    (D) epic : poetry
    (E) sonnet : poem

13. CLIMBER : PEAK ::
    (A) hunter : game
    (B) rifle : bull's eye
    (C) runner : mile
    (D) boxer : glove
    (E) victory : jockey

14. OIL : WELL ::
    (A) water : faucet
    (B) iron : ore
    (C) silver : mine
    (D) gas : pump
    (E) steel : factory

15. PIGMENTS : PALETTE ::
    (A) pigs : farm
    (B) trees : nursery
    (C) chalk : chalkboard
    (D) paints : easel
    (E) painter : artist

16. SIEVE : FILTER ::
    (A) colander : drain
    (B) water : drip
    (C) cigar : smoke
    (D) gold : pan
    (E) mesh : clean

17. INDUBITABLE : CONTRADICT ::
    (A) unhappy : cry
    (B) immovable : budge
    (C) unlikely : like
    (D) false : deny
    (E) breakable : smash

18. STALLION : ROOSTER ::
    (A) buck : doe
    (B) mare : hen
    (C) horse : bird
    (D) foal : calf
    (E) mouse : rodent

19. JUDO : WEAPONS ::
    (A) bridge : aces
    (B) football : helmets
    (C) auto : horses
    (D) golf : clubs
    (E) soccer : hands

20. JUDICIAL : ENFORCE ::
    (A) administrative : veto
    (B) legislative : pass
    (C) elected : appoint
    (D) bench : try
    (E) federal : elect

TEST 6

20 Questions • 10 Minutes

Directions: Each of these test questions begins with two capitalized words that are related to each other in some way. Find out how they are related. Then study the five pairs of words that follow. They are lettered (A), (B), (C), (D), (E). Select the two words that are related to each other in the same way that the two capitalized words are related.

1. RUDDER : SHIP ::
   (A) wheel : car
   (B) motor : truck
   (C) row : boat
   (D) kite : string
   (E) track : train

2. KARATE : FOOT ::
   (A) judo : chop
   (B) bridge : hand
   (C) fencing : foil
   (D) boxing : glove
   (E) baseball : bat

3. LEECH : PARASITE ::
   (A) tree : host
   (B) surgeon : butcher
   (C) worm : turner
   (D) pomegranate : citrus
   (E) mushroom : saprophyte

4. LEAVENING : FERMENTATION ::
   (A) argument : fight
   (B) snow : precipitation
   (C) rain : condensation
   (D) sleet : hail
   (E) sleeping : eating

5. AMUSING : HILARIOUS ::
   (A) grave : melancholy
   (B) smart : genius
   (C) grotesque : odd
   (D) funny : happy
   (E) glad : mocking

6. LIST : ITEM ::
   (A) portrait : person
   (B) constitution : article
   (C) computer : disk
   (D) trial : motion
   (E) tree : bark

7. READ : BOOK ::
   (A) taste : salty
   (B) attend : movie
   (C) smell : nose
   (D) listen : music
   (E) speak : truth

8. PREMIERE : MOVIE ::
   (A) unveiling : statue
   (B) premier : president
   (C) debutante : teenager
   (D) ruler : subject
   (E) show : play

9. PARROT : TROPICS ::
   (A) dog : house
   (B) elephant : India
   (C) roadrunner : desert
   (D) lion : zoo
   (E) zebra : Africa

10. MEDIAN : MIDDLE ::
    (A) center : radius
    (B) angle : measurement
    (C) fashion : designer
    (D) mode : mean
    (E) mean : average

GO ON TO THE NEXT PAGE

11. BONES : LIGAMENT ::
    (A) breakage : elasticity
    (B) muscle : tendon
    (C) fat : cell
    (D) knuckle : finger
    (E) leg : arm

12. DOWN : FLUFFY ::
    (A) elevator : fast
    (B) language : fluent
    (C) satin : smooth
    (D) coat : warm
    (E) board : level

13. BURL : TREE ::
    (A) pearl : oyster
    (B) bronze : copper
    (C) plank : wood
    (D) glass : sand
    (E) pebble : rock

14. YEAST : LEAVEN ::
    (A) soda : bubble
    (B) iodine : antiseptic
    (C) aspirin : medicine
    (D) flour : dough
    (E) bread : roll

15. LIST : CAPSIZE ::
    (A) fail : rise
    (B) careen : crash
    (C) trouble : irk
    (D) lose : discover
    (E) pretend : realize

16. PERIMETER : POLYGON ::
    (A) circumference : circle
    (B) hypotenuse : triangle
    (C) side : square
    (D) degree : angle
    (E) angle : rectangle

17. OMEGA : ENDING ::
    (A) fraternity : sorority
    (B) epsilon : femur
    (C) alpha : beginning
    (D) gamma : ray
    (E) river : delta

18. EXPURGATE : PASSAGES ::
    (A) defoliate : leaves
    (B) cancel : checks
    (C) incorporate : ideas
    (D) invade : privacy
    (E) admit : dissent

19. GERM : DISEASE ::
    (A) trichinosis : pork
    (B) men : women
    (C) doctor : medicine
    (D) war : destruction
    (E) nurse : illness

20. QUASH : MOTION ::
    (A) squeeze : melon
    (B) destroy : building
    (C) quell : riot
    (D) impel : engine
    (E) conduct : voltage

TEST 7

20 Questions • 10 Minutes

Directions: Each of these test questions begins with two capitalized words that are related to each other in some way. Find out how they are related. Then study the five pairs of words that follow. They are lettered (A), (B), (C), (D), (E). Select the two words that are related to each other in the same way that the two capitalized words are related.

1. QUEUE : PEOPLE ::
   (A) gaggle : geese
   (B) pile : pails
   (C) stack : hay
   (D) string : pearls
   (E) file : letters

2. RECRUIT : ENLIST ::
   (A) embalmer : putrefy
   (B) hireling : fire
   (C) heir : disinherit
   (D) army : leave
   (E) employee : apply

3. CONTROL : ORDER ::
   (A) joke : clown
   (B) teacher : pupil
   (C) disorder : climax
   (D) anarchy : chaos
   (E) impulsive : deliberate

4. REMORSE : RUE ::
   (A) pain : cough
   (B) pleasure : enjoy
   (C) sense : commiserate
   (D) senility : age
   (E) rationality : cogitate

5. RETARDANT : FIRE ::
   (A) repellent : infestation
   (B) fertilizer : crop
   (C) disease : vaccination
   (D) accelerant : fumes
   (E) depressant : mood

6. SEWER : SEAM ::
   (A) tailor : thimble
   (B) surgeon : scalpel
   (C) electrician : splice
   (D) seed : spore
   (E) court : plaintiff

7. APOLOGY : ACCEPT ::
   (A) face : feature
   (B) forgiveness : beg
   (C) promise : break
   (D) issue : force
   (E) leverage : earn

8. WOOD : CARVE ::
   (A) trees : sway
   (B) paper : burn
   (C) clay : mold
   (D) pipe : blow
   (E) furnace : melt

9. SPIRE : TOWER ::
   (A) crest : mountain
   (B) frog : pond
   (C) city : state
   (D) man : hat
   (E) church : roof

10. SOLECISM : GRAMMAR ::
    (A) separation : marriage
    (B) foul : game
    (C) incest : family
    (D) race : stumble
    (E) apostasy : dogma

GO ON TO THE NEXT PAGE

11. GRAVEL : CONCRETE ::
    (A) eggs : soufflè
    (B) rocks : stones
    (C) shovel : mixer
    (D) car : truck
    (E) aggregate : congregate

12. APOGEE : ORBIT ::
    (A) pedigree : dog
    (B) detergent : laundry
    (C) apex : mountain
    (D) radius : circle
    (E) perigee : planet

13. WHEELBARROW : TRANSPORT ::
    (A) wagon : pull
    (B) shovel : handle
    (C) ax : hone
    (D) stump : excavate
    (E) lever : lift

14. ASYLUM : REFUGEE ::
    (A) flight : escape
    (B) destination : traveler
    (C) lunatic : insanity
    (D) accident : injury
    (E) hospital : inmate

15. WORRIED : HYSTERICAL ::
    (A) hot : cold
    (B) happy : ecstatic
    (C) lonely : crowded
    (D) happy : serious
    (E) anxious : speechless

16. VALANCE : ROD ::
    (A) pendant : chain
    (B) curtain : raffle
    (C) tic : pleat
    (D) collar : cravat
    (E) choker : necklace

17. TELEMETRY : DISTANT ::
    (A) geology : earthshaking
    (B) optometry : real
    (C) micrometry : tiny
    (D) vision : near
    (E) astronomy : invisible

18. NATION : BORDER GUARDS ::
    (A) state : toil
    (B) property : fence
    (C) mountain : hollow
    (D) planet : satellite
    (E) delta : river

19. TOLERATE : PREJUDICE ::
    (A) survive : food
    (B) swim : cramps
    (C) kill : knife
    (D) estimate : computer
    (E) respect : wife

20. SOLDIER : REGIMENT ::
    (A) navy : army
    (B) lake : river
    (C) star : constellation
    (D) amphibian : frog
    (E) nurse : doctor

ANSWER KEY

TEST 1: GRE VERBAL ANALOGIES

1. E
2. B
3. C
4. C
5. D
6. E
7. B
8. C
9. A
10. B
11. A
12. A
13. D
14. B
15. D
16. A
17. D
18. C
19. D
20. B

TEST 2: GRE VERBAL ANALOGIES

1. D
2. C
3. A
4. B
5. D
6. C
7. C
8. C
9. D
10. C
11. A
12. C
13. B
14. B
15. E
16. C
17. A
18. D
19. C
20. D

TEST 3: GRE VERBAL ANALOGIES

1. B
2. D
3. C
4. C
5. B
6. C
7. D
8. B
9. B
10. D
11. A
12. D
13. C
14. B
15. E
16. A
17. D
18. B
19. B
20. C

TEST 4: GRE VERBAL ANALOGIES

1. C
2. D
3. C
4. B
5. B
6. B
7. C
8. D
9. B
10. D
11. D
12. A
13. A
14. B
15. D
16. E
17. C
18. B
19. B
20. C

TEST 5: GRE VERBAL ANALOGIES

1. C
2. D
3. C
4. D
5. E
6. B
7. A
8. B
9. C
10. A
11. E
12. B
13. A
14. C
15. B
16. A
17. B
18. B
19. E
20. B

TEST 6: GRE VERBAL ANALOGIES

1. A
2. C
3. E
4. A
5. B
6. B
7. D
8. A
9. C
10. E
11. B
12. C
13. A
14. B
15. B
16. A
17. C
18. A
19. D
20. C

TEST 7: GRE VERBAL ANALOGIES

1. D
2. E
3. D
4. B
5. A
6. C
7. B
8. C
9. A
10. B
11. A
12. C
13. E
14. B
15. B
16. A
17. C
18. B
19. B
20. C

EXPLANATORY ANSWERS

TEST 1: GRE VERBAL ANALOGIES

1. **(E)** A gallop is faster than a trot. Only scurry and lope have a similar speed differential.
2. **(B)** A trellis may be used to prop a rosebush, as a pillar is used to buttress a structure.
3. **(C)** A crown is a royal symbol; a crucifix is a religious symbol.
4. **(C)** An island is surrounded by the ocean as an oasis is surrounded by the desert.
5. **(D)** Mathematics is the science of numbers, while numerology is the occult study of numbers; astronomy is the science of celestial bodies, while astrology is the occult study of celestial bodies.
6. **(E)** *Bucolic* relates to rural life and suggests the natural; *urban* implies the manufactured. Mist is a natural occurrence; smog is fog made foul by smoke and chemical fumes.
7. **(B)** To be abhorrent is to be extremely dislikable; to be arduous is to be extremely difficult.
8. **(C)** Wood may be measured by the cord; milk may be measured by the quart.
9. **(A)** One result of a drought is thirst, a possible result of a blizzard is snow blindness. The analogy is one of cause and effect. *Aridity* and *dryness* are synonyms.
10. **(B)** A minaret is a high tower attached to a mosque; a steeple is a high structure rising above a church.
11. **(A)** Chaff is the worthless husks of grain left after the threshing of wheat; dregs are the worthless residue created by the process of making wine.
12. **(A)** A spy must be devious in order to succeed; a farmer, to succeed, must be productive.
13. **(D)** Ebb and wax are opposite motions, as are slacken and grown. *Ebb* and *slacken* connote recession, while *wax* and *grown* connote expansion. Choices A and B reverse the order of the analogy.
14. **(B)** The director is responsible for the production of a drama; the editor is responsible for the production of a magazine.
15. **(D)** A cliché is commonplace; a maxim is terse. The analogy is based on *inherent* characteristics. A pun may be annoying, but it does not have to be.
16. **(A)** To be thrilled is to be extremely pleased; to be drunk is to be extremely tipsy.
17. **(D)** A collection of willow trees may make up a grove; a collection of blackberry bushes may make up a thicket.
18. **(C)** A sin is not moral; a crime is not legal.
19. **(D)** An ellipse is a kind of curve; a square is a kind of polygon.
20. **(B)** Rayon is a manufactured substitute for silk; margarine, made from vegetable oils, is a substitute for butter.

TEST 2: GRE VERBAL ANALOGIES

1. **(D)** To demand is to request in a very strong manner; to crave is to wish in a very strong manner.
2. **(C)** An album holds photographs; a wallet holds money.
3. **(A)** A faucet controls the flow of water; a throttle controls the flow of fuel.
4. **(B)** A holocaust is death and destruction caused by fire; hanging is death caused by a noose about the neck.
5. **(D)** A pendulum oscillates—that is, swings backward and forward; a gyroscope spins.
6. **(C)** Dill is one kind of herb; fir is one kind of conifer, or cone-producing tree.
7. **(C)** The intestine is part of the digestive system; pores are part of the excretory system.
8. **(C)** A flask is a small bottle; a pamphlet is a small book.

9. **(D)** Avarice is extreme desire, even greed, for money; voracity is extreme desire, even greed, for food.
10. **(C)** A lack of hair is baldness; a lack of rain is drought.
11. **(A)** A ship is a large boat; a tome is a large book.
12. **(C)** A scythe symbolizes death; a heart symbolizes love.
13. **(B)** A kennel is a man-made shelter for dogs; a stall, also man-made, is usually employed to house a horse. A stork builds its own nest.
14. **(B)** A carnivore eats meat; a vegetarian eats vegetables.
15. **(E)** Libel is a written defamation of character; slander is a false and defamatory oral statement about a person. Both are forms of defamation. An oak is a deciduous tree; a spruce is a coniferous tree. Both are types of trees.
16. **(C)** An entry is the smallest unit in a dictionary; a note is the smallest unit in a musical score.
17. **(A)** Mauve is a color; basil is a spice. This is a simple part-to-whole analogy.
18. **(D)** To muffle something is almost to silence it; to stymie something is almost to defeat it.
19. **(C)** A whale is an aquatic mammal that superficially resembles a fish; a bat is a nocturnal flying mammal that resembles a bird.
20. **(D)** A verb can name an action just as a pronoun can name a person.

TEST 3: GRE VERBAL ANALOGIES

1. **(B)** A plutocrat is a ruler distinguished by wealth; a theocrat rules on the basis of religion.
2. **(D)** A news report is descriptive of an event; a security guard is protective of an area or person.
3. **(C)** *Prophylactic* means *tending to prevent; therapeutic* means *tending to cure.*
4. **(C)** The rigging on a ship consists mainly of rope; the sails are traditionally made of canvas.
5. **(B)** Matriculation, or enrollment, is the beginning of a process that is meant to end with graduation. Enlistment and discharge are a similar beginning and ending, referring to military service.
6. **(C)** The hydraulic system is operated by means of water; the pneumatic system is operated by means of air pressure.
7. **(D)** Hydrophobia is another name for rabies; rubeola is another name for measles.
8. **(B)** A horse is usually kept and fed in a stable; a hog is usually kept and fed in a sty. The relationship in answer D is reversed. As for answer C, the ram may be confined to the fold for safekeeping at night, but rams and sheep are sent out to graze rather than being fed in the fold.
9. **(B)** A blossom is made up of petals, as a windmill is made up of vanes (also called arms), which catch the wind. A pine tree contains pine cones, but the similarity in configuration between flower petals and windmill vanes makes answer B the better choice.
10. **(D)** An actor plays a role; a ballplayer plays a position.
11. **(A)** *Hamlet* is an example of a tragedy, as the *Iliad* is an example of an epic.
12. **(D)** Fodder or silage for animals is stored in a silo; wine is stored in a cask.
13. **(C)** A kilt is a traditional skirtlike garment worn by a man in the Scottish highlands; a sari is a traditional garment worn by a woman in India.
14. **(B)** The prow is the forward part of a ship; the nose is the forward part of an airplane.
15. **(E)** A tress is a lock of hair, especially the long unbound hair of a woman; a skein is a loosely coiled length of wool or cotton yarn.
16. **(A)** As epoxy may be used to affix or attach objects, a crowbar may be used to pry them apart. The analogy is based upon function or purpose.

17. **(D)** Discipline leads to order; training leads to preparation.
18. **(B)** Something that is overabundant is more than sufficient; something that is absent is more than scarce. The analogy is one of degree.
19. **(B)** Paper, especially fine stationery, may be identified by a watermark; a person may be identified by a birthmark.
20. **(C)** Something that is brilliant is extremely bright; someone who is overjoyed is extremely happy.

TEST 4: GRE VERBAL ANALOGIES

1. **(C)** A xylophone is a percussion instrument; a bassoon is a wind instrument.
2. **(D)** A stallion is an adult male horse, while a gelding is a castrated horse. Similarly, a bull is an adult male bovine, while a steer is a bovine animal castrated before sexual maturity.
3. **(C)** Pliers are tools designed specifically for gripping; a jack is a tool specially designed for elevating.
4. **(B)** A radius extends from the center of a circle to its edge; a spoke extends from the center of a wheel to its edge.
5. **(B)** The zodiac has 12 signs; the year has 12 months.
6. **(B)** Transitivity is an axiom; the Pythagorean theorem is a theorem in geometry.
7. **(C)** To allay fears is to alleviate or subdue them; to pacify an infant is to calm the infant.
8. **(D)** An alcove is a small, recessed section of a room; a cave is a chamber in a mountain.
9. **(B)** The dinosaur is an extinct relative of the crocodile; the woolly mammoth is an extinct relative of the elephant.
10. **(D)** A misdemeanor, though illegal, is not as serious a crime as is a felony. Though something that is cracked is damaged, it is not so seriously damaged as a smashed object.
11. **(D)** Flooding can cause erosion. Pollution can cause contamination.
12. **(A)** A hygrometer is used to measure humidity; a thermometer is used to measure temperature.
13. **(A)** A meal can also be called a repast. A drink can also be called a beverage.
14. **(B)** To cull is to remove what is inferior, or worthless; to select is to pick out the choice, the best.
15. **(D)** A ballad is a type of song; broadloom is a kind of carpet.
16. **(E)** A group of whales is a pod; a group of ducks is a brace.
17. **(C)** An architect's blueprint would show the location of a hallway much as a road map shows the location of a highway.
18. **(B)** A monarch is a ruler; a serf is a peasant. Only *regal* and *lowly* repeat this contrast.
19. **(B)** Someone who is bold is not easily cowed; someone who is demanding is not easily satisfied.
20. **(C)** Milk may be sold by the gallon. The other combinations of goods and measurements are unlikely except for fabric, which tends to be sold by the yard.

TEST 5: GRE VERBAL ANALOGIES

1. **(C)** An article is a form of expository writing; a story is a form of narrative writing.
2. **(D)** A prospector looks for gold; a detective looks for clues.
3. **(C)** Dextrose is a kind of sugar; fat is a kind of lipid. Corn and maize are synonyms, and therefore answer B is incorrect.
4. **(D)** You would expect to see a swarm of bees in an apiary, or collection of hives. You would expect to see a flock of birds in an aviary.

5. **(E)** A latch may fasten a gate, as a buckle fastens a belt.
6. **(B)** Cutting motions have different names depending on the tool used. A stylus is used to incise, but a penknife may be used to whittle.
7. **(A)** The cockpit is an interior section of an airplane; ailerons are on an airplane's exterior, on its wings.
8. **(B)** A vicar is a member of the clergy; a dragoon is a member of the military.
9. **(C)** One would garner (gather) wealth; one would collate (assemble) pages.
10. **(A)** A street is paralleled by a sidewalk, a walkway for pedestrians. A beach is paralleled by a boardwalk, also a walkway for pedestrians.
11. **(E)** A glutton is undiscriminating in his or her love of food; a gourmet is highly selective in choice of food.
12. **(B)** A couplet may be part of a poem; a sentence may be part of a paragraph.
13. **(A)** A climber seeks to reach the peak; a hunter seeks game.
14. **(C)** Oil is extracted from the earth by means of a well; silver is extracted by means of a mine.
15. **(B)** A palette holds a variety of pigments; a nursery contains a variety of trees.
16. **(A)** A colander is used to drain food; a sieve is used to filter.
17. **(B)** If something is indubitable, you cannot contradict it; if something is immovable, you cannot budge it.
18. **(B)** A stallion and a rooster are two different animals of the same sex, as are a mare and a hen.
19. **(E)** In judo, participants use no weapons; in soccer, players (with the exception of the goalie) may not use their hands.
20. **(B)** A judicial function is to enforce laws; a legislative function is to pass laws.

TEST 6: GRE VERBAL ANALOGIES

1. **(A)** The rudder is used in directing a ship; the steering wheel is used in directing a car.
2. **(C)** In karate, the foot is used as a weapon; in fencing, the foil is the weapon. In boxing, the weapon is a fist. In baseball, the bat is a tool, not a weapon.
3. **(E)** A leech is a parasite that gains its sustenance by attaching to and drawing from other living things. A mushroom is a saprophyte, an organism (especially a plant) that lives on dead or decaying matter.
4. **(A)** Leavening is a process that produces fermentation. An argument can produce a fight. Snow is frozen precipitation.
5. **(B)** Something that is hilarious is a more intense form of amusing; genius is a more intense form of smart.
6. **(B)** Just as an item is an entry or unit on a list, an article is a unit of a constitution. Bark is part of a tree, but it is not a unit.
7. **(D)** We read a book and listen to music. For answer B to be correct, the relationship would have to be changed to WATCH : MOVIE.
8. **(A)** The first public showing of a movie is its premiere; similarly, the first public showing of a statue is its unveiling.
9. **(C)** A parrot is a bird found in the climatic region known as the tropics. Only the habitat of the roadrunner in the warm, arid region known as the desert is parallel to complete this analogy. India and Africa are too large to associate with just one type of habitat.
10. **(E)** In this analogy of definition, the median is the middle, having an equal number of items above and below it; the mean is the average.
11. **(B)** Muscles are connected to bones by tendons just as bones are connected to bones by ligaments.
12. **(C)** Down is fluffy; satin is smooth. The analogy is based upon well-known qualities.

13. **(A)** A burl is an outgrowth of a tree that serves no purpose to the tree but that finds utility in its own right when made into a table or craft item. A pearl develops inside an oyster. It serves no useful purpose to the oyster but finds its role in jewelry.
14. **(B)** Yeast is used as a leaven; iodine is used as an antiseptic. These functions are more specific than aspirin's function as a medicine.
15. **(B)** When a boat lists, leans to one side, it threatens to capsize. When a car careens out of control, it may crash.
16. **(A)** The distance around a polygon is its perimeter; the distance around a circle is its circumference.
17. **(C)** Alpha and omega are the first and last letters of the Greek alphabet.
18. **(A)** Passage can be eliminated from a written work by expurgation; leaves are eliminated from trees by defoliation.
19. **(D)** A germ causes disease; war causes destruction.
20. **(C)** To quash a motion (a proposal advanced at a meeting) is to nullify it; to quell a riot is to crush it.

TEST 7: GRE VERBAL ANALOGIES

1. **(D)** People form in a queue like pearls on a string.
2. **(E)** To join the military, one can enlist to become a recruit. To join the work force, one can apply to become an employee.
3. **(D)** Control results in order; anarchy results in chaos.
4. **(B)** To rue is to feel remorse; to enjoy is to feel pleasure. To cogitate does not necessarily result in rationality.
5. **(A)** A retardant protects from fire, as a repellant protects from infestation by insects.
6. **(C)** A sewer uses a seam to connect pieces of fabric. An electrician uses a splice to connect pieces of wire.
7. **(B)** You can accept someone else's apology; you can beg someone else's forgiveness. You cannot break someone else's promise.
8. **(C)** One can create something by carving wood; one can also create something by molding clay.
9. **(A)** A spire surmounts a tower; a crest is the highest point of a mountain. The relationship in answer E is backward.
10. **(B)** A solecism is a violation of the rules of grammar; a foul is a violation of the rules of a game. Apostasy is total rejection of a dogma rather than simple violation of rules.
11. **(A)** Gravel is an ingredient of concrete; eggs are an ingredient of a soufflè.
12. **(C)** The apogee is the outer limit of an orbit; the apex is the upper limit of a mountain.
13. **(E)** A lever helps you lift objects; a wheelbarrow helps you to transport them easily.
14. **(B)** A refugee seeks asylum; a traveler seeks a destination.
15. **(B)** One who is extremely worried may be hysterical; one who is extremely happy may be ecstatic.
16. **(A)** A valance (a short, decorative drapery) hangs from a curtain rod. A pendant hangs from a chain around a person's neck.
17. **(C)** Telemetry is concerned with the distant, and micrometry is concerned with the tiny.
18. **(B)** Border guards protect the boundaries of a nation; a fence protects the boundaries of a property.
19. **(B)** Prejudice can interfere with one's ability to tolerate; cramps can interfere with one's ability to swim.
20. **(C)** A soldier is a part of a regiment; a star is part of a constellation. This is a simple part-to-whole analogy.

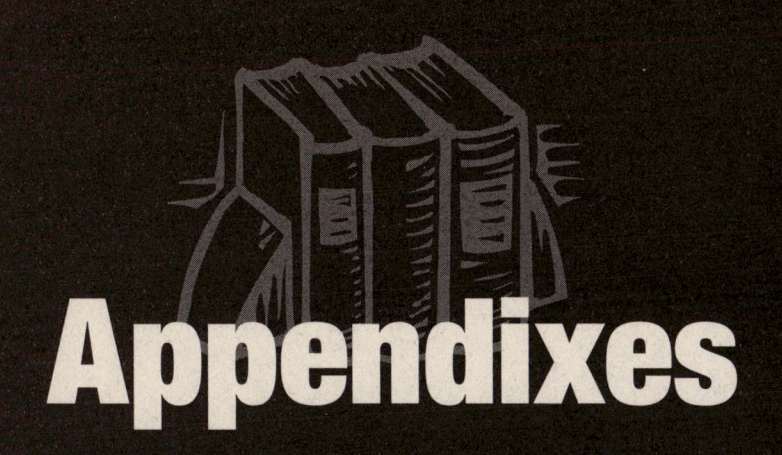

PART 5

Appendixes

PREVIEW

APPENDIX A *Mythology*

APPENDIX B *Nations of the World*

APPENDIX C *Mathematics*

Appendix

Mythology

The Greeks had the most highly developed mythology, in terms of genealogy, personalities, and lifestyles of the gods. Roman mythology closely parallels Greek mythology; many of the gods and goddesses are counterparts of Greek gods. The other highly developed European mythology is Norse mythology, which developed independently from the Greeks and Romans but, because mythology existed to explain the same phenomena in each society, has many similarities.

The Greek gods lived on Mt. Olympus. Roman gods had no comparable dwelling place. The home of the Norse gods was at Asgard, where the dining hall of the heroes was Valhalla and the private dining room of the gods was Gimli.

Kronos and Rhea were parents of the six original Greek gods; their Roman counterparts are Saturn and Ops. The original Greek gods were:

Zeus—King of the gods, comparable to the Roman Jupiter and the Norse Odin.

Hera—Both sister and wife of Zeus and queen of the gods; comparable to the Roman Juno, wife of Jupiter, and the Norse Frigg or Frigga, wife of Odin.

Poseidon—Ruler of the sea and of earthquakes, comparable to the Roman Neptune and to the Norse Njord.

Hades—Ruler of the dead and god of wealth, comparable to the Roman Pluto.

Demeter—Goddess of agriculture, comparable to the Roman Ceres.

Hestia—Goddess of the hearth, comparable to the Roman Vesta.

Parentage of some of the "younger" Greek gods is consistent from myth to myth. Some of the most important gods of consistently acknowledged parentage are these:

Athene or Athena—Goddess who "sprung full-blown from the head of Zeus"; goddess of wisdom, cities, heroes in war, and handicrafts. Her Roman counterpart, Minerva, had the same miraculous birth.

Persephone—Daughter of Zeus and Demeter, goddess of agriculture (like her mother) and queen of the dead; wife of Hades; comparable to the Roman Proserpina.

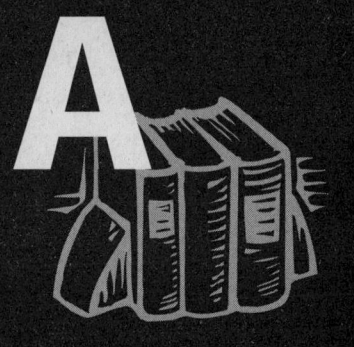

Apollo and Artemis—Twin children of Zeus and Leto. Apollo, god of prophesy, music, and medicine, is a god of purification and giver of oracles. Apollo's name carries over into Roman mythology, where his twin sister is Diana. Apollo's Norse counterpart is Freyr, twin brother of Freya. Artemis is goddess of the moon and of the hunt as well as of woods, meadows, wild animals, and fertility. Artemis has a Roman counterpart in Diana. Freya, goddess of love and beauty, though Freyr's twin sister, is more comparable to Aphrodite.

Hermes—Son of Zeus and Maia; herald of the gods and leader of men, god of trade and eloquence. Hermes' Roman counterpart is Mercury.

Ares—Son of Zeus and Hera; god of war, with a Roman counterpart, Mars.

Dionysus—Son of Zeus and Semele; god of wine and joy, comparable to Roman Bacchus.

Some gods and goddesses of disputed or unknown parentage include these:

Aphrodite—Goddess of sexual love, comparable to the Roman Venus and to the Norse Freya.

Hephaistos—God of fire and thunderbolts, the divine smith and craftsman; comparable to the Roman Vulcan.

Adonis—God of male beauty, vegetation, and rebirth.

Phoebus Apollos—Driver of the sun's chariot in its daily journey across the sky.

Eos—Goddess of the dawn; comparable to the Roman Aurora.

Hebe—God of youth; comparable to the Roman Juventas.

Hypnos—God of sleep; comparable to the Roman Somnus.

Pan—God of woods and fields; comparable to the Roman Faunus.

Thanatos—God of death; comparable to the Roman Mors.

Nike—Goddess of victory; comparable to the Roman Victoria.

Mythology, especially Greek mythology, often makes references to personifications in groups. In some groups, the individuals have distinctive names. Some of the most common are these:

Muses:

Clio—Muse of history.

Euterpe—Muse of lyric poetry and flute playing.

Thalia—Muse of comedy.

Melpomene—Muse of music, song, and tragedy.

Terpischore—Muse of choral dancing and choral singing.

Erato—Muse of love songs and love poetry.

Polyhymnia—Muse of serious poetry and hymns, of mime, and of geometry.

Urania—Muse of astronomy and astrology.

Calliope—Muse of epic poetry.

Fates:

Clotho—Spinner of the thread of life; comparable to the Roman Nona.

Lachesis—Determiner of the length; comparable to the Roman Decuma.

Atropos—Cutter of the thread; comparable to the Roman Morta.

Furies:

Alecto—Unending

Tisiphone—Retaliation

Megaera—Envious fury

Graces:

    Aglaia—Brilliance

    Euphrosyne—Joy

    Thalia—Bloom

Winds:

    Aeolus—Keeper of the winds

    Boreas—The north wind

    Eurus—The east wind

    Notus—The south wind

    Zephyrus—The west wind

Half-people, half-animals:

    Centaur—Head and torso of a man, lower half of a horse

    Harpy—Head of a woman, body of a bird

    Satyr—Head and torso of a man, lower half of a goat

Minor deities of nature:

    Dryads—Tree nymphs

    Naiads—Water, stream, and fountain nymphs

    Napaeae—Wood nymphs

    Nereids—Sea nymphs

    Oceanids—Ocean nymphs

    Oreads—Mountain nymphs

Rivers of the Underworld:

    Acheron—Woe

    Cocytus—Wailing

    Phlegethon—Fire

    Lethe—Forgetfulness

    Styx—The last river that souls must cross

Appendix

Nations of the World

Over the course of history, many nations of the world have changed identities and alliances as well as borders and governments. A brief course in world history and geography is a logical impossibility, but this selective list of some of today's nations and their previous identities and affiliations might prove helpful for the sequential and the language-spoken types of analogy questions.

Current Name	Previous Name or Names
Algeria	Ancient Numidia
Angola	Portuguese West Africa
Armenia	Armenian S.S.R. ...Transcaucasian S.S.R. ...Transcaucasian Federation ... Armenia ... Persia
Azerbaijan	Azerbaijan S.S.R. ...Transcaucasian S.R.R. ... Transcaucasian Federation ... Persia ... ancient Albania
Bangladesh	East Pakistan ... British India
Belarus	Byelorussia ... White Russia
Belize	British Honduras
Benin	Dahomey (French)
Bosnia-Herzegovina	Yugoslavia ... Serbia
Botswana	Bechuanaland (English)
Burkina Faso	Upper Volta (French)
Burundi	Ruanda-Urundi...Belgian Congo...German East Africa
Cambodia	Campuchea...Cambodia...French Indo-China
Central African Republic	Central African Empire ... French Equatorial Africa ... Ubangi-Shari
Chad	French Equatorial Africa
Congo (capital: Brazzaville)	French Congo
Congo (capital: Kinshasa)	Zaire ... Belgian Congo
Croatia	Yugoslavia

Czech Republic	Czechoslovakia...Czechoslovak S.S.R. ...Czechoslovakia... Austria-Hungary
Djibouti	Afars and Issas ... French Somaliland
England	Ancient Albion
Equatorial Guinea	Spanish Guinea
Estonia	Estonian S.S.R. ... Estonia ... Sweden.... Germany
Ethiopia	Ancient Abyssinia
France	Ancient Gaul
Gabon	French Congo
Georgia	Georgian S.S.R. ... Transcaucasian S.S.R. ... Transcaucasian Federation
Germany	Prussia and many independent kingdoms
Ghana	British Gold Coast
Greece	Ancient Hellas
Guinea	French West Africa
Guinea-Bissau	Portuguese Guinea
Guyana	British Guiana
Indonesia	Netherlands East Indies
Iran	Persia
Iraq	Ancient Babylonia and Assyria ... ancient Mesopotamia
Irian Jaya (part of Indonesia)	West Irian ... Netherlands New Guinea
Israel	Palestine ... ancient Canaan
Jordan	Palestine ... ancient Edom and Moab
Kazakhstan	Kazakhstan S.S.R.
Kiribati	Gilbert Islands (English)
Kyrgyzstan	Kyrgyzstan S.S.R.
Laos	French Indo-China
Latvia	Latvia S.S.R. ... Latvia ... Russia ... Poland ... Sweden
Lesotho	Basutoland (English)
Lithuania	Lithuania S.S.R. ... Lithuania ... Russia ... Poland
Macedonia	Yugoslavia ... Bulgaria ... Greece
Madagascar	Malagasy Republic (French)
Malawi	Nyasaland (English)
Malaysia	Malaya and Sabah (North Borneo) and Sarawak
Mali	French Sudan
Moldova	Moldovan S.S.R. ... Turkey ... Romania ... Bessarabia
Mongolia	Outer Mongolia
Mozambique	Portuguese East Africa
Myanmar	Burma ... British India
Namibia	Southwest Africa (English and Afrikaans)
Niger	French West Africa

Oman	Muscat and Oman
Pakistan,	British India
Portugal	Part of Spain
Russia	Leader of the Union of Soviet Socialist Republics (U.S.S.R.), a.k.a. Soviet Union, which at one time included a large number of states such as Armenia, Czechoslovakia, Estonia, Georgia, Kazakhstan, Lithuania, and the Ukraine
Rwanda	Ruanda-Urundi ... Belgian Congo ... German East Africa
Senegal	French West Africa
Slovakia	Czechoslovakia ... Austria-Hungary
Slovenia	Yugoslavia
Somalia	Somaliland (English)
Spain	Ancient Iberia
Sri Lanka	Ceylon (English)
Sudan	Anglo-Egyptian Sudan ... ancient Nubia
Suriname	Dutch Guiana
Switzerland	Ancient Helvetia
Tajikistan	Tadzhikistan S.S.R. ... Afghanistan ... Persia
Tanzania	Tanganyika and Zanzibar
Thailand	Siam
Togo	Togoland (French)
Tunisia	Ancient Carthage
Turkmenistan	Turkistan Autonomous S.S.R. ... Turkmenia ... ancient Persia
Tuvalu	Ellice Islands (English)
Ukraine	Ukraine S.S.R. ... Ukraine ... Rus
United Arab Emirates	Union of the Trucial States, which were: Abu Dhabi, Sharja, Ras al Khaima, Dubai, Ajman, Fujaira, and Umm al Qaiman
Uzbekistan	Uzbekistan S.S.R. ... Uzbek Republic ... ancient Persia
Vanuatu	New Hebrides (French and English)
Vietnam	French Indo-China
West Irian	Netherlands New Guinea
Western Sahara (region)	Spanish Sahara
Yemen	Aden
Yugoslavia (includes Serbia and Montenegro)	Yugoslavia less Croatia, Bosnia-Herzegovina, Slovenia, and Macedonia
Zambia	Northern Rhodesia (English)
Zimbabwe	Rhodesia (English)

Appendix

Mathematics

Some mathematical analogy questions draw upon specific knowledge of algebra, geometry, trigonometry, and calculus. In order to answer these questions, you must have real understanding of the various branches of mathematics. Other mathematical analogies rest upon a more generalized or superficial understanding of the mathematics, with perhaps more complex reasoning required. The following tables compile in one easy reference the general mathematical information you are most likely to find useful.

ROMAN NUMERALS

I = 1	D = 500	$\overline{C}$ = 100,000
V = 5	M = 1000	$\overline{D}$ = 500,000
X = 10	$\overline{V}$ = 5000	$\overline{M}$ = 1,000,000
L = 50	$\overline{X}$ = 10,000	
C = 100	$\overline{L}$ = 50,000	

Rules:

1. A letter repeated once or twice repeats its value that many times. (XXX = 30; MM = 2,000)

2. One or more letters placed after another letter of greater value increases the greater value by the amount of the smaller. (XII = 12; DCX = 610)

3. A letter placed before another letter of greater value decreases the greater value by the amount of the smaller. (IX = 9; CD = 400)

GENERAL MEASURES

Time	Angles and Arcs	Counting
1 minute (min) = 60 seconds (sec)	1 minute (') = 60 seconds (")	1 dozen (doz) = 12 units
1 hour (hr) = 60 minutes	1 degree (°) = 60 minutes	1 gross (gr) = 12 dozen
1 day = 24 hours	1 circle = 360°	1 gross = 144 units
1 week = 7 days		
1 year = 52 weeks		
1 calendar year = 365 days		

THE METRIC SYSTEM

LENGTH

Unit	Abbreviation	Number of Meters
myriameter	mym	10,000
kilometer	km	1,000
hectometer	hm	100
dekameter	dam	10
meter	m	1
decimeter	dm	0.1
centimeter	cm	0.01
millimeter	mm	0.001

AREA

Unit	Abbreviation	Number of Square Meters
square kilometer	sq km or km^2	1,000,000
hectare	ha	10,000
are	a	100
centare	ca	1
square centimeter	sq cm or cm^2	0.0001

VOLUME

Unit	Abbreviation	Number of Cubic Meters
dekastere	das	10
stere	s	1
decistere	ds	0.10
cubic centimeter	cu cm or cm³ or cc	0.000001

CAPACITY

Unit	Abbreviation	Number of Liters
kiloliter	kl	1,000
hectoliter	hi	100
dekaliter	dal	10
liter	l	1
deciliter	dl	0.10
centiliter	cl	0.01
milliliter	ml	0.001

MASS AND WEIGHT

Unit	Abbreviation	Number of Grams
metric ton	MT or t	1,000,000
quintal	q	100,000
kilogram	kg	1,000
hectogram	hg	100
dekagram	dag	10
gram	g or gm	1
decigram	dg	0.10
centigram	cg	0.01
milligram	mg	0.001

TEMPERATURE

Scale	Abbreviation	
Celsius or Centigrade	°C	Freezing Point 0°C Boiling Point 100°C

AMERICAN MEASURES

Length

1 foot (ft or ') = 12 inches (in or ")
1 yard (yd) = 36 inches
1 yard = 3 feet
1 rod (rd.) = $16\frac{1}{2}$ feet
1 mile (mi) = 5,280 feet
1 mile = 1,760 yards
1 mile = 320 rods

Weight

1 pound (lb) = 16 ounces (oz)
1 hundredweight (cwt) = 100 pounds
1 ton (T) = 2,000 pounds

Area

1 square foot (ft^2) = 144 square inches (in^2)
1 square yard (yd^2) = 9 feet

Temperature

Water freezes at 32°F (Fahrenheit)
Water boils at 212°F

Liquid Measure

1 cup (c) = 8 fluid ounces (fl oz)
1 pint (pt) = 2 cups
1 pint = 4 gills (gi)
1 quart (qt) = 2 pints
1 gallon (gal) = 4 quarts
1 barrel (bl) = $31\frac{1}{2}$ gallons

Dry Measure

1 quart (qt) = 2 pints (pt)
1 peck (pk) = 8 quarts
1 bushel (bu) = 4 pecks

Volume

1 cubic foot (ft^3 or cu ft) = 1,728 cubic inches
1 cubic yard (yd^3 or cu yd) = 27 cubic feet
1 gallon = 231 cubic inches

TABLE OF AMERICAN/METRIC CONVERSIONS (APPROXIMATE)

American to Metric	Metric to American	Table of Metric Conversions*
1 inch = 2.54 centimeters	1 centimeter = .39 inches	1 liter = 1000 cubic centimeters (cm^3)
1 yard = .9 meters	1 meter = 1.1 yards	
1 mile = 1.6 kilometers	1 kilometer = .6 miles	1 milliliter = 1 cubic centimeter
1 ounce = 28 grams	1 kilogram = 2.2 pounds	1 liter of water weighs 1 kilogram
1 pound = 454 grams	1 liter = 1.06 liquid quart	1 milliliter of water weighs 1 gram
1 fluid ounce = 30 milliliters	°C = $\frac{5}{9}$ (°F − 32°)	
1 liquid quart = .95 liters	100°C = 212°F	
32°F = 0°C	°C = $\frac{5}{9}$ (°F − 32°)	
212°F = 100°C		
°F = $\frac{9}{5}$ °C + 32°		

These conversions are exact only under specific conditions. If the conditions are not met, the conversions are approximate.

NOTES

NOTES

NOTES

NOTES

NOTES

NOTES

NOTES

Build the skills you need for test success!

Students turn to **ARCO**® for a complete library of targeted test-prep handbooks that have helped thousands of test-takers reach—and even exceed—their score goals. Don't miss these exceptional resources:

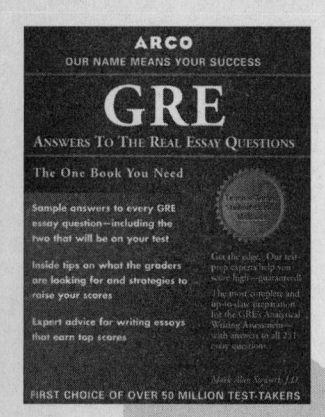

GRE Answers to Real Essay Questions
Instructional tips and detailed review for 251 essay questions that have frequently appeared on the exam.
$14.95

More GRE CAT prep from ARCO!

GRE/LSAT Logic Workbook
In-depth practice for building critical skills for the analytical section of the exam.
$10.95

ARCO
THOMSON LEARNING

www.petersons.com   AOL Keyword: Peterson's

GRE/LSAT/GMAT/MCAT Reading Comprehension Workbook
A targeted handbook packed with all types of reading passages that you'll encounter on the exam.
$10.95

Visit your local bookstore or call to order: **800-338-3282.** To order online, go to **www.petersons.com** and head for the bookstore!

The Graduate Channel at Petersons.com
—Your One-Stop Online Destination for Information on Degree Programs, Financial Aid, and More

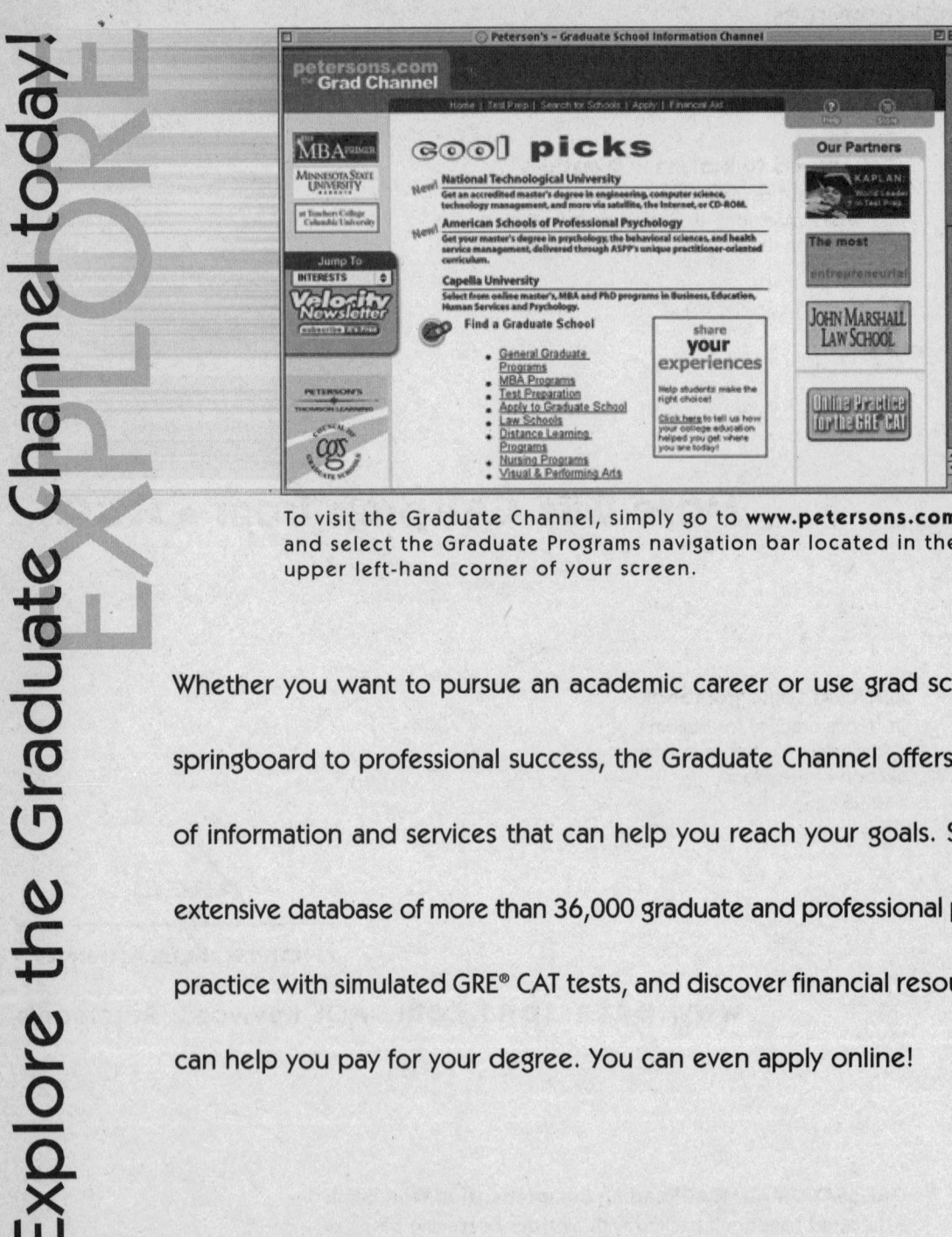

To visit the Graduate Channel, simply go to **www.petersons.com** and select the Graduate Programs navigation bar located in the upper left-hand corner of your screen.

Whether you want to pursue an academic career or use grad school as a springboard to professional success, the Graduate Channel offers a wealth of information and services that can help you reach your goals. Search an extensive database of more than 36,000 graduate and professional programs, practice with simulated GRE® CAT tests, and discover financial resources that can help you pay for your degree. You can even apply online!

PETERSON'S
™
THOMSON LEARNING

www.petersons.com • AOL Keyword: Peterson's • 800-338-3282